The World Encyclopedia of
Musical Instruments

The World Encyclopedia of
Musical Instruments

MAX WADE-MATTHEWS

CONSULTANT: WILLIAM MIVAL
ROYAL COLLEGE OF MUSIC, LONDON

LORENZ BOOKS

First published in 2000 by Lorenz Books

© Anness Publishing Limited 2000

Lorenz Books is an imprint of
Anness Publishing Limited
Hermes House
88–89 Blackfriars Road
London SE1 8HA

Published in the USA by Lorenz Books
Anness Publishing Inc., 27 West 20th Street
New York, NY 10011; (800) 354–9657

A CIP catalogue record for this book
is available from the British Library

Publisher: Joanna Lorenz
Project Editor: Felicity Forster
Editor: Beverley Jollands
Photographer: John Freeman
Designer: Ian Hunt
Jacket Design: Goodall James
Picture Researchers: Cathy Stastny and Daniela Marceddu
Editorial Reader: Kate Sillence
Production Controller: Wendy Lawson

1 3 5 7 9 10 8 6 4 2

Contents

Preface

If music be the food of love, play on!
WILLIAM SHAKESPEARE (1564–1616), "TWELFTH NIGHT"

People have been making music for a very long time, and for most of that time they have invented ways of making sounds with instruments. Music begins in the mind: melody and timbre can find expression through the voice, and rhythm and tempo through clapping, stamping and dancing. But the inventive mind soon looks for other solutions which will produce more volume, new varieties of sound, new challenges.

The evidence of the very oldest music is provided by the remains of instruments. Clappers, flutes and drums have survived from before the last Ice Age, and these are the ancient ancestors of the thousands of musical instruments used in the world today. In exploring the history and development of musical instruments, this book presents a general history of music, for this shows what was played

ABOVE: "Buffalo Dance" from George Catlin's North American Indian Portfolio *of 1844. One of the dancers is keeping the rhythm with a shallow frame drum.*

and how it sounded. The musical instruments of previous ages and different cultures have much to say, not only about music, but about social patterns, technology and skills, ritual and religion.

One of the pleasures of music is playing together, and instruments need to sound good in ensembles as well as in solo playing. The modern orchestra has evolved as a flexible group of instruments that can produce a balanced sound, yet also offer many contrasts of tone and colour. In Europe, medieval and Renaissance instrumental ensembles were generally used to accompany singers, and were confined to wind instruments and strings. The groups were gradually enlarged by the addition of brass and percussion as the orchestra began to take centre stage. By the 19th century, some orchestras had grown to

monstrous proportions and composers were writing on a very large scale, calling for exceptional resources, especially in the percussion section, and even sometimes inventing new instruments to provide the musical effects they wanted.

ABOVE: A 16th-century trio of musicians playing together from a manuscript.

ABOVE: This Italian mosaic from the 2nd century BC shows strolling masked musicians.

ABOVE: A chamber group performing at an outdoor reception.

There is a mutually dependent relationship between performers, composers and instrument makers. Each is limited by the abilities of the others, but also inspired by them. The development of music represents a constant striving to arrest the ear of the audience with sounds that are more beautiful, more interesting or more original than any heard before. In their quest for originality, composers make fresh demands on performers and their instruments. At the same time, performers improve and extend their technique, and call for new music and

ABOVE: Musical instruments such as this double bass and bow have a strong aesthetic appeal.

better instruments to demonstrate their talents. In addition, instrument makers invent new shapes or discover new materials that transform their instruments and offer new potential for musicians. Music develops new sounds because of the interplay between all the different talents needed to produce it.

Even when they are not being played, musical instruments have a strong aesthetic appeal, which stems from their perfect blend of form and function. They are often lovingly made and beautifully decorated, with satisfying, rounded shapes and smooth surfaces that demand to be touched. Those who play them become deeply attached to them as the emotions expressed in music flow through them. There are plenty of folk tales and myths that tell of instruments with supernatural powers: warning drums, magic flutes, diabolical violins and pianos that play themselves. There is no doubting the magic of music, and musical instruments have a share of it.

ABOVE: A painting from the mid 17th century by Jan Havicksz, entitled The Harpsichord Lesson. *Every young lady of "class" was expected to be able to play the harpsichord.*

ABOVE: Playing in an orchestra can be a magical experience for the performers.

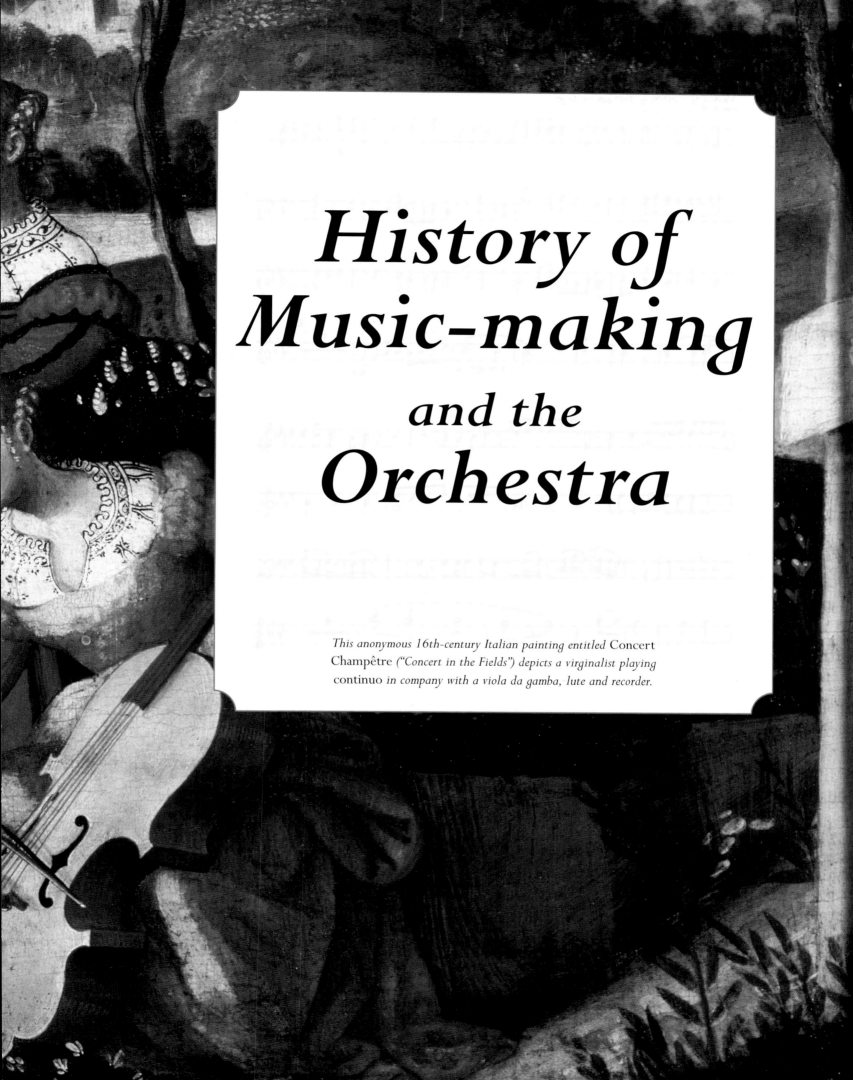

History of Music-making

and the

Orchestra

This anonymous 16th-century Italian painting entitled Concert
Champêtre *("Concert in the Fields") depicts a virginalist playing*
continuo *in company with a viola da gamba, lute and recorder.*

Introduction

Music is the universal language of mankind.

HENRY WADSWORTH LONGFELLOW (1807–82), "OUTRE-MER"

There are few people who do not react to music to some degree. The power of music is diverse and people respond in different ways. To some it is mainly an instinctive, exciting sound to which they dance or move their bodies. Other people listen for its message, or take an intellectual approach to its form and construction, appreciating its formal patterns or originality. Above all, however, there can be hardly anyone who is not moved by some kind of music. Music covers the whole gamut of emotions: it can make us feel happy or sad, nostalgic or energetic, and some music is capable of overtaking the mind until it is oblivious to all else. It works on the subconscious, creating or enhancing mood and unlocking deep memories.

ABOVE: The Amati Quartet led by Attila Balogh was one of the foremost chamber ensembles of the 1980s and early '90s. This picture, taken in 1988, shows the quartet giving one of their recitals.

Music is intimately bound up with important events in all our lives. There is hardly a ceremony, whether personal or national, that is not accompanied by music. It may be as simple as the nightly ritual of a mother singing her baby to sleep or as formal as the playing of a national anthem. It may be a spontaneous outpouring of mass emotion, such as the spectators singing before a football game, or it may be a highly wrought and carefully rehearsed performance of massed bands or choirs at a great state wedding or funeral.

The history of music is a part of the history of humanity. Ethnographic studies of ritual among primitive societies have provided plenty of evidence to show that music-making is a basic and universal instinct. Because it is not a concrete art form, we can have no knowledge of what music sounded like in the centuries before

ABOVE: Instruments that were in use in the Iberian peninsula during the 13th century included a portative organ, cornetts, double bladder pipe, bagpipes, lutes and shawm.

ABOVE: A performance of Carmen *at Blackpool Opera House in 1938. Bizet's most successful opera opened in Paris in 1875, during the last year of his short life.*

ABOVE: *This painting by Anne Vallayer-Coster, entitled* The Attributes of Music, *was completed in 1770, just before the French Revolution and the beginning of the Romantic period in music. The instruments (from left to right) are horn, cornemuse, lute, flute and violin.*

it began to be written down or, much later, recorded. But very early written accounts remain, as well as ancient instruments and pictures or carvings showing them in use, to convey some idea of the importance of music to ancient civilizations.

In the 20th century, there has been an unprecedented interest not only in the written remains of the music of previous generations, but in establishing how such music really sounded. As recently as the 18th century, musicians were expected to provide only new works for concert audiences, whereas modern music-lovers are avid for music from all historical periods, often performed on instruments and in styles that attempt to recreate the

effect intended by the composer. There are many ways in which we try to understand the lives of previous generations in order to set our own lives in a secure context, and music is a powerful way of evoking the past.

At the same time, musicians are constantly seeking new forms of expression. As in every other contemporary art form, originality is highly prized in music, and every new development in technology is explored by both composers and players. Recording techniques have made all forms of music instantly available to a universal audience, but have not diminished the demand for live performance, on a wider range of instruments than ever before.

ABOVE: *At the far left of this 15th-century Spanish painting are three singers reading from sheet music, accompanied by a band of six musicians on the right.*

What is Music?

Musick is a tonick to the saddened soul.

ROBERT BURTON (1577–1640), "ANATOMY OF MELANCHOLY"

When asked "What is music?" people will give various replies. Some will try to be scientific and say that music is a succession of sound waves. But that is also the result of scratching a blackboard with the fingernails, which most people would not describe as music.

The making of music is not restricted to human beings. Many animals, such as whales and birds, appear to use music as a means of communication. Natural music was utilized by the French composer, Olivier Messiaen, who used to go out into the countryside to transcribe birdsong, which he incorporated almost note-for-note into his orchestral and piano music. The American composer John Cage believed that the mechanical background sounds of everyday life could be described as music, and other composers have written works

ABOVE: *Although birdsong is not created for a human audience, it is still music to human ears and one of the pleasures of life.*

requiring all kinds of everyday objects to be used as "musical instruments".

Perhaps an easier question would be "What is not music?", though the answers would be just as varied. To some, the sounds made by a heavy metal rock band constitute music, while to others they are just highly amplified noise. Rock music of the 1950s and '60s, such as the songs of Buddy Holly, Jerry Lee Lewis, the Beatles or the Rolling Stones, was adored by its teenage fans but dismissed as unbearable noise by many of their parents. Many of Berlioz's contemporaries harked back to the "good old days" of Bach, while many early 20th-century music-lovers were none too impressed when confronted with the ground-breaking compositions of Stravinsky.

When André Previn was once asked the difference between popular and classical music, his reply was that there

was no such thing as popular or classical music, there was just good music and bad music. While there are many wonderful "classical" works, there are some that are not worth the manuscript paper upon which they were written. Conversely, as there are many popular songs that end up in the dustbin of history, there are many modern tunes that Mozart would have been proud to have written.

Beauty is in the ear, as well as the eye, of the beholder, and the

ABOVE: *Drums are known to all cultures. This sculpture of a figure playing a small frame drum dates from AD 800, and is of the Peruvian Mochica culture.*

ABOVE: *The military drum was originally used as a means of signalling in battle, and was also beaten to set a rhythm that focused the minds of marching troops.*

ABOVE: Rattles made out of gourds are one of the oldest percussion instruments and have been found in every part of the world.

Listening to music is a psychosomatic experience that, as well as promoting harmony and peace, holds a power for inner reassurance and satisfaction which stems from deep within the human spirit. Many people would count themselves the poorer without it. We do not have to go into the science and philosophy of music to find the answer to our question; we simply need to go into our own souls, for that is where music belongs.

appreciation of a piece of music depends to some extent on the listener's culture and upbringing. To someone born in the West, for example, the music of East Asia is mysterious and possibly difficult to listen to, because its idiom is unfamiliar. However, once its context is understood and Western preconceptions about musical conventions are set aside, it becomes more accessible. Even without understanding, all music has the power to exert an effect on the emotions.

ABOVE: While the ringing of a single church bell might not be classified as music, a peal of three or more certainly is.

LEFT: The Portuguese Quineto de Cristal *in 1882. Crystallophones were a 19th-century innovation and for a while were very popular in Europe and the United States. The glasses were arranged in five octaves and struck with small hammers. In time interest flagged, and crystallophones became historical curiosities.*

What is a Musical Instrument?

Music is the sound of universal laws promulgated.

HENRY THOREAU (1817–62)

Musical instruments and their story have always been part of human history, and the story of music begins with the story of humanity. Music, or sound, stood at the cradle of all religions. When primitive humans struck a piece of rock, stone or skin, or blew into an old bone or hollow branch, they perhaps concluded that what they heard was the voice of the object. They therefore assumed that by awakening the "voice" of the object, they could propitiate the unseen nature of which their life was a part.

The rhythmic articulation of time by means of an instrument of some kind is far older than the construction of a true musical instrument. Any objects that early humans happened to pick up when singing or dancing could become sound-producing "musical instruments". Implements created for use exclusively as musical instruments developed only very slowly and many, if not all, early instruments (such as the pot drum) were merely adaptations

LEFT: Very early in human history it was found that a very loud sound could be produced by blowing into a conch shell.

of artefacts already invented for some other purpose. Instruments are the working tools of music; they are the practical devices by which the acoustic properties of nature are managed for the artistic purposes of music that begin with the player. The musical instrument cannot be separated from the musician. In the hands of an incompetent amateur, the finest Stradivari may as well be a block of wood. However, in the hands of a virtuoso, even a crude violin can sound heavenly.

Obviously, we do not know the world's first "tunes". The development of music predates the invention of writing by thousands of years, and there is no way of knowing what

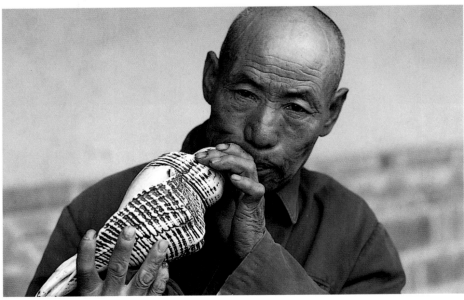

ABOVE: The conch shell is still used as a musical instrument in present-day China; at some temples the shell is blown to announce the beginning of prayers. This conch shell has been fitted with a bamboo mouthpiece.

ABOVE: Rhythm plays an important part in African music. These painted wooden rattles are from Nigeria.

The two elements – the body and the column or box of air – together form a coupled acoustic system.

Other very early instruments include hollow tubes such as reeds and bones, and conch shells, which are believed to have been used as signal instruments. It is possible that these were at first shouted into, until it was discovered that more pleasing sounds could be produced by blowing.

sounds the Neanderthals and early *Homo sapiens* enjoyed. The first "instrument" was certainly the human voice, and ritual chanting is likely to have been accompanied by rhythmic clapping or stamping. This in turn would have led to the striking of an object, such as a convenient log or stone, which could produce a different, and probably a louder, sound.

These early musical instruments, made of naturally sonorous materials, are termed "idiophones". Modern percussion instruments, such as gongs, wood blocks, cymbals and xylophones, are also examples of idiophones. Before long the early musician would have realized that the sound produced by hitting a solid log was different from that produced by a hollow log. The latter is an example of the coupled system of sound production, in which the vibrations are excited in one source with the collaboration of an associated structure – such as the air in the log. This discovery is the foundation of the design of modern wind instruments, such as the horn or oboe, and of the body and soundbox of stringed instruments, such as the violin.

ABOVE: Scrapers are some of the earliest percussion instruments and are known virtually everywhere. These examples from Laos are made from bamboo.

RIGHT: Shakers or rattles come in various shapes and sizes, such as a plastic ball, metal box, wicker basket and natural pod.

ABOVE: Musical bows are known almost all over the world. Often the mouth serves as a resonator while the string is set in vibration by either being tapped with a small stick, as in this example from Colombia, or plucked with a plectrum.

Music of Ancient Civilizations

Provide me now a man that
can play well and bring him to me.

1 SAMUEL 16:17

The earliest archaeological evidence of the use of musical instruments dates from about 3000 BC. By then, the Sumerians, an ancient society living in the fertile crescent of Mesopotamia, had assembled a range of musical instruments, including lyres, harps and reed-pipes, which may have been played as an ensemble. It is also known from written records that they practised antiphonal singing or chanting in their temples. There is no way of knowing what their music sounded like, but it is clear that it was a sophisticated part of Sumerian culture and that it had religious and ceremonial significance.

Egypt

The importance of music in ancient Egypt cannot be overestimated. Music was one of the concomitant joys of life; indeed, as a sign of this, the soundbox of the harp was sometimes fashioned to represent the sacred lotus flower in bloom.

ABOVE: This finely decorated 12th-century BC Egyptian harp is depicted on a tomb painting in Anhour Khaou's tomb in Thebes. In reality the left hand would have played the "back" of the instrument.

From the beginning of the New Kingdom in about 1550 BC, music, which was mainly performed by women, began to play a very prominent part in religious life. Many of the first musicians in the temples were the wives and daughters of priests, the more senior of whom enjoyed a high status second only to that of the king. The instrument of sacerdotal potency and ecclesiastical authority was the *sistrum*, a type of rattle with metal discs strung on a framework of wires, which symbolized divine power. Egyptian temple music was much more than just chanting and jingling. Harps, pandoras and pipes were also used to praise the gods, since it was part of the regular duties of the priest to extol the god in song, and dancing, accompanied by temple musicians, played an important part in many cults.

As time went on and the empire broadened, female slaves from captured nations were brought back to Egypt to serve as musicians. They attended academies of music where they were instructed in both singing and playing instruments. Music in Egypt was of such a high standard that even the Greeks commended it. Instrumental music was important in secular as well as religious life. Musicians played in homes as well as at feasts, in processions and at funeral ceremonies.

The earliest evidence of parallel pipes in Egypt is from about 2700 BC. Divergent pipes came into use — and in

ABOVE: A Theban tomb painting shows a musician playing double shawm pipes and another holding a lute-type instrument.

fact largely replaced the older instrument — in about 1500 BC. The divergent pipes were held with one pipe in each hand, with the proximal ends forming a V. Played exclusively by

ABOVE: This Egyptian wall painting dates from about the 15th century BC and shows a female musician playing an angular harp.

women, each pipe originally had four finger-holes, but later five or six became common. The right hand played the melody while the left pipe sounded a drone accompaniment.

The frame drum arrived in Egypt in about 1550 BC. Also played only by women, the drum accompanied many aspects of Egyptian life, ranging from the cult of Osiris to the dancing of the slaves in the Pharaonic court. Frame drums were similar in

ABOVE: *This Egyptian tomb painting from Thebes, 1425 BC, depicts dancers performing to the music of a double shawm.*

appearance to the modern tambourine, complete with jingling metal rings, discs or pellet bells.

Israel

In ancient Israel, music had a place in almost every activity and at almost every event. The double-headed drum, in the form of the *tof*, is known to have been played in Biblical times, when women used it to accompany their songs and dances. Until about 1000 BC music was the spontaneous outpouring of the people. Later, however, with the establishment of a trained and official body of musicians to lead worship in the temple, it became more formal and more ritualized. Trumpets represented the power of God, and the cantillation of scripture was a potent reminder of the sanctity of God's word, setting it apart from the unsanctified conversation of daily life.

Pipes were also known in Biblical Israel where smaller pipes, called *halil*, were made of cane or metal. The Hebrew prophets plied their trade under the influence of music and were

ABOVE: *A Hebrew coin dating from about AD 135 depicting a lyre.*

often preceded by musicians playing drums, pipes and lyres. (The Latin word *praecinere*, which was used in translations of the scriptures to describe their activity, means both to prophesy and to play the pipes.)

By 200 BC the temple had an established choir of 12 men and a number of boys, who sang to the accompaniment of lyres, pipes and cymbals. Antiphonal singing, which had been a part of Sumerian religious practice and was known to the Egyptians, was adopted by the Jews for the singing of psalms.

ABOVE: *An impression of the Temple of Jerusalem, used as an illustration to a 1732 Bible, showing Solomon dedicating the Temple to the Lord. Music was a feature of the Temple life, and trained musicians were employed to lead the worship.*

ABOVE: *One of the oldest horns still used today is the Jewish shofar. They are made from a billy goat's horn or a ram's horn.*

Classical Greece

That classical Greece was a musical Greece can be seen from the many modern musical words that owe their roots to Greek. Apart from "music" itself, they include "melody", "harmony", "symphony", "orchestra", "organ", "chorus" and "rhythm". The Greek work *mousike* embraced not only what is considered to be music today but also the text and accompanying dance. Greek poets did not just write the words, they also produced the work, trained the singers and dancers (who were mainly amateurs) and directed the accompaniment.

To the Greeks, music, singing and dancing were the main characteristics of a civilized society. They used music for many different purposes, ranging from celebration and the worship of gods to the boosting of morale. Musicians played to workers performing repetitive jobs, such as spinning and weaving, rope-making, grinding corn and treading grapes.

Music also played an important role in military exploits. An essential member of an Athenian trireme's crew was the aulete, or double-pipe player, who played to keep the rowers in time. Spartan armies marched to the sound of the aulos, which kept them at a steady pace without breaking rank. Aulos music also served as a morale booster to the troops, in much the same way as Scottish Highland regiments use the bagpipes today.

Greek contests

The notion of competition was dear to the hearts of the Greeks, and music was no exception. As a focus for competition, the art of *kitharodia* (singing to the self-accompanying of a kithara, or lyre) dates from about 670 BC. Choral contests were instituted about 50 years later, while in 580 BC the Spartans introduced aulos music into their public contests. These festivals were a magnet for performers, who came from great distances to take part.

LEFT: *This Greek terracotta statuette from about 275 BC depicts a female musician playing a kithara. Held at a tilt, the Greeks used the kithara as the primary instrument of classical drama and official cults.*

Kithara versus aulos

During the 5th century BC, musical styles changed radically, as traditions were ousted by new ideas. Plato (c.428–347 BC), who was suspicious of change and denounced the new style as entertaining rather than edifying, complained about the "modern music" of his day, especially the use of the versatile aulos in preference to the kithara, which had also been adapted in an attempt to imitate the aulos and now had an expanded number of strings. Such was Plato's aversion to the aulos that he banned it from his ideal republic, believing that those who could not play the kithara were lacking in education.

Ancient Rome

Music was a rich and constant presence in Roman life. The everyday life of the Romans abounded in songs concerned with all subjects, ranging from reaping to weaving, from weddings to funerals and from love to satire. In the homes of the wealthy, music was often played during dinner, while in the theatre, plays and comedies often included the music of the *tibia* (the Roman version of the aulos) or the hydraulis, or water-pipe. The hydraulis also had a place in the arena, where it was often played with brass instruments, such as the *cornu* and *tuba*, to accompany chariot fights and gladiatorial contests

ABOVE: *That music played an important part in Greek cultural life can be seen from this 5th-century BC vase painting depicting a young man learning to play the lyre.*

ABOVE: *This Etruscan wall painting of the early 5th century BC shows an ambulatory musician playing an aulos, or double pipe. The player was known as an aulete.*

ABOVE: *The Roman Colosseum, seen here as it was in 1835, was a centre of Roman entertainment, much of which was to the accompaniment of music.*

in the arena. Pantomimes, another popular Roman entertainment, regularly incorporated choral singing, instrumental music and dancing.

Cult music in Roman life ranged from elaborate festival performances to accompaniments for the ritual slaughtering of an animal, when the playing of the *tibia* drowned out the cries of the doomed creature. Roman professional musicians had their own associations, which furnished performers for both public and private entertainments: extravagant fees were not unknown for the more popular musicians. Because of their connection with the state cult, these musicians benefited from certain privileges, such as being allowed to roam the streets unhindered, even though they were masked and frequently drunk.

ABOVE: *Second-century Roman mosaic of a hydraulis, the ancestor of the modern organ. Under the pipes was a keyboard that operated perforated sliders. When a key was pressed, a slider was pushed into position to release pressurized air from the wind canal and thereby sound the note. The scene also shows a cornicin, a large and powerful circular horn.*

ABOVE: *First-century BC relief from Denmark depicting Celtic carnyx players. These instruments have a warlike appearance with their bells shaped like grotesque boars' heads.*

India

The origin of the classical music of northern India is shrouded in obscurity. It is a mixture of many ancient cultural influences and the result of a long process of integration of various types of music that makes it one of the world's greatest art forms. The Sanskrit hymns of the *Rig Veda*, composed between the 14th and 10th centuries BC, were – and still are – intoned, and it is possible that the style that is used today has survived virtually unchanged from the time of their composition.

Hindus believe in the power of *samgita*, which encompasses vocal music, instrumental music and dance, to influence the universe and to play a part in freeing the individual from the cycle of birth, death and rebirth.

Raga

The *raag* is the mainstay of northern Indian classical music. There are some 200 main *raga*, each with its own scale pattern and specific rules. Some are linked with specific seasons and times of day, while some are feminine and others masculine.

The performance of a *raag* always follows a set pattern. It begins with the

ABOVE: This 17th-century painting from India depicts lotus-flower dancers performing to the music of a dhola *drum and sitar.*

ABOVE: This painting of Indian marriage celebrations in 1561 shows guests dancing to the rhythm of tambourines, tabla drums, trumpets and cymbals.

alapa, a slow, meditative mood-setter that introduces the notes of the scale in free time and is unaccompanied by drums. This can last several hours, although more usually it is a matter of minutes. The next two sections are the *jorh* and the *jhala*, in which the soloist begins to introduce a rhythmic element and explore complex variations.

The final section, the *gath*, introduces the tabla, a set of two drums played with fingertips and palms. The right-hand drum is the *tabla* and the left-hand one the *bayan*.

Both drum heads are made of skin with a paste of flour and iron filings in the centre. The *tabla* body is made of wood and that of the *bayan* of metal.

Qawwali

Another type of music associated with northern India (and Pakistan) is *qawwali*, a spiritual song that is intended to transport the mystic towards union with the creator. *Qawwali* music can be traced back at least as far as the 9th century, and in its present form to the late 13th century.

A feature of modern *qawwali* is the harmonium, an instrument introduced to India by Christian missionaries around AD 1900. Although the harmonium has the advantage that it does not need constant retuning, it does not meet with universal approval and is banned from All Indian Radio because it does not conform to the traditional flexible intonation of *sruti* music, in which the "same" note can acquire different, but recognizable, pitches in ascent and descent. Neither can the glides and swings of *gamaka*

ABOVE: *The young Indian prince Shri Raga listens to the music of the vina, an instrument characterized by a long string carrier and gourd resonator.*

ABOVE: *This Indian scene depicts the celebrations during the birth of Timur. The musicians are playing instruments such as cymbals, tabla drums and trumpets.*

music be achieved on the harmonium. The celebrated musician Rabindranath Tagore once went as far as to call the harmonium "the bane of Indian music".

Indonesia

The most famous music of South-east Asia is the vibrant, thunderous gamelan, the percussion orchestra, consisting of gong-chimes, metallophones and gongs, which is played in Java and Bali. The tradition goes back well over a thousand years and is believed to predate the Hindu-Buddhist kingdom that was founded in Bali in the 7th century, when the Balinese arrived from Java, having been ousted by the arrival of Islam.

In no other country is music such an integral part of the daily life of the community. There is a greater concentration of orchestras in Bali than

anywhere else in the world. Here, however, as in the rest of the Indonesian archipelago, music does not have a particular religious significance, as it does for Hindus in India.

Spanning over five octaves, gamelan music is like a tree, with some instruments representing the trunk, some the branches and some the flowers. The various instruments of the gamelan include drums, bamboo flutes, cymbals, the *rebab* (an upright fiddle), the great gong, which can be up to 1m/3ft in diameter, and the *trompong* (a row of ten gong chimes set in a wooden frame). One group plays the core melody, while another group stresses this at regular intervals, generally one note in four. A third group expands the core melody with a range of up to three octaves, while a fourth doubles the melody an octave above. As well as these groups, various gongs provide punctuation and drums conduct the rhythmic undercurrent.

Javanese gamelan music is courtly and gentle; the players use padded mallets and the tempo is slow and serene. In Bali, the style is much brighter, louder and more exuberant, using wood or horn hammers and employing a greater dynamic range.

ABOVE: *Balinese gamelan percussion orchestras go back well over a thousand years.* Trompong *players are shown here, with tuned gongs in the background.*

ABOVE: This 18th-century Chinese illustration depicts a man playing a kuchin, *a form of long zither. Traditionally, all dimensions of the* kuchin *have a cosmological meaning.*

China

Chinese music dates back millennia and is one of the oldest and most highly developed of all musical systems. The Chinese concept of music theory is different from that of the West in that the emphasis is placed on the philosophical, cosmological and educational values of music.

Music played an important part in the lives of the ancient Chinese and was closely associated with matters of state and government. To the Chinese, music is part of nature and is organically integrated with the cosmological universe. The earliest Chinese musical notation dates from the 4th century BC, while two centuries earlier Confucius had compiled a book of songs.

Chinese instruments

Since ancient times, Chinese musical instruments have been classified according to their major acoustical material – metal, stone, clay, leather, silk, wood, gourd or bamboo – and how they are played.

The *ch'in*, or classical long zither of China, can be dated back to the T'ang dynasty (AD 618–907). Played with a curved horsehair bow, the modern instrument has no bridges and the stopping places for the ten pairs of silk strings are indicated by ivory discs inlaid into the soundboard. The Thai *chakay*, on the other hand, is played with a single plectrum, usually made of ivory, metal or tortoiseshell.

Another typical traditional Chinese instrument is the *qin*, a seven-stringed

ABOVE: The Chinese yün-luo *gong chimes are of Mongolian origin and consist of between 10 and 24 small bronze bowls suspended vertically in an upright frame.*

zither that has been a favourite subject of poets and painters for over a thousand years. The most delicate instrument in the Chinese repertoire, the *qin*'s ethereal harmonics are a joy to hear.

By the 8th century, the *sheng*, or reed-pipe mouth organ, had 17 pipes. This number became the norm, and today it is tuned chromatically and played polyphonically in triads. Although historically the *sheng* was played at funerals and at court, the *lu-sheng*, traditionally a dance instrument, is now a regular feature of the Chinese orchestra.

The Chinese bronze *bo* cymbal of the Hai Province differs from the Turkish cymbal in that the rim turns out slightly. Used in the Peking opera, these cymbals are about 20cm/8in wide. In the south of the country, in Canton, the cymbal of choice is the *dabo*, held by a small central knob.

Chinese temple and court

The ritual temple music of southern China lives on in the Temple of

ABOVE: Dancers from the traditional Chinese opera in Canton. In spite of the political upheavals in China, Cantonese opera has survived.

ABOVE: *Three female musicians playing Chinese drums and a flute painted on a vase of about 1640.*

Sublime Mysteries in Suzhou. Here the monks play a wide range of music, including pieces for silk and bamboo instruments, flutes and oboes, long trumpets and a whole battery of percussion. In orchestral, ensemble and solo instrumental court music, multipart form dominates. Four stages of court music development are most commonly heard: the introduction, the elucidation of the theme, the transition and the summing-up.

Chinese opera

Kunqu opera, which evolved in the 16th century in Kiangsa province, is a sophisticated opera based on an earlier form of literary drama. Based on written librettos, its tunes are slow-

ABOVE: *A row of Chinese Miao people playing* lu-sheng *mouth organs and long bamboo trumpets.*

moving, with a regular 4:4 rhythm. The principal instruments used in *kunqu* are the *titzu* and *hsiao* (the transverse and end-blown flutes).

In 1790 the visits of various acting companies to Peking, for the 80th birthday celebrations of Emperor Ch'ien-lung, introduced to the capital the operatic styles that were to go on to form the core of "Peking opera". Performed in teahouses, its characters, unlike those of Western opera, are categorized by the kind of person they represent rather than by vocal range. The four main types are: *sheng* (male), *tan* (female), *ching* (warriors and gods) and *ch'ou* (clowns).

ABOVE: *This quintet of Chinese musicans are playing (from left to right) a two-stringed* dutar, paipan *(clapper)*, chettö *(flute)*, sheng *(mouth organ), and* pipa *(lute)*.

ABOVE: *Top row — three trumpets, drum, two* erh-hu *(fiddles)*, kuchin *(zither). Middle row —* yün-luo *(gong chimes)*, lo *(gongs), two* chettö *(flutes), drum. Bottom row — drum, three* pipa *(lutes)*, sheng *(mouth organ)*.

Japan

Japanese musical history can be divided into several stages of development. The first stage is the period up to the 6th century when the country, which had previously been ruled by a number of clans, was developing into an imperial state. Shinto became the state religion, and the music and dance associated with it became the main body of court music. The second stage, which lasted for the next three centuries, saw the introduction of continental Asian music and dance, as well as Buddhism. It was during this time that *gagaku* came into being.

Gagaku court music is the oldest surviving music in Japan and has been preserved at the imperial court and at a few temples. Nearly 20 different types of instrument are used in *gagaku*, including the *sho* (a reed-pipe mouth organ), flute, drums, gongs and chimes. The various types of *gagaku* include *kangan* (instrumental ensembles), *bagaku* (dance music) and the ritual music for Shinto ceremonies.

ABOVE: Japanese girls playing a samisen *(a guitar-like instrument with three strings) and a* koto *(a 13-stringed zither).*

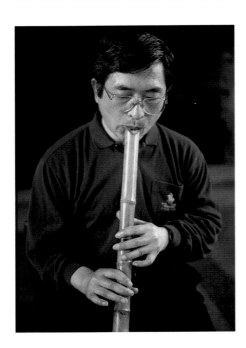

ABOVE: The shakuhachi, *a bamboo end-blown flute with five finger-holes. The instrument originated in China and was taken to Japan by Buddhist priests in AD 935.*

The third stage in the development of Japanese music came in the period between 900 and 1573. It was then that the theatrical form called *noh* was developed. A marriage of drama, theatre, music and dance, the beauty of *noh* lies in its refined symbolism and sophistication.

The last period saw the Japanese version of the zither, the *koto*, come into fashion. The *koto*, which has 13 silk strings that pass over movable bridges, is played mainly by women, who wear three long ivory plectra on the right hand: one on the thumb, one on the index finger and the third on the middle finger. The left hand is used to dampen the strings and change the pitch. Other Japanese classical instruments of the period include the *shakuhachi* (bamboo flute) and the *biwa* (lute).

Korea

The music of Korea can be traced back over 5000 years and is based on two modes, the *p'yongjo* (common in court music, such as *aak*, and folk songs) and the more widely used *kyemyonjo*. The greatest period of musical development in Korea was during the reign of King Sejong (1418–50). Not only did Sejong reputedly devise the Korean alphabet,

ABOVE: A Korean musician playing the koto, *a kind of zither.*

ABOVE: A Korean musician playing the soduang, *a two-stringed instrument with a round resonating box covered with leather at one end and open at the other to admit the neck.*

but he also created an advanced system of musical notation.

Korea treasures its musical heritage, and classical Korean music is actively promoted at the Seoul National Classical Music Institute, where leading musicians are classed as national treasures.

The Korean tradition of *samulnori* drumming goes back at least a thousand years. Played by a quartet of musicians on drums and gongs, *samulnori* originated in the rural farmers' dances that are still performed by dancers wearing hats with long ribbons that swirl into spectacular shapes as the dancers move their heads.

Korea is also known for large orchestras of flutes, oboes and bronze and stone chimes that still play on the first Sunday in May at the ancestral shrine in Seoul. This is a very colourful sight: the massive frames of the chimes are richly decorated with dragons and birds, and contrast with the bold, bright costumes of the musicians.

The *kayagum*, a 12-stringed zither, provides the accompaniment to vocal music and is also played as a solo instrument accompanied by the *changgo* (an hourglass-shaped drum) and the *taegum* (a wooden flute). It has been said that the beauty of *kayagum* music is that when a melody makes a leap down it sounds like a waterfall, and when it reaches the bottom the note vibrates in the same way that water bubbles at the foot of a waterfall.

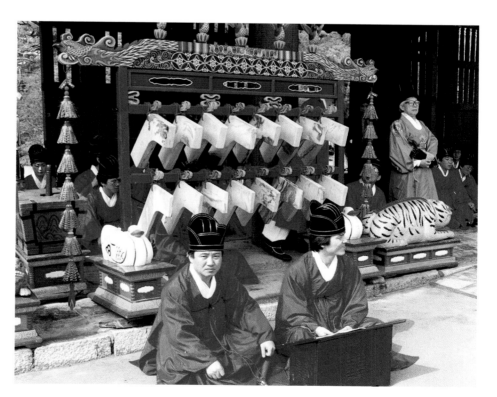

ABOVE: A Korean cholgo, *or temple drum, resting on a wooden stand shaped like a tortoise. In ancient mythology the world was deemed to rest on a tortoise.*

ABOVE: A Korean honga *orchestra playing Confucian ritual music. A feature of the orchestra is the* pyongyong *or stone chimes. Sixteen tuned stones are freely suspended in a wooden frame in two rows and are struck with a mallet made of cow horn; they continue to emit a clear sound for several minutes.*

European Music in the First Millennium

The chime of minstrel music, dulcimer, and harp with many strings,
a pleasant dinning makes to him who heareth not distinct the note.

DANTE ALIGHIERI (1265–1321)

During the first millennium there seems to have been little innovation in Western music, but an exception was the introduction of Gregorian chant in church services. This was a reshaping of the older Roman chant, in which melodies were sung to the accompaniment of a sustained note on, it is believed, a stringed instrument.

ABOVE: *Gregorian church chant from* De Harmonica Institutione *of Benedictine Abbot Regino von Prum,* AD 915.

Pope Gregory I (AD 590–604) is said to have ordered the collection and codifying of the plainsong used in the Roman church, and his name became associated with this form. The chants were written down by monks, using a form of letter notation above the lines of text. The appearance of "neumes" in the 9th century led to a more exact method of defining pitch.

The teaching of the chant was put on an official footing in the church by Pope Vitalian (AD 657–72), who was instrumental in founding the Scola Cantorum, based on the model of the Byzantine court. It was under Charlemagne (AD 742–814) that the Gregorian chant became widely used. With the associated antiphonal psalmody (a liturgical chant that was sung in association with a psalm), it was sung all over Europe.

The chant's system of eight tones was directly related to the eight church modes. It was for unaccompanied voice for, according to St Aloysius, any form of musical instrument was a tool of the devil, while St Augustine expressed concern over the seductive "peril of pleasure" created by beautiful singing. However, in the 9th century Benedictine culture began to include the advancement of music. The monastic revival of the late 10th century saw the gradual introduction of organs into churches, although these were not originally used as an accompaniment to the singing, but rather served for signalling purposes, both to call people to worship and to denote points of the service, like the bell at the elevation of the host.

ABOVE: *This 8th-century illumination shows King David playing the crwth, accompanied by four horns and two dancers. Scribes are writing down the words.*

ABOVE: This drawing from the late 10th century shows Pope Gregory dictating to Deacon Peter.

Secular music

Songs were, of course, also sung outside the church, especially on long journeys such as those to the various crusades and on pilgrimages. It is known that music played a role in the building of Notre Dame (1163–1250), when the workers sang as they worked. Indeed, at this time Paris was the musical centre of the Western world, and its university was one of the first officially to teach music.

One of the leading French musicians of the time was Léonin, who was active in Paris between 1163 and 1190. Léonin played a part in the early development of polyphony, by composing *organum* (a medieval form of part-writing) for two voices taken from the solo portions of graduals and alleluias for all the principal feasts of the ecclesiastical year. The main significance of this work was the introduction of a rational system of rhythm into polyphonic music. After Léonin's death, his work was modified by his pupil Pérotin.

This was the age of the peripatetic musician. There were two main classes: the troubadour (a cultivated travelling musician, generally of noble birth) and the minstrel (a professional entertainer, of more lowly birth). In Germany, the 12th, 13th and 14th centuries saw the heyday of the *Minnesinger*, the German equivalent of the French troubadours. All these singers were both poets and composers of their own songs, for at this time very few sang other people's music.

ABOVE: While peripatetic minstrels were a feature of the medieval landscape, some houses retained their own musicians. This trio is playing a tabor, pipe, small harp and lute.

ABOVE: A group of four early 14th-century German troubadours playing the unusual combination of two trumpets, drum and bagpipes.

Structuring Music

Music is the reaching out towards the utmost realities by means of ordered sound.

RALPH VAUGHAN WILLIAMS (1872–1958)

The Greek mathematician Pythagoras (c.570–500 BC) carried out the earliest known acoustical experiments. Knowing that the shorter the length of a string the higher the pitch will be, Pythagoras demonstrated that pleasing intervals were sounded when a string is divided into certain ratios. When the length is halved, an octave is formed; when it is reduced to two-thirds the pitch is raised by a perfect fifth; when reduced to three-quarters it gives the perfect fourth. The same applies to the length of a column of air in a wind instrument. Over the years the remaining intervals of the scale were filled in with tones and semitones and thus began the gradual progress that culminated in the recognition of

ABOVE: The frontispiece of Franchino Gaffari's Theorica Musicæ *(1492) showing Pythagoras playing instruments such as tuned bells, musical glasses and pipes.*

ABOVE: The number of lines in each staff varied. This music from the Furtmeyer Missal, *written for the Archbishop of Salzburg in 1481, is on a four-line staff.*

tonality, or key. This concept has since remained the basis of musical composition in the West, though smaller intervals, called "microtones", occur in other musical cultures, such as in Indian music, and have been used by some experimental composers of the 20th century.

Harmonic vibrations

It was not until the 17th century that the relationship between the frequency of vibration and the length, diameter, tension and density of the string was established. It was Galileo (1564–1642) who discovered that if either the string's thickness or length is doubled, the frequency of vibration, and consequently the pitch, is halved. For this reason, bass strings can be

made thicker than treble ones – if they were all of the same thickness the lowest string in a piano would have to be about 6.5m/7 yards long.

Notation

The staff originated in medieval Europe as a means of recording plainsong. At first it was a single line around which the neumes, like small ticks, were placed to show the approximate melodic and rhythmic shape. Additional lines were added in the 11th century and the spaces, as well as the lines, were used to position the notes. By the 16th century, today's exactitude of recording pitch was arrived at when a pair of five-line staves became the norm, arranged as a "grand staff" with the top five lines

ABOVE: This 12th-century plainchant from the Missale Romanum *shows the neumatic notation of the day. There is only one line of "notes" which rise and fall.*

ABOVE: This manuscript, entitled Sumer is Icumen In *(c.1240), uses a six-line staff.*

forming the treble clef and the bottom five lines the bass clef.

The *flat* sign, which originally applied only to the B line, originated as a lower case *b*. The natural sign was a square gothic *b* that was later modified to give today's symbol. The *sharp* sign originated as a cancelled *b* with a stroke through it.

Tonic solfa

The tonic solfa had its roots in the 11th century when a monk named Guido d'Arezzo devised a way to help singers learn a new melody by relating its notes to the pitches of certain syllables associated with a well-known tune. The tune he chose was a Latin hymn in which the first syllables of the first six lines were each set one note higher than the previous one. Using the first syllable of each line as his model, he came up with Ut, Re, Mi, Fa, So, La. Apart from the change of Ut to Doh and the addition of Ti, these syllables are still used today.

ABOVE: Guido d'Arezzo (991—after 1033), seen here on the left, is remembered for his development of a system of precise pitch notation through lines and spaces as well as for propagating the method of sight-singing that has evolved into the tonic solfa.

Strings

There's not a string attuned to mirth
but has its chord in melancholy.

THOMAS HOOD (1799–1845)

If we believe Greek legend, it was the twang of a bowstring that first made the god Apollo aware of the musical properties of a vibrating string. The fundamental pitch at which a stretched string, held in tension between two points, is heard, depends upon its length, thickness, weight and tension, together with the properties of the soundbox or soundboard. The frequency at which a given string will vibrate is inversely proportional to its length, proportional to the square of its tension and inversely proportional to the square of its mass, while the amplitude varies with the energy imparted and transmitted.

Materials

A string for a musical instrument may be made of any material that can produce a musical sound when it is held under tension and plucked, bowed or struck. Although most early

ABOVE: *A mid 13th-century fiddler playing with a large arched bow. The stick extends beyond the end of the hair, the projection serving as a handle.*

ABOVE: *These two putti, one playing a small harp and the other the portative organ, are from the frieze of musical angels in the Chapel of Isotta degli Atti in Rimini.*

strings were made out of gut or silk, many other materials have also been used, such as gold wire strings found in Persia dating from the 5th century BC. More recently, nylon or steel strings have become common, and many strings are bound with fine wire.

Gut strings were made from the guts of lambs, from seven to eight months old. After cleansing and pickling in an alkaline solution, the guts were twisted together under tension before being polished with pads made of hair. The final diameter of the string was determined by the number of guts used, which ranged from two for the smallest mandolin string, up to 120 for a double bass.

Methods of string-playing

There are three ways to excite the string: plucking, bowing or striking. Although plucking excites an active range of high harmonics, they are short-lived. Plucking imparts energy by a single impulse and there is no means of maintaining the vibration. The optimum place to pluck a string is about one-seventh of its length from the end, as this will give the best selection of harmonics as well as amplitude. If the string is plucked either with the fingernails or with a plectrum, it is displaced at a sharp angle and a bright sound is produced, as opposed to the duller sound made when it is plucked with the pad of the finger or thumb.

ABOVE: *This 13th-century illustration of King David shows him playing a harp whose arching neck terminates in an open-mouthed zoomorphic head.*

A more solid sound is obtained by striking the string (as on a piano or a dulcimer). A struck string vibrates longer, giving a slower decay in the upper harmonics. However, in the stiffer and tenser lower strings of the piano the vibrations tend not to subdivide indefinitely into the shorter lengths, causing the upper harmonics to be weaker, with most of the energy going into the lower harmonics. Like the plucked string, the struck string has only a single impulse for each note sounded.

One of the more pleasing sounds achieved from a string is by using a bow, which maintains the supply of energy for vibration and thus permits the playing of sustained notes. The sound depends on the position of the bow and the width of the hair brought into operation. Different sounds can be produced by bowing slowly with the full width of the hair, bowing near the centre of the string, bowing swiftly with the edge of the hair, or bowing near the end of the string.

Types of string

TOP ROW, FROM LEFT TO RIGHT: *Until the 1970s many violinists used gut strings exclusively, but as the high-tensioned E string had a tendency to break easily, it was replaced by wire.*

Viola strings are usually made of gut. The lower two, or sometimes all, are wire-wound.

Harp strings are like piano strings, except that they are plucked.

Most classical guitar strings are made of nylon. They are usually sounded with the left side of the fingernails, but some players prefer to use the right side of their nails.

BOTTOM ROW, FROM LEFT TO RIGHT: *Acoustic guitar strings can be made of gut or steel, played with fingers or plectrum.*

Mandolin strings are laid in four courses of two. Tuned to the same pitch as the violin, the strings are played with a plectrum.

The strings of the sitar are carried over two bridges, first the "small" bridge and then the "main" bridge. Tuning is achieved by the pegs, and beads are used for fine tuning.

The strings of a piano range in thickness from very thin top strings to the thickly wound bass strings shown here.

Bows

The Devil rides upon a fiddlestick.

WILLIAM SHAKESPEARE (1564–1616), "HENRY IV PART 1"

The use of a bow as an instrumental accessory originated in the Byzantine Empire but, because of the weak tone of early bowed instruments compared with that of plucked ones, it was considered to be worthy only of the "common people". It was introduced into Europe in the 11th century by the Islamic conquerors of Spain, and within 100 years the bow had become known and was being used over most of western Europe.

Early bows

The form of the early bows, which were in the shape of fully drawn hunting bows, differed greatly from those in use today. As its name suggests, the bow originally had a convex shape, designed to hold a band of horsehair under tension so that it could be drawn across the strings of an instrument to set up a sustained vibration. In time the bowed shape became longer and more slender,

ABOVE: *Detail from Bellini's* Maria with Child and Saints *(1505) showing an angel playing a large viol with a bow that shows the trend for the arch to become lower.*

ABOVE: *Early bows, as the name implies, were similar in appearance to bows used in archery, with a high arched stick.*

though it was still convex. By the 12th century, bows with a curve at one end – a type still occasionally found in eastern Europe – had become popular.

The horsehair was tied directly to the stick at both ends, and the player varied the tension while using the bow, to facilitate the playing of single strings or multiple stopping (drawing the string over more than one string simultaneously). To allow for this, the bow was held in the fist and pressure was exerted on the hair with the fingers.

Early bows differed greatly in size; they could be as small as 20cm/8in. In the 16th century, the violin was becoming a popular instrument for dance music, and short bows of about 35cm/14in were adequate for this purpose. Concert bows were substantially longer, and some were more than twice the

size of the instrument being played. Some bows had sticks that extended well beyond the end of the hair, the projection serving as a handle.

Modern bow

In the second half of the 18th century the bow underwent a number of radical changes, principally to suit the development of the violin as a solo, virtuoso instrument. The new designs were the work of François Tourte (1747–1835) and Wilhelm Cramer (1745–99). Cramer designed a concave bow, which quickly led to the abandonment of the convex version. Tourte widened the ribbon of hair to about 1cm/⅓in, composed of 150–200 strands cut

ABOVE, FROM TOP TO BOTTOM: *The ribbon of the modern violin bow is made of horsehair. The viola bow is similar to the violin bow but is slightly larger.*

ABOVE: *The standard length of the cello bow is about 68cm/27in.*

ABOVE: *The double bass bow is shorter and heavier than the cello bow, and can be held either from above or underneath.*

ABOVE: *The insipid tone of early bowed instruments was due to the bow stick being weak. The player could not tighten the hair and so the strings could not be firmly gripped.*

from white horses' tails. He attached this to a strong, movable frog, so that the tension on the hair could be adjusted and set at the beginning of the performance. The bow could now be held lightly with the fingertips, instead of being grasped firmly in the whole hand. This allowed much greater flexibility and delicacy of playing style, which facilitated the rise of the great 18th and 19th-century violin virtuosi.

ABOVE: *This illustration of 1830 shows the "old" and "new" styles of bowing the violin.*

Bach bow

The Bach bow was created by Knud Vestergard of Viby, Denmark to play the Bach solo violin sonatas "precisely as written", and is associated with the violinist Telmányi. The bow has a very high arch, with as much as 10cm/4in separating the bow stick and the hair at the highest point. When playing on individual strings the bow hair can be tightened by a lever worked by the thumb. By loosening the hair the player is able to encompass all the strings, and thus sustain multiple stops continuously. The creation, however, succeeds in playing Bach's music only as imagined by the bow's 20th-century inventor – not as Bach intended or heard it.

Tourte also fixed the length of the violin bow at about 75cm/30in and the playing hair at about 65cm/25in. To make the stick he chose red Brazilian pernambuco wood for its combination of strength and lightness. These innovations in design established the form of the standard modern bow, which is sometimes referred to as the "Tourte bow".

ABOVE: *Early 14th-century fiddler playing with a high arched bow. The player is gripping the bow where the stick extends beyond the end of the hair.*

ABOVE: *The modern bow, as used by American violinist Isaac Stern (born 1920). Stern's playing – particularly of the Barber and Bruch concertos – has thrilled audiences for over 50 years.*

Reeds

There's music in the singing of a reed.

LORD BYRON (1788–1824)

The sound of a reed instrument is initiated by the vibration of the reed, which sets up the vibration of the air column in the tube of the instrument. Reed instruments fall into two main categories, according to the use of the reed: they are known as "bleating" and "free". The ancient Greek aulos was an early bleating reed-pipe and is known to date back to at least 2800 BC.

Reed preparation

In ancient Greece, cane for making aulos reeds was cut during early summer, when at its most elastic,

and laid out to season in the open. It was scraped and cleaned during the following spring, and cut into segments at the nodes: each internode furnished two reeds. Segments closer to the root were suitable for the left-hand pipe of the aulos and those closer to the tip of the stem were used for right-hand pipes. This is an indication that the left-hand pipe was the lower pitched of the two.

Today, reeds are still cut from the stem of the large semi-tropical grass *Arundo donax* or *Arundo sativa*, commonly, but inaccurately, called cane. The plants are specially cultivated in parts of Spain and southern France. They are now factory-cut, but many players learn to cut their own, a very skilled art. Various attempts to find substitutes for *Arundo donax* have been made from time to time, and materials as diverse

ABOVE: A single reed.

as silver and whalebone have been tried, but have never been successful. A recent development has been the use of manmade fibres, although the general consensus is that artificial reeds sound coarser than those made from natural cane.

Bleating reeds

A reed that beats against a surface is known as a "bleating" reed, and instruments that work on this principle can also be subdivided according to whether they use single or double reeds. The single reed, typified by that

ABOVE: A selection of different types of single reeds (from top to bottom) — clarinet, alto saxophone, tenor saxophone and baritone saxophone.

ABOVE: A selection of oboe double reeds — two baroque, classical, classical oboe d'amore, modern oboe, modern oboe d'amore, two cor anglais and bass oboe.

ABOVE: *The idea for a reed instrument must have evolved from people finding that blowing on a blade of grass produced a sound. This engraving is from Bonanni's* Gabinetto Armonico *(1723).*

ABOVE: *The various stages in making a reed. Top — the cut cane. Middle — the cane is cut in half, split and the scrape is shaped. Bottom — the final stages in shaping, trademarking and packaging the reed.*

of the clarinet, is a narrow slip cut to length, flattened on the inner side, and on the other side scraped down to a feather edge at one end. It is fastened to the mouthpiece of the instrument and vibrates against it.

The double bleating reed, typified by that of the bassoon, is made up of two slips of "cane", hollowed out on the inside until quite thin and again scooped to a feather edge on the outside. The two slips are then bound together and mounted in a short metal tube, known as the "staple".

Free reeds

The free reed is found mainly in certain organ pipes and bellows-blown instruments such as the harmonium and accordion. It is also used in the harmonica (mouth organ) as well as in the traditional Chinese *sheng*. The pitch

of the reeds, which are fastened over slots cut into the metal frame, can be lowered by filing near the fixed end, or raised by filing near the free end. A major development in the history

of the accordion was the introduction by firms such as Höhner, founded in Trossingen in 1857, of high-tempered steel reeds, which helped to ensure the instrument's popularity.

LEFT: *Although most professional oboe players make their own reeds, the process takes time and skill, and ready-made reeds are available.*

Valves

*The irremediable vulgarity of the cornet's timbre
has kept it away from the symphonic orchestra.*

MICHAEL BRENET

In 1815 a notice appeared in the *Allgemeine Musikalische Zeitung* that was to change the evolution of the brass instrument forever. Heinrich Stölzel, a 38-year-old horn player in the orchestra of Prince von Pless in Upper Silesia, announced that he had produced a horn on which a scale of nearly three octaves could be achieved by means of two airtight valves that were pressed down by "piano keys" and returned by springs. Although Stölzel is often regarded as the sole inventor of the valve, it is believed that he was ably assisted by his fellow musician Friedrich Blühmel.

ABOVE: *An 1848 view inside Adolph Sax's factory showing brass instruments being produced.*

Function of the valve

The purpose of the valve is to admit vibrating air into, or exclude it from, auxiliary tubing of sufficient length to lower the basic pitch of an instrument by a certain musical interval. The length of this tubing must be in proportion to that of the main tubing; the length for a whole tone is about one-eighth of the whole and that for

ABOVE: *A trumpet has three piston valves and two finger grips.*

a semitone about one-fifteenth. On a three-valved instrument the depression of the first valve lowers the pitch of the instrument a semitone; depression of the second lowers it a whole tone; and the third an extra semitone. This combination, with different harmonics obtainable by altering the pressure of the lips, allows a complete scale to be played.

Once the valve has been depressed and released it is instantly returned by a spring; the most common method is to have the spring push the valve back up from the bottom.

Although valves are traditionally made of brass, sometimes plated with silver or nickel, other materials have been used. The Boosey "Solbron" was made of bronze while, for its

tubas, the Swiss Hirstbrunner Company produces the "Trypen" valve, which is made from a combination of brass and plastic. The most efficient valves, however, are those made from "Monel", which is a copper-nickel alloy.

Piston valve

In the years between 1820 and 1840, various experiments resulted in the production of two different types of valve: piston and rotary. In 1835 Wilhelm Wieprecht produced his robust short-stroke Berliner Pumpen

LEFT: *The piston valve is returned to its open position by means of the spring, while the coquilles connect with and admit air into the additional tubes that change the pitch of the instrument.*

ABOVE: Each piston valve has its own tuning slide; the further out the slide is pulled, the lower the note produced.

valves. These had horizontal passageways and were used on all types of brass instruments. In 1839 this was improved upon by Etienne-François Périnet, who made a lighter and narrower valve, in which the coquilles were positioned obliquely in the piston. The main advantage of this valve was that it could be worked faster and the air column moved around a curve instead of, as with Wieprecht's valve, around a 90° bend.

ABOVE: Tuba valves are, of necessity, bigger than trumpet valves and as such take longer to return to the open position after being depressed. This means that as a rule the tuba does not play fast music and is usually not expected to play notes shorter than semi-quavers.

ABOVE: The flugelhorn uses piston valves to produce the different pitches required.

Today, many euphoniums and tubas have four valves. The extra valve not only helps to keep the instrument in tune, but also allows the musician to play lower harmonics. Most makers place the extra valve at the back of the instrument, where it is operated by the first finger of the left hand. However, the Yamaha Company of Japan positions its four valves together, parallel with the bell, and all are operated by the fingers of the right hand.

Rotary valve

Although several people experimented with rotary valves, Joseph Riedel of Vienna produced the design that is used in modern horns. Riedel's valve, which was patented in 1832, has two passageways that pass through the rotor, one on each side of a central spindle. When the valve is operated the cylinder rotates through 90°, directing the air into the valve tube much as water flows through a tap.

ABOVE: Close-up view of the rotary valves on a French horn. Rotary valves were invented by Joseph Riedel in 1832.

Drum Heads and Sticks

The noisy drum has nothing in it, but mere air.

THOMAS FULLER (1608–61)

When a drum is struck, the membrane vibrates in both a circular and a segmental pattern, producing a fundamental tone and various harmonic overtones, the number and strength of which affect the timbre of the instrument. The timbre and apparent pitch of the drum also vary according to the type of beater used, the degree of hardness or softness of the beater and its contact area on the drum head. Hard beaters produce high overtones while light ones have virtually none.

The sound of the drum is also influenced by the place where the membrane is struck. If this is at the edge, high overtones will be elicited, while if it is hit at or near the centre, deeper tones will predominate. Percussionists get to know their instruments and know the place on the membrane (the "beating spot") that is best to strike.

Drum heads

The first drum heads were made of hide, but animal skin reacts strongly to changes in atmospheric humidity,

RIGHT: *One of 12 musical angels painted by the Italian painter Fra Angelico in 1433. This one is playing a drum with a parchment head.*

ABOVE: *The Indian* dhol *has two indefinitely pitched heads, each with a loud, deep sound. The drum is used to herald public announcements and to lead processions.*

so today artificial materials such as plastic are used. Early side drum heads were tensioned with ropes drawn into V-shapes, with leather buffs at the point of each V which were drawn to tighten the ropes and thus increase the tension. Other methods were introduced later, the most usual being rods with screw nuts. Until World War II, most drums were single-tensioned, with one screw working on both heads. However, as most players prefer to have one head tighter than the other, double-tensioning was introduced, whereby each head is separately controlled by rods that screw into blocks halfway down the shell.

Drum sticks

There are three main types of beater head: hard, medium and soft. The choice of suitable sticks or beaters depends on the tonal effects required, as different types of stick or beater will influence the sound of the drum in three ways: volume, tone and attack. The harder the head of the beater, the louder the sound will be.

All drums have a sound-spectrum: they will produce a wide range of different sounds. A thin, hard-headed stick will bring out the higher sounds, causing the drum to sound bright and clear. A soft-headed beater, on the other hand, will elicit the low tones, producing a mellow, muffled sound. Hard beaters will produce a crisp,

ABOVE: *The military side drum is covered with a head of either calfskin or plastic.*

Timpano, timbale and bass drum heads

ABOVE: A timpano with a plastic head. The timpanist tunes the head to the required pitch by means of a foot pedal, a device that was invented in 1881 by Carl Pittrich.

ABOVE: The screw-tensioned heads of timbales are made of plastic and usually tuned a certain distance apart. They are usually played in pairs with wooden sticks.

ABOVE: This military bass drum has a plastic head. Plastic, unlike organic hide, is not affected by moisture and is therefore suitable for use in military parades in wet weather.

well-defined attack, while soft beaters, which tend to have larger contact areas, will give a less distinct delivery, the sound being smothered by the spread of the beater head at each contact with the drum.

In general, hard wooden sticks are used for snare drums, while sticks with hard to medium rounded heads (of wood, woven yarn, plastic or hard rubber) are used for playing xylophones and vibraphones. Instruments such as the marimba are played with soft-headed beaters, while timpani can be played with sticks in three degrees of hardness, according to whether the core is covered with soft, medium or hard felt. Some timpani sticks are double-ended, with felt heads on one end and wooden ball-shaped heads on the other, so that the sticks can be quickly reversed as required by the music.

BELOW, FROM LEFT TO RIGHT: Sticks for the bass drum, glockenspiel, vibraphone, rototom, timpani and xylophone.

ABOVE: A percussionist may need a number of different sticks and beaters for a given performance. A selection of sticks is shown here in a container suitable for travelling.

Keyboard Keys and Hammers

Seated one day at the organ I was weary and ill at ease,
And my fingers wandered idly, Over the noisy keys.

ADELAIDE A. PROCTER (1825–64), "A LOST CHORD"

Early European keyboards were simple devices with heavy levers operated with the hands rather than the fingers. The spacing between the keys on early organs, the oldest keyboard instruments, was the same as that for the pipes, sometimes as much as 10cm/4in. Up to the 13th century keyboards were diatonic, with C as the first key. When the B flat was added, this was not intended only for the playing of melodies but also as an aid to transposition. Used solely to accompany plainsong, early keyboards had a range not exceeding two octaves – matching that of the voices of the monks. In the 14th century, with the development of polyphony, the keyboard compass began to widen, and

ABOVE: *Detail from* Court Concert at Prince Bishop's of Lüttich in Seraing Palace *by Paul Delcloche (1753). This finely decorated piano still lacks a pedal.*

by 1330 most of the chromatic keys that we know today had been added.

Closed-case keyboard instruments, in which the tuned strings are held taut above a sounding board, include those in which the strings are plucked, such as the harpsichord and spinet, and pianos, in which they are hammered. Since the harpsichord player cannot control the force with which the strings are plucked, larger instruments frequently have a second keyboard that can be used to add variety in weight and sound quality. Both piano and harpsichord keyboards have the keys for the diatonic notes at the front, with the keys for the other five notes of the chromatic scale (the black keys) arranged between and a little behind them. The modern full-size piano keyboard has 88 notes.

ABOVE: *The piano keyboard consists of white and black keys. The white keys are the natural notes while the black ones cover the sharps and flats.*

ABOVE: *Detail of the strings of a grand piano made by the Berlin firm of Bechstein.*

ABOVE: The piano hammers hit the strings from underneath. Over the strings is the row of dampers that stop the sound.

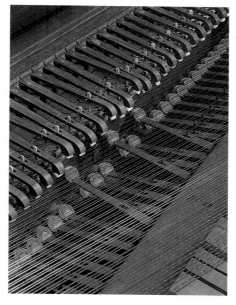

ABOVE: The hammers of a square piano, in which the strings are arranged horizontally in a rectangular box-like case.

ABOVE: Interior view of an upright piano.

Hammerheads

Several materials have been used for covering piano hammerheads. Early German pianos used buckskin, but this suffered from variations in thickness and elasticity. Early 19th-century leather-covered hammers were light, but as the mass and tension of the strings increased, makers tried to increase the weight of the hammers by loading them with lead. This, however, also increased the effort required to play the instrument and the method was quickly abandoned. In England, a coarse woollen cloth was tried, but it was clear that a softer, more durable

material was needed and in 1826 Jean-Henri Pape patented felt hammers that were a blend of sheep's wool and rabbit fur. This material remained in contact with the string for longer before rebounding, thereby producing a fuller, rounder tone than that achieved by leather.

Bass hammerheads, which are much thicker and heavier than those that strike the treble strings, are pricked with holes to give them a softer texture. The softer the felt the more slowly it rebounds from the string, thus preventing unwanted high overtones. If the felt is untoned it produces an uneven tone, many of the notes sounding duller or brighter than their neighbours.

Piano action

In a grand piano the hammers strike the strings from underneath and fall back by gravity, the action being, therefore, more responsive than in the upright piano, which has to rely on springs to return the hammers. For this reason the quick repetition of notes on the grand piano is generally

more efficient than on the upright. Quick repetition is also facilitated by the escapement, which allows the hammer to rebound from the string and be ready for the same note to be struck again. By catching the hammer before it reaches its original position, the note can be repeated more quickly than would be possible if the hammer travelled the full distance.

ABOVE: Clavichord hammers are responsive to the force of the player's finger movements.

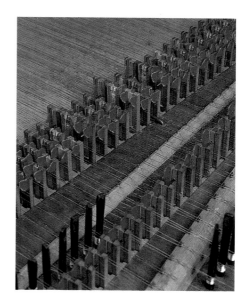

ABOVE: Interior view of a harpsichord, showing the jacks under the strings.

Evolution of the Orchestra

Musicke is said to be the rejoycing of the heart:
Musicke comforteth the mynde and feareth the enimie.

JOHN FLORIO (1553–1625), "FIRST FRUTES"

The word "orchestra" comes from the Greek, and originally meant the place where the Greek chorus sang and danced. In the Roman theatre, this space was reserved for the seats of senators. Later it was applied to the stage itself. The term was revived in the late 17th century, and by the early 18th century it had been applied in France to the players themselves.

The roots of the modern orchestra go back to the 16th-century consorts employed in noble households, and to the groups of instrumentalists

ABOVE: *Five musical angels from a triptych by Hans Memling painted in about 1480. The instruments depicted are the psaltery, tromba marine, lute, sackbut and tenor shawm.*

ABOVE: *Fifteenth-century Italian fresco of an angel playing a sackbut — a standard instrument in civic bands at this time.*

especially assembled for important occasions such as royal weddings and funerals. During the 17th century the composition of orchestras varied from place to place: strings were preferred in Italy, France and England, whereas the German courts preferred brass ensembles.

Municipal consorts

Musicians were employed by European civic authorities from as early as the 13th century. The first town known to have availed itself of a regular musician was Brunswick, Germany, in 1227. Florence in Italy and Ypres in Belgium had civic musicians by 1291 and 1297 respectively. In Germany, town musicians were known as *Stadtpfeifer* (town pipers) and in England as waits.

The duties of these official musicians were many and varied, ranging from civic functions to church festivals and celebrations.

English waits

The word "wait" derives from either Anglo-Saxon *wacian* or Old High German *Wahta*, both meaning "watch" or "guard". In time the word began to be used for the shawm, the instrument played by the watch, which was generally dubbed the "wait pipe". Many English towns possessed waits at an early date, York (1272) and Norwich (1288) being among the first recorded. The musical part of the waits' duties grew and by the mid 14th century three waits were included in the Royal Band of Edward III. By the

15th century most towns employed waits, whose main function it was to attend the mayor on ceremonial occasions and, in some towns, to play in the streets at night.

Most bands of waits performed only in their local area, but some travelled farther afield. In 1589 Sir Francis Drake employed five Norwich waits, equipped with their shawms, trombone and recorder, to provide shipboard entertainment for his expedition to Lisbon – forming what must have been the first ship's band.

German Turmmusik

Although Germany had had *Stadtpfeifer* since the 13th century, in the 16th century a phenomenon known as *Turmmusik* (tower music) became common. This was music played from the church or town-hall tower. The repertory of these bands consisted in the main of harmonized chorales but also included occasional *Turmsonaten*, which were played by instruments such as cornetts, trombones and trumpets, in four or five-part harmony.

ABOVE: Detail from a mural The Nuremberg Town Band, *painted in about 1500 by Albrecht Dürer. Pictured are two trombones, two cornetts, two shawms and a drum. Later that century a greater variety of instruments was in use, including recorder, viol, fiddle, cornett, guitar, lute, bandora and bagpipes.*

Sixteenth-century consort

The main instrument of a medieval consort was the shawm, a double-reed woodwind instrument that was first used in western Asia for dance and ceremonial music, and was brought to Europe by returning crusaders in the 12th century. The forerunner of the oboe, it had a piercing, brilliant tone, which made it especially suited for playing outdoors. It was initially used in folk music, and much later in opera.

Like its eastern prototype, the eight-holed European shawm was made from a single, conically bored piece of hardwood, terminating in a bell.

By the beginning of the 16th century shawms were being used in consort, and several sizes were made. The type instrument was the seven-holed treble, which was about 66cm/26in long. The shrill-toned soprano shawm was tuned a fifth above the treble and was about 48cm/19in long. The alto shawm, tuned a fifth below the treble, was about 76cm/30in long. The tenor shawm, which was tuned a fifth below the alto, was 112cm/4ft long and had a long S-shaped staple on which the reed and pirouette were mounted.

The bass instrument, which was known as the "bombarde" due to its resemblance to the newly invented artillery piece, was tuned an octave below the tenor and was 1.8m/6ft long. It had two keys at the front and two at the rear. There was also a giant bass shawm of about 3m/10ft in length which when played was passed under the musician's arm with the bell resting on the floor behind him.

ABOVE: A 15th-century consort consisting of musicians playing small kettledrums, fiddle, horn, triangle, lute and bagpipes.

Baroque Orchestra (1600–1750)

*Handel's entertainments are calculated for the Quality only,
people of moderate fortunes cannot pretend to them.*

THE ENGLISHMAN'S JOURNAL, 1738

In the 17th century, instrumental music was still the privilege of the great aristocratic and royal households that had the means to employ full-time orchestras and composers. Indeed, the only way that a composer could earn a living was to be employed as a servant by some wealthy patron, either a leading church dignitary or a member of the aristocracy.

A feature of Baroque music was the *basso continuo*, or figured bass, and most music was written for strings and a harpsichord. The harpsichord shared the bass line with the cello, but also added chords that helped to thicken the harmonic texture.

Italy

One of the first orchestras resembling those of today was formed in 1607 by Claudio Monteverdi (1567–1643).

ABOVE: Jean-Baptiste Lully (1639–87) is seen here with the score of Armide et Renaud, *which he composed in 1686.*

Language

By the early 17th century Italian composers had begun to write expression marks into their music, which is why today Italian is still, by convention, the language of Western music. Indeed such was the influence of Italy that some 19th-century English musicians adopted Italian versions of their plain English names, believing – not without good reason – that this would impress their public. The composer John Cooper (c.1570–1627) became Giovanni Coprario, and the Irish tenor and friend of Mozart, Michael Kelly (1762–1826) called himself "Ochelli". Charles Dickens satirized this curious affectation in his story *The Dancing Academy*, in which the dancing master is a certain Signor Billsmethi.

Employed by the Duke of Mantua at one of the richest courts in Italy, Monteverdi was able to use a 40-strong band of strings, flutes, cornetts and trombones for his opera *Orfeo*. The fusion of brass and strings – as opposed to the earlier orchestration of strings and woodwind only – had been adopted by many bands in northern Italy, particularly that of St Mark's, Venice, where Monteverdi ended his career.

This was a period when opera flourished in Naples in the hands of Alessandro Scarlatti (1660–1725). However, in Italy instrumental music also began to be played in its own right, independently of opera, and the concerto came into being. Two of the foremost Italian composers of this form were Arcangelo Corelli (1653–1713) and Antonio Vivaldi (1675–1741). Both wrote *concerti grossi*, characterized by the interplay between a large and a small group of instruments.

France

The *Vingt-quatre Violons du Roi*, which confusingly sometimes numbered 25, was set up to provide music at the court of Louis XIII (1601–43). It served as a training ground for the most brilliant players in France, as well as establishing a stylized method of playing dance music. The band, which had the reputation of decorating and embellishing everything it played, played from memory and as a result some of its performances were nothing short of disastrous. However, when Jean-Baptiste Lully became Louis XIV's *Compositeur de la Musique Instrumentale* he set up his own band, the *Petits Violons*. This band, whose members were the first to wear a uniform and to use their bows in the same direction, was greatly admired and soon became a model for the rest of Europe.

Public concerts

Although music had been banned in England during the Commonwealth (1648–60), on his return from exile in France it was not surprising that Charles II was quick to introduce French music and customs to the English court. One of the Royal violinists was John Banister who, in 1672, started organizing musical performances at his home, which an invited audience would pay to hear.

At the beginning of the 18th century, public concerts as we know them today were still unknown, and musical performances were restricted to the homes of the nobility. However, as the standard of living gradually rose, so did the mercantile class, whose new opulence stimulated a desire for novelty in all forms of artistic expression, including music. It was, however, still music by the upper classes for the upper classes.

Some of the earliest public paid-entry concerts in France were the *Concerts Spirituels*, which began in 1725 in a hall in the Tuileries, Paris.

ABOVE: The Concert *(1690) by A. D. Gabbiani shows seven Modena court musicians playing violins, cello and harpsichord.*

These were primarily performances of sacred music, sung in Latin, which took place on holy days in the church calendar (when the opera was closed). The difference between these events and those organized by Banister in England was that whereas Banister's audience consisted solely of invited guests, there were no restrictions on admission to the Paris concerts.

ABOVE: In the middle of the 18th century the rich still employed musicians to perform in their homes. This painting shows a group of patrons listening to a singer accompanied by a chamber band consisting of a harpsichord, two violins, viola and cello.

ABOVE: Johann Sebastian Bach performing on a piano before his patron Frederick the Great in May 1747.

Classical Orchestra (1750–1830)

Orchestral music is one of the glories of the world.

GEORG SOLTI (1912–97)

The love of orchestral music had become so widespread by the year 1775 that it was said that even "common servants" could be met who pretended "as much judgement of an opera tune as my Lady Duchess". It was also a period when professional performers began to make large fortunes and composers were able to make an independent living, without having to tie themselves to any one court or church. Two of the first truly independent composers were Wolfgang Amadeus Mozart (1756–91) and Ludwig van Beethoven (1770–1827).

ABOVE: London's 18th-century Vauxhall Gardens were the centre of social intercourse for the upper classes. Anybody who was anybody spent time there chatting to the background music of the house band.

Instrumentation

Mozart wrote his early symphonies for the forces he had available, namely strings, two oboes and two horns. By 1782, however, he was independent and began writing for his ideal orchestra, which included flutes, clarinets, bassoons, trumpets and kettledrums. It was, however, Franz Joseph Haydn (1732–1809) and Beethoven who established the nucleus of the modern symphony orchestra; by 1800 the average size of the orchestra was about 40.

Mannheim

One of the first "modern" symphony orchestras was founded by Johann Stamitz (1717–57) at the court of Duke Karl Theodor at Mannheim, Germany, in 1742. The Mannheim orchestra consisted of 50 virtuoso players, making it the largest regular ensemble in Europe at that time. "Its *forte* was like thunder, its *crescendos* like mighty waterfalls, its *diminuendos* like a gentle river disappearing into the distance, its *pianos* like a breath of spring." When a long *crescendo* began it was not unknown for the audience gradually to rise from their seats. This *crescendo* became known as the "Mannheim Steamroller", while an expressive falling phrase was the

ABOVE: Mozart was one of the few musical child prodigies whose genius developed with maturity. By the age of two he was already discovering chords on the keyboard and, by the time he was five, was performing on and composing pieces for the instrument. As well as 18 masses, 21 concertos and 41 symphonies, Mozart also wrote 12 operas, two of the most popular being The Marriage of Figaro *and* The Magic Flute.

"Mannheim Sigh", and various interpolated woodwind trills and turns were "Mannheim Birdies".

Subscription concerts

By the end of the 18th century concerts were being held frequently. Although they were now public events rather than private parties held in the homes of the nobility, they remained an exclusive form of entertainment due to the high price of subscriptions, which had become established by 1760. By charging in advance in this way, promoters of concerts knew just what money was available and thus were able to hire the finest performers they could afford. It was not until the middle of the 19th century that there was a change from subscriptions to the selling of tickets at reasonable prices.

In the days of Mozart and Haydn the audience did not sit quietly as (in theory) they do today, but engaged

ABOVE: Beethoven, who had received his early musical education from his father, became a professional musician at the age of 11. Over the next few years he took lessons from Mozart and Haydn. Soon his aristocratic patrons recognized the worth of his work and gave him financial support for the rest of his life.

ABOVE: The band of strings and horns at the San Beneto Teatro. The musicians are placed in two serried ranks at the side of the hall in Venice.

in many activities, including eating, drinking, chattering to their friends and falling asleep. It is said that Haydn wrote his Symphony No. 94, nicknamed the "Surprise", to wake them up.

Music festivals

A phenomenon unique to British society during the Classical period was the music festival. Lasting two or three days, these were held in many provincial towns in aid of local charities, drawing in the famous musical names of the day to give local people a chance to hear what London audiences were able to enjoy on a regular basis. The annual *Three Choirs* festival, held in Gloucester, Worcester and Hereford, was one of the first to be founded, in 1724. Leicester held two such festivals in 1771 and 1774 and, in July 1803, just over the border in Warwickshire, Nuneaton held a two-day event. In 1823 and 1825 York held two very successful festivals and, in 1826, under royal patronage, over £2400 (US$1485) was raised in Birmingham, a town that had been holding triennial festivals since the 1790s. The forward march of

ABOVE: By the early 19th century renowned opera singers such as Giuseppe de Begnis were performing virtuoso parts full of technically difficult vocal pyrotechnics.

19th-century musical life in Britain continued in 1813 with the founding of the London Philharmonic Society, whose main aim was to perform the great orchestral works of the day.

Romantic Orchestra (1830–1910)

*It is scarcely credible that a distinct Romantic school
could be formed in music, which is in itself romantic.*

ROBERT SCHUMANN (1810–56)

By the 1850s the orchestra was increasing in size, and by 1880 it was not unusual to see an ensemble of 100 or more instrumentalists. Composers were beginning to treat the orchestra as a homogeneous whole rather than as diverse sections, with an increasing awareness of the importance of internal balance.

One of the greatest Romantic composers was Richard Wagner (1813–83) who, unlike earlier composers, was not content simply to write for the instrumental forces already present in the orchestra. As well as introducing existing instruments to the orchestra, he even specified the making of new ones, such as the bass trumpet and the Wagner tubas for *The Ring*. Hector Berlioz (1803–69) was also an

ABOVE: A scene from the première of Wagner's Rienzi, *performed at the Dresden Hoftheater on October 20, 1842.*

ambitious composer, and in his *Requiem* he called for a chime of 16 timpani. Gustav Mahler (1860–1911) wrote on an equally grand scale, and his Eighth Symphony was written for a chorus of 500, as well as 350 children's voices, seven soloists and an augmented orchestra – not for nothing was this work nicknamed the "Symphony of a Thousand".

On June 17, 1872 the largest orchestra ever formed took part in a concert at the World Peace Jubilee in Boston, Massachusetts. The orchestra of 1000 instrumentalists and choir of 20,000 voices were conducted by Johann Strauss the Younger, who was on a tour of the United States. Armed with a long illuminated baton and 100 assistant conductors, he led the band (as Strauss later recalled) in an "unholy racket" such as he had never before or since heard.

Larger orchestras meant higher overheads and, as many orchestras no longer had royal patronage, it was only through the efforts of the rich music-lovers who sponsored events that most orchestras survived. Bigger concert halls were built to accommodate the large paying audiences that were needed at concerts to make the orchestras viable.

Promenade concerts

The concept of the promenade concert originated in France, where successful concerts were mounted in Paris by Philippe Musard and Louis Antoine Jullien. The format was brought to Britain, and the first London promenade concert was held in December 1838. Unlike promenade concerts today, where the audience is static, those attending these early events literally did promenade, chatting to their friends as the concert progressed. Music was a secondary

ABOVE: Richard Wagner, one of Europe's finest Romantic composers, is seen here conducting the Siegfried Idyll *on the steps of his house as a surprise for his wife Cosima on the morning of her birthday in 1870.*

ABOVE: The cover of the sheet music for the Promenade Quadrille *showing the Covent Garden Orchestra in London, 1870.*

concern, as the audience used the opportunity to show off their fashions.

Orchestral tours

By the 1840s, large musical groups were beginning to tour, both nationally and internationally. This was mainly due to the advent of the railways, which were able to transport large numbers of people (and baggage) much faster than horse-drawn coaches. At last people in the provinces were able to see and hear what those in the capital cities had been enjoying for many years. This led to a resurgence of interest in music, and many towns throughout Europe formed their own amateur bands and choirs.

The music of preceding generations began to be revived. In contrast to the 18th century, when most of the music played was contemporary, during the 19th century the works of

dead composers, such as Beethoven, Mozart and Handel, found a place in almost every concert.

It was not only bands that were taking advantage of the better transportation; composers and soloists such as Franz Liszt (1811–86), Niccolò Paganini (1782–1840) and Felix Mendelssohn (1809–47) also began to make provincial tours, to the delight of those who were unable to travel to hear them play in the big cities.

ABOVE: A scene from a performance of Wagner's Tannhäuser *at the Bayreuth Festival of 1972.*

ABOVE: An early 19th-century performance in London's Vauxhall Gardens. A feature of the band are the two black musicians — one with a tambourine and the other with a Turkish crescent. An important development during the 18th century was the adoption by European bands of "Turkish" or "Janissary" music. The instrumentation depended heavily on percussion, and a feature of these bands was that percussion instruments were usually played by young black men. Dressed in the most exotic manner, they performed incredible acrobatics as they played.

RIGHT: An illustration of an English orchestra from the early 19th century.

Modern Symphony Orchestra

There are two golden rules for an orchestra:
start together and finish together.

THOMAS BEECHAM (1879–1961)

After World War I the cost of mounting such colossal works as Mahler's Eighth Symphony became prohibitive and composers turned their pens to smaller combinations. One such composer was William Walton (1902–83) whose *Façade* was greatly influenced by jazz, as was *The Rio Grande* by Constant Lambert (1905–51). The divide between "serious" music and jazz narrowed, with jazz idioms also coming to the fore in Walton's *Belshazzar's Feast*, in which the squeaking flute sounds like a slate pencil scraping on a hard stone wall. Another composer who used both new and old musical forms was Michael Tippett (1905–98), who

ABOVE: The modern symphony orchestra usually consists of over 90 players, requiring a large concert hall for its performances. The Philharmonia Orchestra is shown here performing at the Royal Festival Hall in London.

ABOVE: For maximum volume, modern composers may include a large choir and percussion section in their compositions. The Bournemouth Symphony Orchestra and Choir are seen here under the direction of Kees Bakels. Founded in 1893, this orchestra has become one of Britain's foremost provincial orchestras and has been conducted by many great maestros.

incorporated motifs from spirituals in *A Child of Our Time* and blues and boogie-woogie in *Songs for Dov*.

In the 1950s the idea developed among composers that each separate instrument should be distinctly audible playing its individual part, rather than hearing the orchestra as an entity, a single giant instrument. Players now had to work much harder than before to give richness or beauty of tone-colour to the music.

Conductorless orchestra

The post-revolutionary Pervyi Simfonicheskii Ansambl (First Symphonic Ensemble) was formed in the USSR in 1922. The unusual aspect of the orchestra was that, believing that in the ideal Marxist state all men are equal, its members felt that there was no need to be led by the dictatorial

baton of a conductor; instead they were led by a committee. Although it was a partial success, the principal difficulty with the concept was in changing tempo. The orchestra survived for ten years and had to be disbanded only when the individual talents began to rebel against the rigid control under which they were expected to play.

New instrumental techniques

Twentieth-century orchestral practice provided composers with a vast range of techniques. One composer who developed a remarkable effect was the Spanish composer Roberto Gerhard (1896–1970), who devised the ethereal ringing tone produced by stroking the edge of a cymbal with a double bass bow. Another novel use of the orchestra was that produced by Pierre Boulez (born 1925) in *Don* from *Pli selon Pli*, where he used the orchestra not as families of woodwind, brass and strings, but as three groups of high, medium and low-voiced instruments, irrespective of their colour.

ABOVE: *A modern symphony orchestra stands to acknowledge the audience's applause.*

Some composers, although writing music for the instruments of a conventional orchestra, arranged the instruments in unusual combinations. In his *Music for Strings, Percussion and Celeste*, Béla Bartók (1881–1945) divided the strings into two chamber groups placed on either side of a piano, harp, celeste and percussion section.

Another composer who experimented with new effects was Claude Debussy (1862–1918). His symphonic sketch *La Mer*, composed in 1905, was finished while he was staying at the Grand Hotel at Eastbourne in England, overlooking the sea, and is a well-known example of his impressionistic approach to composition. Although Debussy used large forces for his orchestral works, it was less to enhance volume than to create colour in his music.

Other new orchestral effects have been created by the woodwind deliberately overblowing, brass players being instructed to whisper, shout or yell into their mouthpieces, and string players being asked to produce harsh, grating sounds by bowing between the bridge and the tailpiece of their instruments. Compositions like these are set to continue breaking all the rules well into the 21st century.

ABOVE: *A large symphony orchestra accompanying a group of jazz soloists.*

Authentic Music

The tragedy in the interpetation of music of the past lies in the fact that it is confined to concert halls, congresses of musicology, or conservatory classes. Music needs air, sunlight and liberty to be alive.

WANDA LANDOWSKA (1877–1959)

It has recently become fashionable to perform music with an authentic orchestra, using the number and type of instruments that the composer would originally have intended. Players and scholars alike have investigated early music and instruments in an attempt to discover just what was played and on what instruments, how it sounded and how it was performed. Indeed, such is the current situation that a concert of early music is likely to attract a larger audience than one of modern music.

There are special problems confronting the performer of authentic music, and each of these must be considered before calling a performance truly "authentic". Design and colour cannot be separated. In the same way that an outline drawn by Raphael could not be coloured in with Cézanne's palette, a modern violinist will not play in the same manner as Corelli. Even if he is playing on a 300-year-old instrument, he still has to know how the music was intended to be played.

Although modern composers use instruments which, by name at least,

ABOVE: Authentic music performances can be a living history experience. In this case a Salzburg violinist is dressed in 18th-century costume to enhance the period effect.

would have been familiar to Haydn and Beethoven, the style of playing and the sounds produced are totally different. Orchestral sounds changed completely with the introduction of Boehm flutes, Triébert oboes, Klosé clarinets and Heckel bassoons, not to mention valved horns and electronic instruments.

Another factor to bear in mind is the size of the orchestra's string section in relation to the wind section. In the 18th century it was unusual for an orchestra to have more than eight violins, 12 being rare. By the time of Beethoven's death a violin section of 32 had become common. However, there was no relative increase in the woodwind section. It follows therefore

RIGHT: A modern group of musicians dressed in late 18th-century costume recreating an orchestra playing Mozart's Te Deum.

LEFT: *A chamber group of musicians performing in the style of the early 19th century.*

Johann Stein to tune Mozart's piano had a frequency of 422Hz – half a tone lower than modern pitch. From 1800–50 the pitch in France rose from 423 to 446Hz. In 1880 Steinways were tuning their pianos to 457Hz – a quarter-tone above the present pitch.

The first attempt to fix a standard was made in 1834, but had no success. In 1889 it was decided to stabilize the pitch at 435Hz and by international agreement in 1939 "concert pitch" was fixed at a frequency of 440Hz.

that a work by Mozart played by a modern orchestra will not sound like the sonorities Mozart heard – the wind being lost under a mountain of strings. Unless the orchestra plays with the correct numerical relationship between the strings and wind, as the composer understood it, the sound will never be "authentic".

Any instrument that is used over a period of time undergoes changes. These changes invariably alter the sound produced and, as composers score for instruments according to how they perceive the sound they make, so does the way they write for them. Elgar did not write for the horn in the same way that Beethoven or Purcell did.

Pitch

It is not only the instruments, but also the pitch that has altered. From 1762–89 the tuning-note (A) varied between frequencies of 377 and 428 cycles per second, or Hertz (from a minor third to half a tone below the modern standard). Apart from this variation, musicians in different regions tuned to different pitches at the same time. France preferred a low, Germany a middle and England a high pitch. The tuning fork used in 1780 by

LEFT: Performers of early brass instruments playing Turmmusik (tower music). The narrow bore of the two trombones indicates that these instruments are related to sackbuts.

ABOVE: The Academy of Ancient Music was founded in 1973, and its ensemble is dedicated to giving authentic performances on period instruments of a mainly 18th-century repertoire.

Chamber Music

*Chamber music concerns itself as a world of sound
that has external boundaries but no internal ones.*

HANS WERNER HENZE (BORN 1926)

Originally, the term "chamber music" described intimate music for small groups of solo instruments performing in a drawing room before either a small audience or with no listeners at all. Chamber music differs from other orchestral music in that generally only a single instrument performs each part, whereas in an orchestra the parts are played by groups of instruments.

Although there had been a lot of small-scale ensemble music in the Middle Ages, the medieval court was a place of public exhibition, with very little opportunity for domestic music-making. However, with the rise of instrumental music and an increasing interest in amateur vocal and instrumental music-making in the 16th century, music began to play an important part in the homes of the well-to-do.

Many great houses maintained one or more professional musicians and in 17th-century Italy some princely establishments appointed musicians who had special responsibility for the performance and composition of chamber music. Monteverdi held such a post in the household of the Duke of Mantua, and his contemporaries in similar posts included Enrico di Foggia and Sigismondo d'India.

ABOVE: A painting by Max Buri (1868–1915) showing a group of German village musicians in about 1910.

Another development of the period was the tendency to arrange vocal music for instruments. From the mid 16th century consort music for viols flourished, with compositions being circulated in manuscript copies. Some were published by composers such as Michael East (c.1580–1648) and William Byrd (1543–1623), who issued their collections in 1610 and 1611 respectively. During the 16th and 17th centuries many consorts were formed, the music of which led to the invention of new dances such as the slow, stately pavan and the quicker galliard, as well as the musical forms of *ricercare* and *canzona*, which in turn led to the development of the 17th-century sonata and fugue.

In the 17th and 18th centuries chamber music was encouraged in Germany by the flourishing *collegium musicum*, in Italy by the spread of music academies and in England by the formation of music clubs.

Eighteenth-century chamber music began to include wind instruments, especially in France where music for

ABOVE: A Musical Evening *by Michel Ange (1680–1730). The painting shows a chamber ensemble (harpsichord, cello, violin and flute) performing to a group of friends.*

ABOVE: *This painting by Pieter Fabris shows a group of mid 18th-century chamber musicians playing in Lord Fortrose's apartment in Naples, Italy.*

ABOVE: *One of the finest musicians of the 20th century, Yehudi Menuhin, with his sister Hephzibah and the French cellist Maurice Gendron.*

various combinations of violin, flute, oboe, bassoon and harpsichord was first published. This flexible instrumentation, much of which included a fully written-out harpsichord part, as opposed to the *continuo* required hitherto, seems to have been a development prompted by publishers rather than composers.

In the homes of the nobility regular music evenings were held, at which small groups of musicians played for the family and their guests. Some of these groups were professional musicians who were sponsored by the family. One such ensemble was the Rasumovsky Quartet in Vienna, which was founded and paid for by Count Rasumovsky, the Russian ambassador to Vienna, who played second violin in the group. It was considered one of the best in Europe and even Beethoven wrote pieces especially for it.

New instrumentation

In early 20th-century France there was a proliferation of works for combinations unknown before 1900.

There was a concentration on the flute and the harp – uncommitted instruments that suited the impressionistic age. Examples include the enchanting *Introduction and Allegro* by Maurice Ravel (1875–1937) and Debussy's trio, Sonata for Flute, Viola and Harp.

Another French chamber composer who went in for unconventional instrumentation was Pierre Boulez, who scored *Le Marteau sans maître* for flute, viola, guitar, vibraphone or xylophone and percussion. Igor Stravinsky (1882–1971) was also an innovator and his *L'Histoire d'un soldat* (1918) was scored for clarinet, bassoon, cornet, trombone, violin, double bass, three actors and a dancer.

However, it will take a lot to beat Schoenberg's scoring of *Pierrot Lunaire*

ABOVE: Florilegium *was founded in 1991 to play the music of the 17th and 18th centuries. The group is one of the most exuberant chamber ensembles in Europe.*

ABOVE: An 18th-century string quartet playing at double music desks that are reminiscent of the double prayer desks of two centuries earlier.

specialized individuals, and might offer little to the amateur performer, who instead takes refuge in more accessible works from earlier eras.

String quartet

This chamber group was evolved by Joseph Haydn while he was employed by the Esterházy family at Eisenstadt near Vienna in the late 1750s. For the first time, chamber music abandoned the harpsichord and the new ensemble may have been used for outdoor serenades, for which it was too much trouble to carry the harpsichord outside. Altogether, Haydn wrote over 70 quartets, most of them in sets of six.

One of the novel features of the string quartet was that all the instruments had an equal share of the tunes, and for this reason the music was fun to play.

ABOVE: The San Francisco-based Kronos Quartet was founded in 1973 and exclusively devotes itself to playing music of the 20th century and beyond.

in 1912. This extraordinary work was written for flute, clarinet, bass clarinet, violin, viola, cello, piano and a narrator. The inflexions of the latter's voice are included in the score.

Modern chamber music

In the 20th century a reaction against the large Romantic orchestrations of the 19th century led to a renewed interest in chamber music. This was not the chamber music of the past, such as piano trios, string quartets and quintets, but small groups with new sounds and unusual combinations of instruments, with an emphasis on mixed ensembles of wind and strings and often also with vocal as well as percussion elements.

Modern chamber music has moved from the private house to the concert hall, and organizations such as the Library of Congress and the Dutch Donemus Foundation, or wealthy

individuals such as Walter Cobbett have been, and still are, active in promoting it.

The original social function and context of chamber music has now wholly disappeared. Much modern chamber music can be both difficult to play and demanding to listen to. It is often written for highly skilled and

ABOVE: Although piano duets using one or two pianos are common, it is most unusual for more than two to be played together. This photograph from a 1920s advertisement shows four musicians, each playing a Bechstein grand piano.

ABOVE: An early 19th-century quartet playing at a quadruple music desk especially designed for quartets.

This is still the case today: the sign of a good string quartet is a sense of equality.

The string quartet (like the brass band) suffers from a lack of colour contrasts – but this can be overcome not only by the differences in tone between the instruments, but by the way they are played. For instance, the instruments can be either played with the bow (*coll'arco*) or plucked with the fingers (*pizzicato*). The violin player may play notes on the G string that would normally be played on other strings. This gives a warmer quality to the sound.

Another trick to thicken the sound is the use of double-stopping, in which more than one string is played on an instrument at the same time. Two composers who used double-stopping to great effect were Debussy and Grieg. Contrasts can also be achieved by resting instruments before bringing them all in together for a climax. Haydn, Mozart and Beethoven were all masters of the string quartet and often doubled instruments for special effects.

In the 18th century it was taken for granted that music should be composed with amateur capabilities in mind. However, if a composer writes simple music today it is sometimes frowned upon and regarded as fit only for learner musicians. Although Mozart, Beethoven and Schubert all enjoyed writing string quartets, the form died out in the 19th century, but was revived in the 20th century, notably by Bartók and Shostakovich. Other 20th-century composers who are noted for their string quartets are Schoenberg, Hindemith, Walton and Tippett, whose five quartets included influences from the 16th-century madrigal.

Chamber orchestras

After World War I, economic factors saw an end to some of the large orchestras that had been dominant at the beginning of the 20th century, and composers increasingly wrote for smaller combinations of instruments. In the decades between the two World Wars a number of chamber orchestras were founded, the best known of which was the Basle Chamber Orchestra, which was set up in 1926 and was conducted by Paul Sacher.

In London, the Boyd Neel String Orchestra was founded in 1933. In an attempt to get the best of both worlds, it adopted an 18th-century repertoire and instrumentation while at the same time encouraging contemporary composers to write new works for it. In an attempt to stimulate interest in chamber music, similar orchestras, such as the Swiss Melos Ensemble, were founded all over Europe.

ABOVE: The English Chamber Orchestra was founded by Arnold Goldsbrough in 1948. One of its prime engagements was under Benjamin Britten at the Aldeburgh Festival.

ABOVE: The Austrian Alban Berg String Quartet was founded in 1971 and has won international distinction with its recordings of the complete Bach, Brahms, Berg and Webern quartets. They are seen here playing at the Royal Festival Hall, London, in 1998.

European National Music

The 19th century was a period of European nationalism, not just in military matters but also in the arts, including music. For two centuries, the dominant musical figures in Europe had been German – from Bach to Beethoven – but the Romantic movement, which stressed personal feelings, led to composers striving to express their own traditions, and drawing on the musical influences of their own countries.

United Kingdom

Since the death of Henry Purcell in 1695, the United Kingdom had not produced a major composer, but the successful career of Arthur Sullivan (1842–1900), composer of the Savoy Operas, revived British music and paved the way for a generation of recognizably "English" voices, notably Edward Elgar (1857–1934) in whose music a mixture of nobility and nostalgia defined the British spirit at the end of the Victorian era. Frederick Delius (1862–1934) wrote works full of pastoral lyricism, and Ralph Vaughan Williams (1872–1958) rediscovered and reworked the rich vein of English folk music.

Czechoslovakia

One of the first orchestral composers to compose works with a definite national character was Bedřich Smetana (1824–84). Although he seldom used actual folk songs in his music, unlike his close friend Antonin Dvořák

(1841–1904), Smetana's work was unmistakably Czech. Absorbing the traditions of Berlioz and Liszt, Smetana was also an excellent pianist in the style of Clara Schumann. In 1861 he was appointed head of the Department of Music in the newly formed Prague

ABOVE: Scandinavian scenery inspired composers such as Sibelius and Grieg.

Society of Arts and it was during the tenure of this office that he wrote his most famous opera, *The Bartered Bride*. After suffering for some time from a whistling in his ears, in 1874 Smetana suddenly became stone deaf, but, like Beethoven before him, went on composing, including arguably his best work, *Má Vlast* ("My Country"), a set of six musical landscapes.

Finland

Another 19th-century composer whose music is evocative of his country is the Scandinavian Jean Sibelius (1865–1957), who was born in the

ABOVE: Sir Edward Elgar was England's greatest national composer of the 20th century. His work includes such typically English compositions as the four Pomp and Circumstance *marches and the* Enigma Variations. *A great friend of Adrian Boult, Elgar fixed a sign on his cottage gate, "Please Boult the Gate".*

Finnish town of Hämeenlinna. Although intended for a legal career, he soon abandoned his law studies to devote himself entirely to music. In 1892 a performance of his first large-scale orchestral work, the *Kullervo* Symphony, created such a sensation that he soon became established as Finland's leading composer. One of his most popular works is the tone poem *Finlandia*, which he composed in 1899 and which was banned by the Tsar because it roused such nationalistic fervour. Although his inspiration was intimately connected with Finnish landscape and literature (such as *Kalevala*, the national folk epic), Sibelius's achievements lie principally in his remarkable mastery of form.

Norway
Edvard Grieg (1843–1907) turned to his native folk music for inspiration, having learnt the folk songs of Norway from his mother. One of his most popular works is his incidental music to Ibsen's play *Peer Gynt*, in which he evokes trolls, mists and mountains in a work that is unmistakably Scandinavian.

Germany
One of the most obvious examples of overt nationalism in 19th-century orchestral music must be the work of Richard Wagner (1813–83), whose love of everything Aryan was to make him the darling of the Nazis, who conveniently forgot his Semitic ancestry. Wagner drew inspiration from

ABOVE: *In the 18th and 19th centuries Prague was one of the main musical capitals of Europe. This scene of the Old Square is as it was in the days when Mozart walked its streets, and would have been familiar to Czechoslovakia's two great national composers, Dvořák and Smetana.*

ABOVE: *The Battle of Polotsk, 18 August, 1812. One of the compositions that most brings to mind "Mother Russia" is Tchaikovsky's 1812 Overture, which describes in music the day when Napoleon's army was finally defeated. The work has many musical effects, from the roar of cannon to church bells ringing out the news of victory.*

the legends and myths of Germanic folklore, producing epic operas such as *Tristan und Isolde* and *Tannhäuser,* as well as the renowned *Der Ring des Nibelungen*.

France
Camille Saint-Saëns (1835–1921), as president of the Société Nationale de Musique, declared himself in favour of the "essential French qualities of logic, reason and clarity", and imparted these qualities to his huge musical output, including operas, choral and orchestral works, organ and chamber music. Gabriel Fauré (1845–1924) was a pupil of Saint-Saëns, and composed ravishing songs and choral works of great delicacy and elegance.

Russia
Russian music is full of the sounds of "Mother Russia", from Tchaikovsky's patriotic *1812 Overture* to the folk-based compositions of musicians such as Mikhail Glinka (1804–57). Glinka was regarded as the "father" of Russian music, and inspired a group of composers, known as "The Five", who set out to develop a pure Russian style. They included Alexander Borodin (1833–87), whose opera *Prince Igor* relates the story of the 12th-century struggles of the Russians against the Polovtsy invaders, and Modest Mussorgsky (1839–81) whose masterpiece is the opera *Boris Godunov*, based on Pushkin's drama about the 16th-century Tsar.

Folk Music

*The best way to get to knowing any bunch of people
is to go and listen to their music.*

WOODY GUTHRIE (1912–67)

While most music tends to cross boundaries, folk music differs from area to area. The folk music of Northumberland is different from that of southern England; the music of Hamburg is different from that of Munich or the Tyrol; in Russia, the folk tunes in the west are different from those in the east. The workers on the American cotton plantations sang songs that were unknown in the industrial cities of Boston and New York. The words and tunes of folk songs were transmitted aurally, and might have existed in several versions in different places, as they were subtly altered over the years.

In Britain, most songs were traditionally sung only by men. Women exercised their vocal chords only while working or in the home, and were very rarely heard in public.

ABOVE: This print from the 1830s shows a party of villagers folk-dancing outside an inn in Süd Tirol, Austria, now part of northern Italy.

Work songs

Many traditional songs were about work, especially the hard conditions associated with occupations such as working in the fields, down the mines or on ships. Singing made hard work easier and many songs were of the call and response type, in which the leader or shantyman would sing out the story and the rest of the workers would join in the chorus. Another type of work song was the street cry, with which street vendors advertised their wares.

Ballads

The ballad was a song that told a story, and might be based on contemporary news events of the day, such as a battle or a mining disaster, or on legends or fictional tales. In the days before radio or television, when few working people were able to read newspapers, singing or listening to these ballads was one way to escape briefly from the

ABOVE: The composer Béla Bartók travelled extensively all over Hungary and neighbouring states, making recordings of folk songs.

daily grind. There were also many shorter songs, which might be pithy and humorous or lyrical and romantic.

Instrumental accompaniment

At work in the fields, or in the home, most folk music was sung unaccompanied. In Biblical Israel songs were sung to the accompaniment of the harp, while in classical Greece the singer was accompanied on the kithara. In medieval Europe folk songs were sung to pipe and tabor and later to the hurdy-gurdy or bagpipes. Bagpipes were purely a folk instrument, being thought to be crude and fit only for the tavern, in contrast to the viol, favoured by the more well-to-do.

Dancing

Feast days and their associated rituals have invariably included both music and dancing, such as the May Day Morris dancing of southern England and the sword dances of the north. These two very different traditions of folk-dancing reflect the Viking occupation of the north-east of Britain.

Originally, dances like these were performed only on certain occasions, and were part of religious ceremonies to celebrate the passing of the seasons and to bring good luck to the harvest. Though the original significance of these dances has been lost, they are

ABOVE: *Before radio and television people made their own amusements, and one of the few pastimes available for the "labouring poor" was dancing. This print of 1804 shows a Polish man dancing before his friends.*

ABOVE: *One of the joys of life in the southern states of America is when the family play their instruments on the porch.*

ABOVE: *Morris dancing is thought to be associated with fertility. There are many groups who try to recreate England's past.*

still performed on festive occasions, such as village fête days.

Some folk dances have become popularized far beyond their point of origin. The waltz originated as a peasant dance in southern Germany, but has become known – in its more refined state – all over the world. Another genre that has become popular way beyond its native shores, due both to migration and, latterly, to a film and stage show, is Irish dancing.

As with folk songs, the instruments that provided the music for these dances were small and portable, such as the fiddle. The accordion, invented in the early 19th century, became popular as an accompaniment for open-air dancing, and a 20th-century innovation in Morris sides is the inclusion of the concertina.

Contemporary folk music

In the 1960s, with the growth of the American civil rights movement and the increasing aversion of young people to America's involvement in the war in Vietnam, folk songs experienced a revival of interest as a means of political protest, sung by professional folk singers such as Joan Baez (born 1941), Pete Seeger (born 1919) and Bob Dylan (born 1941). Many of Bob Dylan's "protest" songs of the mid '60s have become folk classics, such as *Masters of War*, *The Times They are A-changin'* and *With God on our Side*. Country Joe McDonald's chorus, "And it's one, two, three, what are we fighting for?" has become the universal anti-war anthem.

ABOVE: *One of the new-style folk singers of the 1960s was Bob Dylan, whose songs relate to the protest movement of that time.*

Revolutionary Music of the 20th Century

Think nothing. Wait until it is absolutely still within you.
When you have attained this begin to play.

KARLHEINZ STOCKHAUSEN, INSTRUCTIONS TO PERFORMERS OF "ES"

As the 20th century dawned, some composers turned away from the hitherto accepted rules of harmony and composition and ventured out into the realms of polytonality, atonality and microtones.

Atonal music

In 1908 the Austrian composer Arnold Schoenberg (1874–1951) changed the whole basis of harmony. He abandoned

By numbers

A composer who drew inspiration from unusual sources was the Russian Joseph Schillinger, who emigrated to the United States in 1930. At one concert he asked his audience which composer the new work he had just played reminded them of. Suggestions included Mozart, Bach and Beethoven; however, nobody could guess Schillinger's actual source, which had been the stock-market quotations. Schillinger had plotted the figures on a sheet of graph paper and given each a proportional musical value. Schillinger also taught music, and amongst his pupils was Glenn Miller, whose *Moonlight Serenade* was written as an exercise set by Schillinger.

ABOVE: Arnold Schoenberg decided to abandon tonality in 1907 when he wrote his Second String Quartet, a work in which the keys are not stated but "sensed".

the idea of the central keynote and regarded every semitone of a chromatic scale as being of equal importance. One of his early atonal compositions was the opera *Expectation*, a work for soprano and orchestra. Although some listeners admired Schoenberg's work, many more found it unintelligible, preferring tonal music that was more pleasing to the ear.

Microtones

Another innovation of the 20th century was the use of microtones. Although microtones were, and still are, common in eastern music, and are found in some eastern European folk music, the smallest interval generally used in European music was the semitone. The main promoter of microtones in Europe was the Czech composer Alois Hába (born 1893), who divided the notes of the scale into intervals of one-third, one-quarter and one-sixth of a tone. Due to the construction of European wind instruments, such music is only easily playable on strings and trombones.

Polytonal music

Polytonality is the use of two keys simultaneously. Again, to most listeners this is very grating on the ear, but the genre did find some early supporters. One of these was Charles Ives (1874–1954), an insurance salesman who wrote music in his spare time. Some of his music is very complex to perform: in its original form, his Fourth Symphony, for instance, needs four conductors to

ABOVE: Charles Ives was the first American composer to break away from the German style that had influenced most American music during the late 19th century.

ABOVE: *Dimitri Shostakovich was greatly influenced by his compatriots Rimsky-Korsakov, Tchaikovsky and Prokofiev.*

keep the players together. Another exponent of polytonality was Igor Stravinsky. His music for the ballet *The Rite of Spring* begins with a bassoon solo that is scored deliberately at the top of the instrument's range because he wanted the player to strive to reach the note to give the sound the quality of struggle. At its first performance in Paris in May 1913 the audience almost caused a riot. At one point the manager of the theatre, in an attempt to restore calm, was heard to say "Listen before you boo." When the composer Camille Saint-Saëns heard the work, he just kept repeating *"Il est fou."* Yet the work has since become an established and popular part of the orchestral repertoire.

Aleatoric music

Some of the music of Karlheinz Stockhausen (born 1928) never sounds the same twice over because it is aleatoric: it includes the improvisatory elements of chance and free choice. Stockhausen has abandoned conventional notation altogether and writes "text scores" in which he explains in words how the music should be played. In *Gold Dust*, for instance, he even suggests that the musicians should starve themselves for four days and nights before the performance.

Another composer who explored the operation of chance was John Cage (1912–92), whose *4' 33"* consists of

four minutes and 33 seconds of silence, the idea being that the music is created by the sounds provided by the natural environment at the time. This work was satirized by the musician and humorist Gerard Hoffnung, who in the mid 1950s announced that he had written a work that included three bars of silence. The first and third bars, so Hoffnung explained, were in 5:4 time, but the second bar was in 3:4 time, "thereby giving the whole work a quasi-Viennese flavour".

ABOVE: *Karlheinz Stockhausen abandoned both conventional musical notation and instrumentation, utilizing "instruments" such as iron chains and shortwave radios.*

ABOVE: *Igor Stravinsky had a rich and diverse musical output. Here he is shown conducting a 1951 rehearsal of his opera* The Rake's Progress *in Venice, Italy.*

Many of Cage's works for dance companies and concert performances exploited his invention of the "prepared piano", in which he created percussive effects by placing objects such as rubber bands and paperclips between the strings. He also wrote *HPSCHD*, a piece for seven harpsichords and 51 tape machines, and *0'00"* which was for any musician playing any instrument in any way.

ABOVE: *The composer and pianist John Cage was a pupil of Schoenberg. His music exploits a variety of percussive and novel sound effects produced by orthodox instruments, modified instruments such as the "prepared" piano, and objects such as radio receivers, chairs and even dead fish.*

Brass Bands

The brass band contest is the one and only
successful rival to the football match.

GEORGE MILLER

Brass bands came into existence in England and Wales in the 1830s as a result of the philanthropic efforts of factory owners to enrich the lives of their work forces. They saw brass bands as valuable adjuncts to their works, and in an era of increasing leisure, the bands became a popular pastime.

Improvement in the manufacture of brass instruments at around this time made both fingering and blowing easier, and the advent of the railways made travel feasible for working people. It was not long before bands began to compete with one another in friendly rivalry.

ABOVE: *Brass baritones from an Austrian town band giving an outdoor performance in Salzburg, Austria.*

Contests

The first known brass band contest, at which five bands took part, was held at Burton Constable, near Hull, in 1845. In those early days the participating bands were restricted to 12 players (as opposed to 25 today) and played arrangements of works by composers such as Weber, Rossini and Mozart.

The most distinguished of these early bandsmen was Enderby Jackson, a conductor and arranger who, in 1854, established the principle that all participating bands in a contest should play the same test piece.

Today the British National Brass Band Contest, held in London at the Royal Albert Hall, is the highlight of the British bandsman's year. Since 1978 the more ambitious British bands have also been able to compete with their European counterparts at the European Brass Band Championships.

United States and beyond

Brass bands became popular in the United States almost as early as they did in Britain. One of the first bands to be formed in the United States was the Brass Band of New York, established by Alan Dodworth in 1834. Brass band

ABOVE: *The "Besses o' th' Barn" band from Whitefield, Lancashire, was one of England's foremost brass bands. It was founded in 1818 and is seen here during its successful tour of France in 1905.*

concerts soon became a part of the American way of life. It was truly music for the people, with bandstand gazebos in almost every park. Some of these, such as that in New York's Central Park, were paid for by the railway company as a way of increasing fare income by transporting out-of-town concertgoers into the city. On Boston Common, concerts were so well attended that some are said to have attracted crowds of up to 10,000 people.

By 1900 the brass band movement had reached its zenith in England and Wales, with some 20,000 brass bands. Although their number declined after World War II, there was a revival of interest from the 1960s. This resurgence occurred not only in Britain, Australia, New Zealand and the United States but also in Europe, where British-style brass bands were formed in the Netherlands, Sweden, Switzerland, Norway and Belgium.

Repertoire
Brass bands play a mixture of transcriptions of orchestral works and original compositions. Notable early

ABOVE: The Durham Miners' Gala is one of the most eagerly anticipated events in the British brass bandsman's diary. Many bands take part in the event, both marching through the town and giving static concerts.

arrangers of music for bands include J. Ord Hume, Samuel Cope and William Rimmer. As well as orchestral composers such as Arthur Bliss, Gustav Holst and Sir Edward Elgar, all of whom wrote for brass band, the brass band's repertoire has been greatly enhanced by men such as Eric

Ball, Geoffrey Brand and Granville Bantock. At first, some of this new music was treated with suspicion, and it was not unknown for band conductors, unaccustomed to anything but the harmonies of marches and hymn tunes, to change "wrong notes" to their own satisfaction. It is reported that one conductor with a limited knowledge of Italian went into a music shop after receiving a new score with the intention of buying "some of those new-fangled *senza mutes*".

These days, band concerts in the park are still enjoyed by thousands of people who like nothing better than relaxing in the sunshine listening to a "good drop of music".

LEFT: The continued survival of brass bands in Britain depends on young people taking up brass instruments to fill the ranks of older musicians. The presence of so many youth bands in the country assures the future of the brass band movement.

Military Bands

Explain it as we may, a martial strain
will urge a man into the front rank of battle.

Henry Theodore Tuckerman (1813–71)

Soldiers of the world have always marched to music, even if it was only the rhythmic tread of their own feet. By 1600 BC Egyptians were marching to trumpet and drum, and a thousand years later Roman trumpeters played on the march. Trumpets were an integral part of Caesar's army and on that fateful day, while standing by the bridge crossing the Rubicon, the trumpets blew a thunderous blast. In 6th-century Persia the regiments marched to bands of drums, pipes and trumpets. Four hundred years later their descendants were still enjoying the stirring music of large bands of drums, cymbals, trumpets and other wind instruments.

European military bands

Military bands came to the attention of western Europeans during the Crusades from the 11th to 13th centuries, when they encountered Saracen bands consisting of *surnay*

LEFT: A Prussian military band shown on the sheet music for Preussicher Zapfenstreich *by H. Saro, published in 1885. A feature of the band is the Turkish crescent surmounted by the Prussian Eagle.*

(oboes), *nafir* (trumpets), *buq* (horns) and *naqqara* (kettledrums). During the late Middle Ages European armies began to copy these bands loosely, employing combinations of shawms, bagpipes, trumpets and drums. The duties of the musicians were mainly to play at tournaments and to accompany the soldiers on campaign.

Janissary bands

An important development during the 18th century was the adoption by European military bands of "Turkish" or "Janissary" music. The instrumentation of these bands included oboes, fifes, side drums, kettledrums, cymbals, triangles, Turkish crescent and bass drum. Such was the fad for this type of music that some regiments in Poland, Russia and Prussia even imported whole bands, complete with musicians, from Turkey. Today, remnants of the Janissary era live on in the leopardskin apron worn by bass drummers and the shape of the lyre glockenspiel.

The trend was reversed in the early 19th century when, in 1826, the Sultan of Turkey disbanded his corps of Janissaries and invited Giuseppe Donizetti (brother of the composer) to reorganize Turkish bands on the lines

ABOVE: Russian horn bands were a feature of the late 18th and early 19th centuries. Such was the popularity of these combinations with the Russian nobility that they often sold them to one another — players as well as horns.

ABOVE: For centuries, armies have used drums to keep their marching troops in step. Here an 18th-century side drummer leads a platoon of troops past the National Theatre in Prague.

ABOVE: Brightly dressed army side drummers playing at the Battle of Fontenoy in 1745.

of European ones. Persian bands followed suit and adopted Western instrumentation in about 1840.

New instruments

By the end of the 18th century military bands were increasing in size, mainly as a result of adding extra percussion instruments, which in turn made it necessary – for purposes of audibility – to increase the wind section. Clarinets, both B flat and E flat, were introduced into military bands and soon

outnumbered any other instrument. Performing the same role as the violins in the symphony orchestra, there were two main reasons for the clarinet replacing the oboe in military bands. First, it is much easier for a marching musician to play the single reed clarinet than the double reed oboe and

second, the softer sound of the oboe tends to become lost when playing with modern brass instruments.

American Civil War bands

During the American Civil War military bands proliferated on both sides of the conflict and were heard on all occasions, from ceremonial parades to battle marches. A good band was a source of tremendous pride and was long remembered by those fortunate enough to witness the "dawn of peace".

Sometimes Union bands played in competition with their southern counterparts. One such impromptu concert happened during a lull in the Battle of Spotsylvania in 1864. Each side brought their band to the front line where, for an hour or so, the bands played alternate tunes. The concert ended with the Confederate band bringing tears to the eyes of the battle-hardened men of both sides with their heart-rending rendition of *Home Sweet Home*.

ABOVE: Members of military bands often "double" on stringed instruments. The bands of the Austrian Empire were no exception and here Johann Strauss the Younger is seen conducting a military orchestra at a royal ball in Vienna.

Military schools of music

A major event in the evolution of European military bands was the celebration of peace at the end of the Crimean War in 1856. Military bands of all the allied nations took part, giving the bandsmen an opportunity to hear each other play and compare standards. In the wake of the British bands' poor showing (particularly embarrassing when they played the national anthem in different keys), the Royal Military School of Music was founded at Kneller Hall in Twickenham, near London.

At this time British military bandmasters were still mainly civilian musicians and – more surprisingly – were in many cases foreign. Three examples were Francis Ptacek, a member of the Prague Conservatoire who was director of the band of the Leicestershire Militia; Herr Sawerthal,

ABOVE: *Marching bands are popular in the United States, Australia and, to a lesser degree, Britain. This Sydney annual marching band festival takes place in Australia every August.*

the bandmaster of the Royal Engineers; and Karl Tieke, the composer of the evergreen march *Alte Kameraden*, who was the director of the band of the Royal Irish Dragoon Guards.

It was not until 1887 that an army bandmaster, Dan Godfrey, the director of the band of the Grenadier Guards, received a commission. Today all directors of full-time military bands are of officer rank.

Civilian "military" bands

During the 19th century the term "military band" became something of a misnomer as it began to be used more loosely, referring also to civilian bands using military band instrumentation for public concerts. One of the most popular of these civilian bands was the renowned Jullien Band.

Jullien

Louis Antoine Jullien (1812–60) was the son of a military bandsman. After a period of study at the Paris Conservatoire, he began promoting concerts of dance music at the Jardin Ture, where he became known as the "Napoleon of Music".

ABOVE: *Almost every school in the United States has its own band. This one is proudly playing on the steps of the Capitol building in Washington DC.*

ABOVE: *The drum corps of the Grenadier Guards playing at the annual "Trooping of the Colour" in London.*

ABOVE: One of the best-known annual events in Germany is the Oktoberfest. *Held in Munich, this beer festival is enlivened by the many bands that perform.*

In 1840 he moved to England, and made his debut in Drury Lane in June.

Thanks to a spotless white waistcoat, as well as his ambrosial curls, superb moustache and the magnificent air with which he wielded his baton, Jullien was the object of unsparing ridicule.

ABOVE: Jullien's concerts were always sold out well in advance. Despite this, he was never able to pay off the debts he had amassed in Paris, and he died bankrupt.

He was a devotee of Beethoven, and whenever he conducted works by that composer he would have a new pair of white gloves presented to him which he would wear while he conducted.

Each year Jullien tried to bring some novelty into his concerts. In 1849 he introduced the *monstre* ophicleide (a brass instrument later superseded by the tuba) which at that time was the largest wind instrument ever made. In 1851 he toured with a French drum corps, which appeared in full military uniform by permission of Prince Louis Napoleon. In the same year, appreciating the discomforts, if not the dangers, of passive smoking, Jullien requested that his concerts be non-smoking events.

Sousa

Another famous civilian wind band was that formed by John Philip Sousa (1854–1932) in 1892. Sousa was born in Washington DC, and from the age of six he learnt to play the violin, as well as studying various band instruments, harmony and musical theory. In 1867 he followed in his father's footsteps and became a professional trombonist, but later turned to the violin and conducting. Between 1868 and 1892 he built up a promising reputation as bandmaster of the United States Marine Corps Band. In 1892 he left the service to form his own famous band, which toured Europe several times as well as making a two-year world tour in 1910–11. Sousa, who is justly called the "March King", composed 136 marches, including *The Washington Post*, *The Stars and Stripes Forever*, *Liberty Bell*, *High School Cadets* and *El Capitan*. Sousa is also remembered for the redesigned helicon first made for his band in 1899, now known as the sousaphone.

ABOVE: Sousa was justly known as the "March King" — he composed 136 marches. His band became famous worldwide and he made a two-year world tour in 1910–11.

Country Music

You got to have smelt a lot of mule manure
before you can sing like a hillbilly.

HANK WILLIAMS (1923–53)

For many, country music is summed up as songs about orphaned children, lost mothers, betrayed lovers, train wrecks and coal-mining disasters. However, there is actually a lot more to country music than sentimentality and sickly patriotism. It is not just "hillbilly music" but has a century of tradition, with many styles evolving and co-existing over the decades. It is a blending of the two distinct traditions of the American settlers: European ballads, story songs and dance music, and African-American blues and work songs.

ABOVE: *Hank Williams was America's greatest honky-tonk performer, whose early death ensured him a permanent place in country music's pantheon of stars. One of his best-known songs is* Cold, Cold Heart.

The commercialization of this blend came in the mid 19th century with the minstrel shows that were created by white performers parodying black manners. These shows gave birth to two distinct forms of entertainment. In the North they evolved into vaudeville, while in the South they nurtured home-grown banjo and fiddle players.

Another seedbed for country music was the southern rural church where singing was – and still is – a central part of the service. Although the white and black churches had different styles, they merged into a tightly harmonized music called "bluegrass". An early example of this type of music was that sung by the Carter Family from Virginia, whose songs were based on the ultimate embodiment of home and family values. Their unornamented, nasal, simple four-square harmonies were entirely white with no black influences whatsoever.

In marked contrast to the "home harmonizers", there were more progressive singers, such as Jimmie Rodgers (1897–1933), who sang a combination of jazz, blues and country. Although he recorded with many bands, his most moving performances were those in which he was accompanied only by his guitar – songs such as the autobiographical *T. B. Blues*, *T. for Texas* and *Waitin' for a Train*, which is one of the most popular train songs ever.

ABOVE: *The fiddle is one of the most popular instruments with country musicians. It is used in many types of country music, from bluegrass to the sentimental tones accompanying the songs for which the genre is famous.*

ABOVE: *This country fiddle player is being accompanied by an accordion player.*

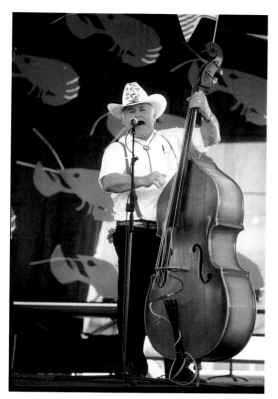

ABOVE: Before the advent of the electric bass guitar, every country band had a string bass. Some bass players were very versatile and were able to produce remarkable effects on their instrument.

pianos and a strong string section, became known throughout the world. Nashville remained the bastion of country music throughout the 1960s, but remained very conservative, both artistically and politically. In the '60s and early '70s there was, for example, an unhealthy number of songs supporting America's involvement in the Vietnam War, notably Merle Haggard's *Okie from Muskogee* and *The Fightin' Side of Me*, which cemented his stardom but enraged liberals everywhere. The slushy sounds of Nashville were rejected by singers such as Waylon Jennings (who had played with Buddy Holly) and Willie Nelson. They left Nashville and went to Texas where they established what has become known as "outlaw country". During the 1980s and '90s mainstream country music has become more and more like pop, so that in many cases it is hard to spot the difference.

Rodgers influenced many country singers, including the legendary Hank Williams (1923–53). Williams sang in the first person and dealt head-on with issues such as adultery and alcoholism. His many songs are still part of almost every country singer's repertoire and there is hardly ever a country music concert anywhere that does not include at least one Hank Williams song.

Grand Ole Opry

Country music spread into the homes of Americans via radio programmes, in particular Chicago's *National Barn Dance*, the *Louisiana Hayride* from Shreveport, and WSM Radio's *Grand Ole Opry* from Nashville, Tennessee. In the mid 1950s Nashville became the centre of country music and the "Nashville Sound", featuring tickling

ABOVE: Willie Nelson (born 1933) is one of the most influencial songwriters and singers country music has ever known. His laid-back style of singing once led one reviewer to announce that by the time Nelson had sung one line, Dolly Parton would have sung a complete song! One of Nelson's best-known albums is Tougher than Leather, *which deals with the effects of fate on life.*

ABOVE: Many solo country singers have teamed up with a colleague to produce duets. One of the most successful of such pairings is Dolly Parton and Kenny Rogers.

Jazz

Jazz is a truly American music, being a combination of that country's two dominant cultures – African and European. As a genre it is almost unique in embodying both rural and urban sounds, as well as ranging from the raw sounds of New Orleans Dixieland bands to the sophistication of New York cool jazz groups.

New Orleans

Dixieland jazz evolved from the ragtime music of the late 19th century, which was epitomized by the work of Scott Joplin, composer of piano rags such as *The Entertainer*. Finding the steady ragtime 2:4 time monotonous, some musicians doubled the time to 4:4 and began to play the melody just a little ahead of or behind the beat, which gave an unevenness to the pulse.

ABOVE: Louis Armstrong single-handedly transformed jazz from a collective art to one of solo expression. His clear, ringing trumpet-playing was impeccable.

These subtle rhythmic changes increased the swing of the music, producing the fast, happy, high-energy music now known as traditional jazz.

One of the earliest exponents of the genre was Buddy Bolden (1877–1931), who is remembered for his blues songs, such as *Careless Love*. Another of the early traditional players was Jelly Roll Morton (1885–1941), a brilliant pianist, arranger and composer, who is best remembered for his *Tiger Rag*.

Another early New Orleans bandleader was "King" Oliver (1885–1938), who moved to Chicago in 1918 and formed his own band, the Creole Jazz Band, in 1922. One of the musicians Oliver invited to join him was Louis Armstrong (1901–71), who had started his professional life playing trumpet in the red-light district of New Orleans for 15 cents a night. Armstrong, a master of improvisation, formed his own band in 1925 and revolutionized jazz for all time. He was the first to create solo improvised melodies that complemented the basic theme, and thus established the central role of the soloist in what had previously been an ensemble form. His technical virtuosity was breathtaking – he was, for instance, able to hold high notes effortlessly for three or four bars at a time.

Chicago "traditional" jazz

Influenced by what was happening in New Orleans, the Chicago of the early 1900s was also a centre of jazz. Led by Nick LaRocca, the Original Dixieland Jazz Band – which was composed

ABOVE: When one thinks of jazz, one automatically thinks of New Orleans, a city where almost every bar and club has its own house band.

ABOVE: As well as being a comedian and film maker, Woody Allen is an enthusiastic jazz clarinettist, his favourite being New Orleans jazz. He is seen here guesting in a band show.

melodic improvisation is very free in cool jazz and players often use counterpoint to play two improvised melodic lines at the same time. Two of the best-known exponents of cool jazz are Miles Davis (1926–91) and the Dave Brubeck Quartet.

ABOVE: Thelonious Monk was one of the greatest jazz pianists. Born in New York City, he began playing at his local Baptist church. Although he had his own big band, he is better known for his jazz quartet.

solely of white musicians – made the first ever jazz recordings in 1917. One man who was inspired by the band was the legendary Bix Beiderbecke (1903–31) who, after hearing a recording by LaRocca, persuaded his parents to give him a cornet. He formed his own band – the Wolverines – in 1923, but by 1925 he had gone solo and was performing with various touring bands. Although he died at only 28, Beiderbecke was the man chiefly responsible for introducing Dixieland jazz to a white audience, and without him the genre would never have become so popular.

Bebop and cool jazz

An offshoot of classical jazz is bebop, which developed in Harlem in the early 1940s. The onomatopoeic name was coined by young musicians including Dizzy Gillespie (1917–93), Charlie Parker (1920–55) and Thelonious Monk (1917–82) to describe the style that emerged during their jam sessions, characterized by upbeat rhythms, fast tempo and improvisation. Bebop later became accepted as the nickname for the

whole wave of new jazz that exploded after World War II.

Cool jazz ("modern jazz") musicians take a more intellectual approach to their music. Disdaining any kind of showmanship, they often play with their backs to the audience. The rhythm is muted, the drummer simply keeping the beat, on which the players stay rather than syncopating. The

ABOVE: Dizzy Gillespie, trumpeter, composer and bandleader, was responsible for giving jazz a whole new style that included whole-tone scales and altered chords.

Big Bands

To swing is to affirm.

FATHER G. V. KENNARD

In the mid 1920s the move began to form larger jazz bands, which were in fact small orchestras. Two of the early dance bands of the era were those led by Paul Whiteman (1890–1967) and Fletcher Henderson (1897–1952).

Whiteman, a classically trained violinist, formed his first (all-white) small band in 1919. In 1924 he organized the first ever concert of jazz music at New York's Aeolian Hall, at which the highlight was George Gershwin playing his *Rhapsody in Blue* for the first time. Whiteman's orchestra was so successful that at one time there were no less than 28 different "Whiteman" bands touring the United States.

Fletcher Henderson, whose band consisted of all black musicians,

ABOVE: *Glenn Miller formed his band in 1938, and within a year his trademark sound of soothing reeds — for example in* In The Mood *— had become world famous.*

played at New York's Roseland Ballroom. However in 1923, after Louis Armstrong had played for a short time with the band, Henderson changed his style from polite dance music to swing jazz. Henderson is remembered especially for his revolutionary "call and response" arrangements, which split the band's instruments into two groups, the first group stating a melody and the second responding to it.

Instrumentation

One of the important innovations of the big band was the introduction of the saxophone. One of the first jazz saxophonists was Coleman Hawkins (1904–69), who introduced the instrument to Henderson's band in

1923. Between the 1930s and '60s, saxophones were to feature strongly in the "big band" orchestras led by people such as Glenn Miller and Duke Ellington in the United States, Henry Hall in England and Bert Kaempfert and James Last in Germany.

Big band leaders

One of the most talented jazz musicians was Duke Ellington (1899–1974). His compositions are still standard works in most bands' repertoires and include classics such as *Satin Doll* and *Mood Indigo*. Ellington, whose band was at its peak during the 1930s, introduced the "jungle style", in which growling trumpets and wailing clarinets gave the music an unmistakable African feeling.

ABOVE: *George Gershwin was one of America's most versatile songwriters. With his brother Ira he wrote musical comedies, such as* Funny Face *and* Tiptoes.

ABOVE: *Duke Ellington: pianist, bandleader and composer.*

ABOVE: *Noted especially for his minimalist piano style, which he had perfected by the end of the 1930s, Count Basie was one of the finest jazz pianists of the 20th century.*

Another jazz man to hit the scene in the 1930s was the clarinettist Benny Goodman (1909–86). Goodman was well known for his sight-reading skills and was the first white jazz musician to break the colour barrier and work with black colleagues. Goodman's band, which was noted for being the best rehearsed and most precise, played the "pop" music of its day.

Kansas City swing

Count (William) Basie (1904–84), who became the leader of Kansas City swing, began his career as pianist in the Bennie Moten band, one of the first to feature the combination of five brass, four reed and four rhythm players. After Moten's death in 1935, Basie began to build his own ensemble from the remnants of his mentor's band. He soon became one of the most successful jazz bandleaders, and led his band until his death in 1984. The band was noted for its "head arranging", in which riffs were improvised during performances, the other musicians having hastily to adjust their parts.

Western swing

Western swing is a combination of string-band music with jazz styles that developed in the late 1920s. One of the first bands to feature the new type of music was the Light Crust Doughboys, which featured the fiddler Bob Wills (1905–75). Wills soon left to form his own band, the Texas Playboys, which became the epitome of western swing. Wills incorporated old-time country fiddling, jazz, blues, boogie-woogie and the Tex-Mex sounds that became so popular in the 1960s.

ABOVE: *Although the early days of Basie's band were exhilaratingly wild, under his leadership they became the most disciplined and sleek big band of the era.*

ABOVE: *Benny Goodman, the "King of Swing", was at home in jazz and classical music.*

ABOVE: *Duke Ellington was the master of swing and endured long after the period was history. He led arguably one of the greatest swing bands of all time.*

Rock and Pop

You have to blame Thomas Edison for today's rock 'n' roll.
He invented [sic] electricity.

STAN GETZ (1927–91)

Rock music evolved from the blues. After the end of World War II many African-Americans from the Deep South moved to northern cities such as Chicago, in search of work and to escape the racialism that was — and to some extent still is — rife in the former Confederate States. Here, musicians created an urbanized rhythm that served as a foundation for pioneer rock 'n' rollers such as Little Richard and Chuck Berry.

Electric guitar

Although the first solid-body electric guitar was built by Les Paul, it was first mass-produced by Leo Fender, and became a key element in rock 'n' roll. Fender, a California-based guitar and

ABOVE: *Elvis Presley was the foremost and most influential popular singer of the 1950s and '60s. His style ranged from country to rock and mainstream.*

ABOVE: *The Beatles, who began their musical career in a nightclub in Liverpool, became the world's top pop group with hit records such as* She Loves You *and* A Hard Day's Night.

amplifier manufacturer, had often been asked by musicians if he could give more volume and at the same time eliminate screech and feedback from the electrified instruments of the time. He came up with the solid-body guitar that he developed just after World War II. His first model, the Broadcaster, entered mass production in 1948, and its sharpness and attack made it an instant success, especially with country musicians. In 1950 its name was changed to the Telecaster, and it was this instrument that gave the rock of that decade its distinctive sound. In 1951 Fender introduced his solid-body bass guitar and, five years later, his futuristic Stratocaster.

One of the pioneers of electric guitar-playing was Muddy Waters (1915–83), who moved up to Chicago from Mississippi. In 1944 he bought his first electric guitar, one made by Fender, and within two years had formed his first electric combo.

African-American music

The importance of African-American music cannot be overestimated. From the Motown sound of the 1960s, through soul and disco to the rap of the 1990s, the exciting sounds of black music have dominated and led the way in many popular music trends. More than anything else, rock music has helped to integrate black and white America, breaking down the racial barrier that has plagued the country.

The 1950s

Many of the young white singers of the 1950s derived their inspiration from black music, including Elvis Presley (1935–77), who became one of the most influential rock 'n' roll singers of the 20th century. Born in Tupelo, Mississippi, as a boy Elvis was always in demand for singing at church services and revival meetings, and was greatly influenced by black blues singers. Indeed, when people who did not know him heard him singing, they could not believe that he was white. Presley's romantic, suggestive ballads, which were matched by his gyrations on stage, made him one of the first mass idols of American adolescent culture (as well as getting him banned from many television stations).

ABOVE: *The legendary rock guitarist Jimi Hendrix, born in Seattle, had his first hit in Britain with* Hey Joe *in 1967.*

Another pioneer was Buddy Holly (1936–59), whose short career was the inspiration for many singers of the 1960s, including Mick Jagger. Holly was a shy, bespectacled youth from Texas whose life was tragically cut short in a plane crash in 1959.

Rock 'n' roll was synonymous with rebellion and no one was more rebellious than Jerry Lee Lewis (born 1935), who shocked the morality of the age by marrying his 13-year-old cousin. It was not until the mid 1960s that Lewis once again gained public approval.

ABOVE: *Abba, whose name was taken from the initial letters of the members' names, were one of the few pop groups outside America or Britain to gain international stardom.*

Pop music

The 1960s have been rightly dubbed the "Swinging Sixties", and musically they were dominated by the Beatles and the Rolling Stones. Whereas the Beatles based their music on the rock of the 1950s, the Rolling Stones were rhythm-and-blues-based. Both bands had great success, and in one way or another have influenced almost every other rock band since.

While many bands were conventional, some performers mirrored the violence of the time (especially the United States' involvement in Vietnam). One of these was Jimi Hendrix (1942–70), who was one of the greatest guitarists of the '60s and had been a member of James Brown's backing band, the Famous Flames. His erotic stage actions, suggestive lyrics and guitar-smashing antics brought him much criticism — on one occasion he doused his guitar with lighter fuel and set it on fire. Other like-minded bands included The Who and the Sex Pistols.

ABOVE: *Frank Zappa (1940–1993) started writing music at high school, inspired by the rhythmic experimentation of the avant-garde composer Edgar Varèse.*

ABOVE: *Vanessa Mae (born 1976) became one of the youngest musicians to play with the London Philharmonic and took the music world by storm with her album* The Violin Player.

Another band of the 1960s and '70s, Frank Zappa's Mothers of Invention, was used as a vehicle for band-audience involvement. Music was only a part of the performance, which also included satire and comedy. Anything could happen, from a bag of vegetables being opened and examined to "dead air", when the band stopped and completely ignored the audience. On one occasion, when the audience had become unsettled and angry, Zappa approached the microphone saying, "It brings out the hostilities in you, doesn't it?" Zappa went on to become a film producer and classical composer, and died in 1993.

There was a respite from "heavy metal" when in 1974 a breath of fresh air entered the pop charts with Abba. This Swedish quartet, who depended more on television and radio than live concerts to build an image, achieved their breakthrough by winning that year's Eurovision Song Contest with *Waterloo*, a song that became a top-ten hit in many countries and many languages.

Famous String Players

*To play great music you must keep
your eyes on a distant star.*

YEHUDI MENUHIN (1916–99)

The idea of a stringed instrument being a virtuoso instrument emerged during the Baroque period, when composers such as Arcangelo Corelli, who was a violinist, began to exploit the strings' expressiveness in *concerti grossi* and solo sonatas. Eighteenth-century refinements in stringed instrument design allowed for increasing technical brilliance by a number of great Italian virtuosi, culminating in the talents of the violinist Niccolò Paganini (1782–1840), who confirmed the star status of the soloist. He was also an expert on the mandolin, guitar and viola.

Violin

The great violinists of the Romantic period included Rudolphe Kreutzer (1766–1831), for whom Beethoven wrote his *Kreutzer Sonata*, and Joseph Joachim (1831–1907), to whom Brahms's Violin Concerto was dedicated. Fritz Kreisler (1875–1962) showed an early talent for the violin and by the time he was 15 had

ABOVE: *Yehudi Menuhin was one of the most respected musicians who has ever lived. His violin-playing inspired young players.*

ABOVE: *David Oistrakh coupled the technical brilliance of Heifetz with the warmth of Menuhin. He can truly be said to be one of the greatest violinists of all time.*

achieved worldwide success. His playing epitomized Viennese lilt and warmth, while his almost constant vibrato made him one of the founders of the modern school of violin-playing.

As well as being the foremost composer of his generation, Paul Hindemith (1895–1963) was also an outstanding viola player, playing in the Rebner and Amar Quartets, and the Opera Orchestra in Germany from 1915–23. Also an accomplished violinist, it was said he could play every instrument in the orchestra.

Yehudi Menuhin (1916–99) began his career as a child prodigy, and was at home in all types of music, achieving a unique tone and mastery of rhythm. He will always be remembered for his playing of the Elgar Violin Concerto under the direction of the composer, and as a humanitarian for the schools he founded for musically gifted children in England and Switzerland.

David Oistrakh (1908–74) achieved national recognition in the former Soviet Union after performing Glazunov's Violin Concerto in 1927. The Soviet authorities prevented him from performing outside the USSR until the early 1950s, but from then on he took the international stage by storm. He remained a Soviet citizen all his life and was committed to contemporary Russian composers such as Prokofiev and Shostakovich.

The Israeli violinist Itzhak Perlman (born 1945), although a victim of poliomyelitis at the age of four, was giving public recitals when he was ten years old. In his subsequent career, Perlman's charismatic stage presence, combined with his instinctive directness of musical expression, brilliant technique and a concern for refinement of detail, has brought him international recognition.

ABOVE: *Mstislav Rostropovich was a close friend of Benjamin Britten, who wrote several cello works for him.*

ABOVE: The charismatic Jacqueline du Pré made her debut at the age of 16.

Cello

As the cello took a more prominent role in chamber music during the 18th century, composers such as Liugi Boccherini (1743–1805) began to recognize its potential as a solo instrument. An early British virtuoso, Robert Lindley, began playing when he was five years old. His technique was said to be so brilliant that he was able to play first violin parts on his cello. In 1794, aged 18, Lindley played before the Prince Regent and, by 1826, had become lead cello with the Italian Opera in London.

Pablo Casals (1876–1973) probably did more for the cello than any other player. Although he is mainly remembered for his masterly playing of the Bach solo cello suites, Casals was also a conductor and a member of a chamber trio, and founded an annual festival of chamber music in France. Another influential cellist of the 20th century is Mstislav Rostropovich (born 1927), who has been immensely successful in playing the works of composers such as Shostakovich, Prokofiev and Britten.

The talent of Jacqueline du Pré (1945–87) was recognized at a very early age. She launched her professional career in 1961 with a concert at London's Wigmore Hall, at which she played a cello of 1672 by Antonio Stradivari. One of the great musical icons of the 20th century, she was admired by her audiences for the love she radiated in her playing, which was noted for its instinctive feeling for style as well as its technical proficiency. In 1973 her career was suddenly interrupted by the onset of multiple sclerosis, but she continued to teach.

Harp

Nicholas Bochsa (1789–1856), though a skilful player of almost every instrument, was best known for his expertise on the harp, an instrument on which he was constantly discovering new musical effects. Harpist to Louis XVIII, in 1817 he had to leave his native France hurriedly, due to his part-time business in forged documents. One of Bochsa's favourite pieces was his *Fantasia for Harp and Violin* which he often played with

ABOVE: Since making her London debut in 1963, Marisa Robles has become a professor at the Royal College of Music.

ABOVE: John Williams is a very versatile guitarist, playing classical, jazz and pop music — he founded the pop group, Sky.

Nicholas Mori, who was said to have handled his violin as tenderly as a mother her child, but as playfully as the child its toy.

The Spanish harpist Marisa Robles (born 1937) is one of the foremost players of the 20th century, noted for the quicksilver quality of her playing.

Lute and guitar

The eminent Spanish guitarist Andrés Segovia (1893–1987) was largely self-taught, but championed the guitar as a concert instrument, commissioning many new works. One of his pupils was Julian Bream (born 1933), who also took up the lute and quickly became a leading performer on it. In 1971, Bream began giving encouragement to guitar and lute makers by inaugurating the Semley Festival in Wiltshire to promote rare chamber music.

John Williams (born 1942) also studied guitar with Segovia. As a composer, he is particularly active in crossover projects, using tapes and electronics in his music and drawing on non-Western influences.

Famous Woodwind and Brass Players

*It takes perhaps a thousand poor musicians
to produce one virtuoso.*

RALPH VAUGHAN WILLIAMS (1872–1958)

As with other orchestral instruments, the expansion of the solo repertoire for woodwind and brass went hand in hand with technological advances that enabled the instruments to be played with far greater range and expressiveness.

Flute

Although Vivaldi and Mozart wrote for the solo flute, it was neglected during the 19th century, but found favour with French impressionists such as Debussy, and many modern composers have since written for it. The virtuoso James Galway (born 1939) is widely known as a popular soloist, but also spent many years as an orchestral player, including a period as principal flautist with the Berlin Philharmonic under Herbert von Karajan. A strong advocate of contemporary music, Galway's bright tone and twinkling

vibrato has brought him thousands of fans all around the world.

Jean-Pierre Rampal (born 1922) was an all-round musician of astonishing versatility. His repertoire ranged from Baroque to contemporary, while his playing was noted for its pure tone, subtle dynamics and exquisite phrasing.

Oboe

The sweet tone and expressive playing of Leon Goossens (1897–1988) set new standards for the instrument. Principal oboe with Henry Wood by the time he was 16, Goossens's phrasing, superlative finger technique and breath control were to influence many composers to write concertos for the oboe.

Another leading 20th-century oboist is the legendary Heinz Holliger (born 1939), who is an eminent exponent of sounding chords, double trills and

ABOVE: *Leon Goossens was one of the finest oboe players of the 20th century. A member of a very musical family, he was brother to the conductor Eugene and the harpists Sidonie and Marie.*

glissandos. He is not shy of experimentation; his work with sounds produced by a microphone placed within the bore of his instrument encouraged composers such as Hans Werner Henze to write for the oboe.

Clarinet

One of the 20th century's finest clarinettists was Benny Goodman (1909–86), a musician who was equally at home in classical music and jazz. He formed a 12-piece jazz band in 1934, but did not forsake his classical roots, for he later recorded the Mozart Clarinet Quintet with the Budapest Quartet, as well as commissioning works from Aaron Copland and Paul Hindemith.

ABOVE: *One of Ireland's most popular musicians, James Galway has entertained millions with his flute-playing, performing both classical music and popular songs.*

ABOVE: *Barry Tuckwell studied horn technique with the virtuoso Dennis Brain (1921–57) on his arrival in England in 1950. He was Professor of Horn at the Royal Academy of Music (1963–74), launching his solo career in 1968.*

Horn

Barry Tuckwell (born 1931) began his musical career in Melbourne, Australia, at the age of 15 and played with the Sydney Symphony Orchestra. He was principal horn with the London Symphony Orchestra from 1955 to 1968, in which year he founded the Tuckwell Wind Quintet. The leading horn player of his generation, Tuckwell is famed for his outstanding ability to make light of extreme technical and musical difficulties, achieving his marvellous tone by playing a large-bore Holton double horn, rather than the lighter-toned instrument preferred by many of his contemporaries.

Trumpet

One of the finest trumpet players was Louis Armstrong (1901–71), a man who almost single-handedly transformed jazz from a collective art to one of solo expression, exemplified in a series of 1920s recordings known as the "Hot Fives" and "Hot Sevens". His clear ringing trumpet sound

influenced many modern trumpet players, both jazz and classical.

The innovative player Maurice André (born 1933) has brought the trumpet to a whole new audience. One of his main contributions to trumpet-playing has been his pioneering of the small, four-valved piccolo trumpet. He has transcribed for it many Baroque compositions originally written for other wind instruments.

Another champion of modern trumpet music is Håkan Hardenberger (born 1961). He has had various works written specially for him, including Harrison Birtwistle's trumpet concerto *Endless Parade*. A master of musical effects, Hardenberger's playing combines technical brilliance with a great beauty of sound.

Wynton Marsalis (born 1961) comes from New Orleans, and is chiefly known as one of the most famous jazz trumpeters of his generation. However, such is his catholic taste that he is as much at home with Haydn's trumpet concertos as he is with the

ABOVE: *Håkan Hardenberger is one of the world's top trumpet players, famous for his flawless technical ability and the beautiful quality of his tone.*

ABOVE: *The great jazz trumpeter Louis Armstrong in a scene from* High Society.

Lincoln Center Jazz Orchestra. He is also a composer, and in 1997 won a Pulitzer Prize for his operatic piece *Blood on the Fields*.

Trombone

Many technical developments of the 20th century have been due to the influence of jazz musicians. One of the foremost jazz trombonists of the second half of the century is the German virtuoso Albert Mangelsdorff (born 1928). He played with various German jazz groups before forming his own band in 1958. In 1964, influenced by his recent tour of Asia, he started introducing eastern elements into his playing. His main claim to fame, however, is that he was the first trombonist to succeed in playing three and four-note chords on his instrument, a feat that he achieved by a skilful combination of lip and vocal sounds.

Famous Keyboard and Percussion Players

The great pianists have nothing to show save technique and affection.

LUDWIG VAN BEETHOVEN (1770–1827)

The harpsichord had a major role in the Baroque ensemble as a continuo instrument, but other keyboard instruments, from majestic church organs to the domestic spinet, have largely been used as solo or accompanying instruments, or in chamber music. The modern piano is capable of suggesting the range and richness of an entire orchestra, and has a vast solo repertoire. It is sometimes used in modern orchestral music, but is treated like a special member of the percussion section.

Keyboard

One of the most remarkable keyboard players of the 18th century was William Crotch (1775–1847). Born in Norwich, the son of a carpenter, he was a child prodigy without parallel in the history of music. By the time he was two he was able to pick out tunes on an organ, and a year later his mother took him on a series of concert tours throughout England. As well as the piano Crotch also played the violin, which he did standing on a chair so as to be seen by his audience. In 1822 he was appointed principal of the newly established Royal Academy of Music.

Frédéric Chopin (1810–49) soon established himself as a pianist, making his public debut when he was eight years old. He arrived in Paris in 1831, where he was introduced to the artistic circle of Romantics such as Liszt, Berlioz and Bellini. Brought up on the

ABOVE: Clara Schumann, the wife of the composer Robert Schumann, was a fine performer and teacher and became one of the foremost pianists of the late 19th century.

music of Bach, Chopin was an intellectual who forged his own forms. His unique music is unmistakable, and he is recognized as one of the greatest composers for the piano.

Born in Hungary, Franz Liszt's (1811–86) early promise was rewarded by a subscription from five noblemen, which enabled him to study piano in Vienna. There he met Beethoven, who prophesied an excellent future for him. In 1831, on hearing Paganini's first concert in Paris, Liszt resolved there and then to become the Paganini of the piano. From 1838–47 he toured Europe, where the amazing strength of his fingers, which enabled him to execute the most rapid passages with amazing force, won him his reputation as the greatest piano virtuoso of his

ABOVE: Franz Liszt was the most popular pianist of his day. This caricature shows him being ecstatically received by his adoring female fans.

day. One of the outstanding musical personalities of the 19th century, Liszt created a brand new style that carried piano-playing technique further than ever before.

Clara Schumann (1819–96) was born in Leipzig, and was taught the piano by her father, the composer Friedrich Wieck, who also taught Robert Schumann. Clara made her musical debut in 1828, but after her marriage to Robert Schumann in 1840 she largely abandoned touring until after his death. Her playing was characterized by her seriousness and restraint, and her repertoire concentrated on Schumann, Beethoven, Chopin, Bach and Mozart. As well as editing many of her husband's works, she also composed many piano pieces of her own. She was also a famous and influential teacher.

The next generation of piano virtuosi included Ignacy Paderewski (1866–1941), who also became, briefly, prime minister of Poland in 1919; Sergei Rachmaninov (1873–1943), best known for his piano compositions in the Romantic style; and Artur Schnabel (1882–1951), an outstanding interpreter of Beethoven.

The Canadian pianist Glenn Gould (1932–82) performed on the concert

ABOVE: Evelyn Glennie, now a full-time solo percussionist, has collaborated with indigenous performers in many parts of the world to further audiences' understanding and appreciation of world music.

platform for only ten years, but was renowned for his charismatic recordings of the keyboard music of Bach. Alfred Brendel (born 1931) is known for his interpretations of Mozart, Beethoven, Schubert and Liszt. Vladimir Ashkenazy (born 1937), who was joint winner of the 1962 Tchaikovsky Piano Competition, was born in the former Soviet Union but left in 1963 and now lives in Iceland. A passionate pianist, he is equally known as a conductor.

Percussion

In Western music the percussionist has acquired virtuoso status in the 20th century, as composers have begun to use percussion more prominently and many new instruments from around the world have been added to the percussion section. The British player James Blades (1901–98) was a world-renowned orchestral player and an authority on percussion, who lectured and broadcast for many years. He influenced Evelyn Glennie (born 1965), who, although she partially lost her hearing at the age of eight,

was introduced to percussion when she was 12. Glennie made her solo debut at the Wigmore Hall in 1986. In 1989 she was the first solo percussionist to perform at the Proms. She has since toured with major orchestras and has had many pieces composed especially for her.

ABOVE: Russian-born Vladimir Ashkenazy shared first prize in the Tchaikovsky Piano Competition of 1962 with the British pianist John Ogdon (1937–89).

ABOVE: Although an infrequent piano performer, Mitsuko Uchida's inspired repertoire includes Mozart, Schoenberg, Birtwistle and Debussy.

Court Composers

*Music must be supported by the king and the princes,
for the maintenance of the arts is their duty.*

MARTIN LUTHER (1483–1546)

Before the 18th century, musicians and composers worked for princes and kings. Such was the prestige of top organists that Paul Hofhaimer (1459–1537), imperial organist to the Holy Roman Emperor Maximilian I, travelled with his royal master in his own special chariot. Maximilian's contemporary in England, Henry VIII, was also greatly interested in music and maintained a private band of 40 instrumentalists and singers.

Secular music was composed for private – not public – performance. Before 1750, professional musicians copied their music by hand, and even towards the end of the century Mozart often prevented his music from being widely circulated, as he feared it would be copied. As there was no protection of copyright or performing rights, patronage was the only way composers had of securing an income.

ABOVE: *An autographed manuscript of Mozart's Symphony No. 8, written in brown ink on thick cream paper.*

Lully

One of the most musically influential courts in Europe was that of Louis XIV (1643–1715). Jean-Baptiste Lully (1632–87) was born in Florence but had moved to France when he was 14, working first as a servant, then as a violinist. He entered royal service in 1652 and attained the post of Royal Composer in 1662. He developed the French operatic style, favouring short, simple songs rather than the florid arias so popular in Italy, and made a large fortune by obtaining a monopoly over French opera production.

Haydn

In 1761, Franz Joseph Haydn (1732–1809) entered the employment of the Hungarian Count Esterházy, with whom he spent the next 30 years. Although Esterházy's musical establishment was disbanded in 1790, Haydn retained his salary when he returned to Vienna. His long service with the family gave him great scope for composition, and he earned a reputation across Europe for his symphonies and string quartets, two forms for which he established the classical style. He then spent two years in London, where he wrote the last 12 of his 104 symphonies.

ABOVE: *Lully went to Paris as a servant but his musical talents soon came to the attention of Louis XIV. He transformed music from a mere court pastime into a national art.*

On his return to Vienna, he gave some lessons to a young German named Beethoven. Haydn was a prolific composer, and a humble and genial man who was well loved by the musicians he directed.

Bach

Orphaned at the age of ten, Johann Sebastian Bach (1685–1750) was brought up by his older brother, who taught him to play the organ, but his musical debut was as a choirboy at Lüneburg when he was 15. In 1703 he was appointed organist at Armstadt, but displeased his employers when he immersed himself in innovative organ music while neglecting his routine duties as choirmaster.

In 1708 he was appointed Kapellmeister to the Duke of Cöthen.

ABOVE: Signed copy of the first movement of Bach's Sonata in G Minor for solo violin.

ABOVE: The one certain way for musicians to make a living in the 18th century was by having a royal patron: Mozart's father introduced his son to various European courts.

As the Duke was a Calvinist, he required little music in his religious services, and Bach was able to concentrate on secular compositions and recitals. However, as a devout Lutheran, he wished to return to church music and in 1723 he accepted a more lowly post as cantor at the

ABOVE: In 17th-century England the main patron of music was the king. William III was no exception and encouraged his composers.

Thomasschule in Leipzig, where he remained for the rest of his life.

Bach, who once said that it was his purpose to dispel sadness and bring joy, could turn his skills to almost any kind of music, although, in his own day, he received greater recognition as an organist than as a composer. His major standing as a composer was achieved only with the 19th-century revival of interest in his works.

Handel

George Frideric Handel (1685–1759) was born in Germany, but became a naturalized English citizen and one of England's greatest composers. Although he showed an early taste for music, Handel entered the University of Halle as a law student. However, after a short period as organist at the cathedral, he gave up his studies and went to Hamburg. It was here, in 1705, that his first operas *Almira* and *Nero* were produced. Five years later he became Kapellmeister to the Elector of Hanover. His period in Hanover was short, for by 1712 he was in London and in good favour with

Queen Anne, who gave him a life pension. In 1714 Anne died and his former master, the Elector, became King George I. Without doubt, Handel's greatest work is the *Messiah*, which he wrote in three weeks. It was first produced in Dublin in 1742, with a choir of about 30.

ABOVE: One of the most influential English composers of the first half of the 18th century was George Frideric Handel.

Modern Composers

My music is best understood by children and animals.

IGOR STRAVINSKY (1882–1971)

While the Romantic composers of the 19th century believed that the prime function of music was to express emotion, those of the 20th century were more likely to see it as a search for new sounds and, consequently, new instruments on which to produce them.

United States

Aaron Copland (1900–90) used American jazz and folk idioms, as well as special effects, such as the orchestral reproduction of a gunfight in *Billy the Kid*. Other works by Copland that use folk music include *Rodeo* and *Appalachian Spring*. Another 20th-century American composer is Leroy Anderson (1908–75), whose light classical music gained wide popular appeal. His music was a blend of infectious melodies, popular dance rhythms and novel effects, such as the pizzicato strings in *Plink, Plank, Plonk*, the percussion in *The Syncopated Clock*, and unconventional "instruments" such as a typewriter and sandpaper.

John Cage (1912–92) was as much an inventor as a composer. A pupil of Schoenberg, Cage relegated harmony and pitch to a secondary role and gave priority to rhythm and noise. He drew up large charts on which he plotted rhythmic structures to compose works such as his *Concerto for Prepared Piano*. In *Music of Changes* the progressions all depend on the tossing of a coin.

Russia

Dimitri Shostakovich (1906–75) graduated from Petrograd Conservatory in 1925. His First

ABOVE: Although Shostakovich ran foul of the Russian state in 1948, he was politically rehabilitated in 1956 and his work greatly influenced young Russian composers.

Symphony, composed while he was still a student, won international acclaim in 1926, but his Fourth was withdrawn in 1936 during rehearsal when the Stalinist authorities objected to his opera, *Lady Macbeth of the Mtsensk District*. Although he attempted to ingratiate himself with his Fifth Symphony, his relationship with the government remained uneasy, and in 1948 he was denounced for "formalism" and fired from his teaching post at the Leningrad Conservatory. He undertook to bring his work nearer to "folk art", and finally regained his job in 1960.

Shostakovich wrote 15 symphonies and several operas and ballets, as well as chamber, choral and piano music, and his work had a great influence on younger Russian composers.

ABOVE: Aaron Copland's use of the jazz and folk idioms of his native land in his music cannot fail to stir up images of the America of the late 19th and early 20th centuries.

ABOVE: *In his youth Messiaen used to write down birdsong, which he included in his music. Taken prisoner by the Germans in World War II, his* Quartet for the End of Time *was written in a concentration camp.*

France

Paul Dukas (1865–1935) achieved worldwide success for his orchestral work of 1897, *L'Apprenti sorcier* and, although he wrote some successful music for the stage, it is virtually by this work alone that Dukas is remembered. His severe self-criticism reached such a pitch that he refused to publish any new composition, eventually going as far as to burn everything not yet published. His surviving work includes the opera *Ariane et Barbe-bleue* (1907), *La Péri*, a ballet published in 1912, and a sonata for the piano in E minor.

One of Dukas's pupils at the Paris Conservatoire was Olivier Messiaen (1908–92). Messiaen, an organist as well as a composer, was greatly influenced by Indian and eastern music, and his orchestral compositions display great rhythmic complexity.

Electronic music

The *ondes Martenot* ("Martenot waves"), one of the earliest successful electronic instruments, was patented by the French cellist and radio engineer, Maurice Martenot (1896–1980) in 1928. Using oscillating valves as the sound source, the pitch was controlled by moving one hand along a wire, while the other hand operated a number of "expression" keys. Later a keyboard was added for pitch orientation. The *ondes Martenot* was first used in an orchestra for a performance of Messiaen's *Turangalíla* Symphony in 1947. Arthur Honegger (1892–1955) and Pierre Boulez also wrote music for the instrument.

In 1949 an electronic music studio was set up in Paris to further the work of Pierre Schaeffer (born 1910), a radio technician and the founder of *musique concrète*, a term he coined to describe a form in which pre-existing real sounds were manipulated in various ways and combined into a kind of sound collage. Other composers to use the studio included Stockhausen, Messiaen and Boulez.

Jean-Michel Jarre (born 1948) became a pupil of Schaeffer in 1968. He combines electronic music with melodic orchestration to produce commercially successful recordings such as *Oxygène* (1977) and *Equinoxe* (1978). He has mounted a series of live performances on a huge scale, culminating in a Bastille Day celebration in Paris in 1990 that was attended by 2.5 million people.

ABOVE: *Boulez is a great exponent of avant-garde music. He once said that his music, like fashion, was self-destructive so that it could be replaced by a new collection.*

ABOVE: *Jean-Michel Jarre studied counterpoint, fugue and harmony at the Paris Conservatoire and released his first electro-acoustic recording,* La Cage, *in 1969.*

Role of the Conductor

It is better to conduct with the ear than with the arm.
The rest follows automatically.

GEORG SOLTI (1912–97)

Although the role of the virtuoso conductor was a 19th-century phenomenon, there had always been one member of an ensemble whose duty it was to direct the others and so ensure a uniformity of performance. In ancient Greece the "giver of time beat with his stave up and down", while in Rome, time was indicated by the leader stamping his feet. In 17th-century France it was the custom to beat time loudly on the floor with a large staff – which on one occasion had fatal consequences. In 1687, while conducting a *Te Deum* to celebrate the king's recovery from sickness, Jean-Baptiste Lully brought his long staff down on his foot instead of the floor and died of the subsequent gangrene poisoning. The staff survives today both as the conductor's baton and in the mace carried by drum majors

leading military bands. During the 15th and 16th centuries some choral conductors kept time by waving a rolled-up sheet of music.

Until the 18th century it was usual for the conductor to be the composer. He generally directed the band from his seat at the harpsichord, although in France it bcame fashionable for the first violin to direct. This was also the case with the Mannheim orchestra, an ensemble that was greatly influenced by French practice.

Although Beethoven is known to have conducted his own works, his methods were far from conventional. When conducting from the piano, he bent lower to indicate that he wanted the music played softly. When the music came to a *crescendo*, he raised

LEFT: *The modern conductor's baton – used for beating time and indicating expression – is a thin tapering stick about 50cm/20in long. Although first seen in the late 18th century, batons did not come into general use until the 1820s.*

himself by degrees and, upon the commencement of the *forte*, would spring bolt upright. To increase the *forte* even more, he would often join in with a shout to the orchestra.

From the late 18th century music became more complex, with each instrumental section having more solo music to play. Although Carl Maria von Weber (1786–1826) conducted an orchestra with a baton in 1817, the first man to conduct an orchestra in the modern sense – moving his hands and arms without making a sound himself – was the German violinist Louis Spohr (1784–1859), leader of the orchestra of the Theater an der Wien, who conducted the Philharmonic Society of London in 1820.

In Vienna, the directors of the new waltz orchestras of the early 19th century, such as Johann Strauss the Elder (1804–49) and his rival Joseph Lanner (1801–43), led while playing the violin, beating time with the bow. This custom is sometimes resurrected by the conductors at the annual New Year's concert in Vienna.

Nineteenth-century conductors took on more and more responsibility for the performance. They established the speed and helped players come in at the right time. They decided how the

ABOVE: *After making his conducting debut in 1943 with the New York Philharmonic, Leonard Bernstein (1918–90) conducted many famous orchestras, including La Scala, the Vienna Philharmonic, the Israel Philharmonic and the London Symphony Orchestra.*

ABOVE: *The custom in the 18th century was for the leader of a musical band to conduct from the keyboard. Here Bach is seen conducting an ensemble from the clavichord.*

music should be played and phrased. They were also more necessary because orchestras were growing larger. Although he never achieved his dream, Berlioz's ideal orchestra size was 465. Conducting soon came to be regarded as an important profession in its own right and, as the 19th century progessed, a conductor cult grew. It became usual for composers to conduct not just their own works but also those of others.

In opera it was customary for the conductor to concentrate on the singers rather than the band, and to this end he was placed immediately in front of – and facing – the stage, with the orchestra behind him, following his beat as best they could. It was not until 1897, when Gustav Mahler (1860–1911) became conductor of the Vienna State Opera, that the podium was moved to the back of the orchestra pit.

ABOVE: *Some conductors use very subtle gestures, in which even minor movements of the forearm can cause the players to respond instantly.*

Conducting with style

ABOVE AND LEFT: *Many conductors are showmen, relishing their position in the limelight, and their antics sometimes seem intended more to impress the audience than direct the orchestra. These photographs show just a few of the hundreds of gestures and instructions made by a conductor within the context of a performance.*

Famous Conductors

You must have the score in your head,
not your head in the score.

Hans von Bülow (1830–94)

In his *Notes for Conductors*, Richard Strauss advises a conductor to put his left thumb in the armpit of his waistcoat and lead the orchestra with the right. It is, so Strauss advises, the audience and not the conductor who should sweat. One man who followed Strauss's advice to the extreme was Arthur Nikisch (1855–1922), who certainly allowed the baton to do all the work. He never distracted the orchestra or the audience with elaborate gestures, and conducted almost solely from the wrist down. Indeed, any minor movement of his forearm would so alarm the players that they would instantly respond with a massive *fortissimo*. Amongst Nikisch's disciples were Fritz Reiner (1888–1963) and Adrian Boult (1889–1983).

ABOVE: Arthur Nikisch, seen here with the Berlin Philharmonic Orchestra, was known for conducting the orchestra in a subtle manner, moving his arms only slightly.

ABOVE: The English conductor Sir Thomas Beecham founded the London Philharmonic Orchestra in 1932. He was especially known for his interpretations of Delius's music.

Thomas Beecham (1879–1961) never had a technique! His baton did whatever the state of the performance prompted. He disdained to be seen beating anything less complex than phrases, but at the same time he discreetly beat time by opening and closing the fingers of his left hand. He was renowned for his dry wit: during one rehearsal he remarked that the second trumpet was too loud. The embarrassed leader had to explain that the second trumpet player had telephoned to say that he would be

a little late. Unperturbed, Sir Thomas replied: "Well, when he comes, tell him he is too loud."

The qualities of a conductor as a personality are always important. That some have more pleasant personalities than others is a fact of life, and some, however musical they are, leave a lot to be desired. Arturo Toscanini (1867–1957) was notoriously temperamental. At one rehearsal of Verdi's opera *Falstaff*, he threw the score at four different women soloists, alleging that they had not learnt their parts. At another rehearsal he threw his gold watch to the floor and stamped on it. His disregard for other people's feelings was legendary and on one occasion, when a red carpet was laid from the stage entrance to the podium as a mark of respect for him, Toscanini refused to enter until it was taken up, growling "*Non sono un cardinale.*"

Most great conductors have, however, been more amenable and well respected by the musicians with whom they work. The British conductor John Barbirolli (1899–1970), who succeeded Toscanini as conductor of the New York Philharmonic in 1937, was vivacious and charming. He returned to Britain in 1943 to become permanent conductor of the Hallé Orchestra in Manchester. Another well-loved figure was Malcolm Sargent (1895–1967). Particularly noted for his choral work, from 1928 he was the conductor of the Royal Choral Society. Sargent was noted not only for his

ABOVE: The son of an émigré Italian violinist, Barbirolli became one of Britain's foremost conductors. For his services to music, he was knighted in 1949.

immediate grasp of a complicated score and for his extraordinarily effective "stick technique", but also as a "showman". In 1950 he succeeded Adrian Boult as conductor of the BBC Symphony Orchestra. Sargent, the natural successor to Henry Wood as principal conductor of the Promenade Concerts, was equally at home with classical and modern music, and many young and inexperienced players gained much confidence by his support.

Herbert von Karajan (1908–89) was a far less accessible man and personified the image of the conductor as star. Between the 1950s and '70s he was the dominant figure in European music. While presiding over the Berlin Philharmonic for 35 years, his influence also spread over the Vienna State Opera, the Salzburg Festival, the Vienna Symphony Orchestra, the Philharmonia Orchestra in London and La Scala in Milan. Karajan was an

imperious, stubborn and demanding conductor who worked only on his own terms. Throughout his career he continued to question and rework his own musical interpretations, but his intimate knowledge of the players of the Berlin Philharmonic and his belief in their potential enabled him to turn it into one of the world's finest orchestras.

His predecessor in Berlin had been Wilhelm Furtwängler (1886–1954), whose conducting was characterized by a curious wavering beat that often confused those who were not used to him. He was particularly associated with the music of Wagner, at a time when it came to stand for the ideals of the Nazi regime in Germany. Otto Klemperer (1885–1973), on the other hand, was denounced by the Nazis and left Germany to become an American citizen. Another leading conductor of his time, his performances were notable for their attention to detail, especially in the woodwind section.

An outstanding figure of the new generation is Simon Rattle (born 1955). At the age of 16 he took lessons in conducting from Pierre Boulez, and in 1974 won first prize in the Bournemouth International Conducting Competition. In the same

ABOVE: In 1980 the British conductor Sir Simon Rattle was appointed principal conductor of the City of Birmingham Orchestra, which he transformed into a world-class ensemble. He has a deep solidarity with his orchestras.

year he was appointed assistant conductor of the Bournemouth Symphony Orchestra. In 1980 he became principal conductor of the City of Birmingham Symphony Orchestra, which he transformed into a world-class ensemble. In 1999 it was announced that he would replace Claudio Abbado as chief conductor of the Berlin Philharmonic in 2002.

ABOVE: Herbert von Karajan was one of the most respected conductors of the 20th century. He was principal conductor of the Berlin Philharmonic for 35 years.

ABOVE: Sir Georg Solti studied under notables such as Bartók and Kodály, and was Musical Director of the Chicago Symphony Orchestra until his death in 1997.

Famous Concert Halls and Orchestras

...For we must have music, We must have music
To drive our fears away.

NOEL COWARD (1899–1973)

Until the 18th century, public concerts as they are known today did not exist. One of the first rooms to be devoted to formal concerts was that opened in London by Thomas Hickford in 1711. From then on other custom-built concert halls and opera houses gradually started to appear all over Europe.

German patrons of music built concert halls on a grand scale. At Schwetzingen, the Elector of Palatine built a new opera house capable of holding an audience of 5000, while Duke Karl Theodor of Württemberg bankrupted his entire principality to provide sensational opera productions at Mannheim.

The Berlin Opera House was built by Frederick the Great of Prussia (1740–86). A notable flautist and patron of music, Frederick was deeply immersed in French culture and maintained a French-speaking court. Opened in 1773, the Opera House, which employed singers from Italy and dancers from France, was equipped with parking space for 1000 carriages. The staircases were so wide that sedan

ABOVE: *This painting by Ludwig Edward Lutke shows the German State Opera House in Berlin, c.1845.*

ABOVE: *The Amsterdam Concertgebouw Orchestra was founded in 1888. Its hall is renowned for its magnificent acoustics.*

chairs could be carried up to the fourth tier of the boxes, and three enormous chandeliers illuminated the whole auditorium.

In London, purpose-built concert halls included Carlisle House, Soho Square (1764); the Pantheon, Oxford Street (1772); and the Hanover Square Rooms (1775). Halls were also opened in some major provincial centres, such as Bath, which, thanks to its spa, was the centre of English fashionable society in the 18th century.

Throughout the 19th century the orchestras involved in London concerts contained so many of the same players that it would be difficult to describe each orchestra as different. Players had little or no

financial security and were engaged for each concert, not for the entire season. The custom of sending a deputy to the rehearsals, or even the concert, had become established, meaning that the composition of the orchestra was constantly changing.

One of the first conductors to recruit musicians for an entire season was Charles Hallé (1819–95). Hallé had made his reputation in Paris, but was driven to England by the revolution of 1848 and eventually settled in Manchester, which had an influential German community. He threw himself heartily into the town's musical life and in 1857 founded what was to become the celebrated Hallé

ABOVE: *The New York Metropolitan Opera House was founded in 1883 but was rebuilt after a fire destroyed the original building.*

Orchestra. Its members were always present at both rehearsal and concert, making the orchestra the most disciplined and efficient band in the country. They never sounded, as did so many other orchestras, like a bunch of instrumentalists thrown together for a single event.

During the 20th century several great orchestras have been founded in London, including the London Philharmonic, which was founded in

ABOVE: Musical events held at the Royal Albert Hall in London range from brass band contests to rock concerts.

1932 by Thomas Beecham, and the BBC Symphony Orchestra, which was founded in 1930 and was the first orchestra to offer an annual salary and paid holidays.

As the 20th century progressed, orchestras faced the problem of financial support. The Boston Symphony Orchestra was founded in 1881 by the financier Henry Lee Higginson. He gave his conductors absolute artistic freedom and kept the orchestra at the highest level of achievement. Its financial future was assured by Higginson's creation of a body of 300 guarantors. Further south, the New York Philharmonic was founded in 1842. For the first 66 years of its existence it was run by an internal committee of musicians.

However, in 1908, due to financial difficulties, the orchestra was taken over by a syndicate.

The Berlin Philharmonic Orchestra, which acquired its high international reputation under the directorship of Herbert von Karajan, is funded by the city of Berlin, and has its home in an acoustically brilliant concert hall affectionately known as the "circus tent". Although it has a capacity of 2000, the seats virtually surround the orchestra, giving the hall a feeling of intimacy.

The audience at the Royal Albert Hall in London is seated in a vast ellipse, but had to suffer poor acoustics until they were remedied in the 1960s. The brick and glass building was built from 1867–71, and is universally known as the venue for the annual Henry Wood Promenade Concerts, which have been performed there since World War II when their former home, the Queen's Hall, was destroyed.

The Sydney Opera House on Bennelong Point is one of the city's most notable features. Designed by

ABOVE: Kurt Masur conducting the New York Philharmonic Orchestra in 1999. Masur made his United States debut in 1974.

Jørn Utsen, the building was largely financed by the Australian lottery and was opened in 1973. Its programme offers 16 different operas a year and there is a performance almost every night during the winter.

The world's largest opera house is the Metropolitan Opera House at the Lincoln Center in New York, completed in 1966 with an audience capacity of 4065.

ABOVE: Looking like something that has just emerged from the sea, the main features of the Sydney Opera House in Australia are its nine flying roofs, the highest point of which is 67m/220ft above sea level.

Encyclopedia
of
Musical
Instruments

The modern symphony orchestra consists of around 20 different musical instruments. These can be categorized into four main groups: strings, wind, percussion and keyboards.

Introduction

The noise or sound which musicians make while they are tuning their instruments is nothing pleasant to hear, but yet is a cause why the music is sweeter afterwards.

FRANCIS BACON (1561–1626)

Musical instruments can be categorized in various ways. The most straightforward system (used in this book) is to divide them into four main groups: strings, wind, percussion and keyboards (with the voice as a fifth category, although perhaps not strictly an "instrument"). The categories are not necessarily mutually exclusive. Some instruments in the keyboard category, for example, are related to those in other groups: the piano could also find a home in the string section, while the organ, which is operated by a system of pipes, could easily fit into the wind section. To these main groups could be added electronic instruments. However, as most of these feature keyboards, they can be found in this book with the other keyboard instruments.

Musicologists classify instruments according to the way in which the sound is produced. "Idiophones" are

ABOVE: This segment of a string section shows the first and second violins in the foreground.

those in which the body of the instrument vibrates when struck to produce the sound. They include bells, rattles, cymbals and xylophones. The group called "membranophones"

consists entirely of drums, in which the skin is struck and vibrates. "Chordophones" include all stringed instruments, such as the violin, guitar and piano, and "aerophones" are wind instruments, such as the trumpet, clarinet and organ, in which a column of air vibrates. In "electrophones", such as the electric organ or synthesizer, the sound is produced electronically.

Instruments can also be listed in two groups depending on whether the musician forms a unity with his instrument, or a duality. The former group includes wind instruments that are played by combining a vibrating column of air – produced by the player's breath – with the tube of the instrument. The second group represents a slightly more advanced stage of musical development and includes stringed instruments, in which the player produces the

ABOVE: The woodwind section consists of flutes, oboes, clarinets and bassoons.

vibrations in the soundbox by exciting the strings with a bow or his fingers.

There are many musical instruments that are widely used but are not part of the standard orchestra. Some are folk instruments, such as the concertina and the bagpipes, or traditional instruments from Africa and East Asia. Others are early instruments that fell into disuse but in recent years have been revived to play the early music that was written for them.

The 17th and 18th centuries saw many improvements in musical instruments, especially in extremes of pitch, achieved by innovations in design and engineering, such as the addition of extra holes and keys. As technical advances were made, players were able to refine their technique and composers were prompted to write more challenging and expressive music. This often led, in turn, to the need for further refinements in the design of the instruments.

The industrial revolution was a springboard for sophisticated improvements in instrumental mechanics. The development of

ABOVE: Percussion sections may include a wide variety of instruments. This set-up shows xylophones, tubular bells, gong, and a collection of drums and cymbals.

the cast-iron frame turned the piano into a high-tension, high-performance instrument. Work by people such as Jakob Grundmann and Carl August Grenser, who increased the number of keys and provided alternative fingering on the oboe; Heinrich Stölzel and Adolphe Sax, who did so much work on developing valved instruments; and

ABOVE: An orchestral brass section.

the German goldsmith Theobald Boehm, who improved the flute, resulted in much greater versatility in the use of wind instruments. Yet the creations of the great 17th-century violin makers have never been equalled, and many attempts to introduce new materials have resulted in the makers returning to traditional methods that have proved unbeatable.

ABOVE: The keyboard instrument most often seen on the concert platform is the piano.

❖ *Strings* ❖

How Stringed Instruments Work

What can be more strange, than that the rubbing of a little hair and
cat-gut together should make such a mighty alteration in a man.

JEREMY COLLIER (1650–1726)

Although the orchestral term "strings" is used only for the violin family, there are many other stringed instruments, played with or without a bow, that come under the general term "chordophone". In every case, the mechanics are the same.

One group of stringed instruments, which includes the harp and lyre, is played with open strings – each string producing only one note. The other group, into which most other stringed instruments fall, consists of those played with "stopped" strings: each string can be held down, effectively changing its length, so that it will produce a range of notes.

Sound production

There are two distinct types of construction of stopped-string instruments, each with its own acoustic implications. The lute is a perfect example of one type, with a flat soundboard and a bowl-shaped back, with no connecting ribs or soundpost. Instruments of the second

ABOVE: *Detail of two violins, showing the f-holes and parts of the bridges.*

type, by far the most common, have flat soundboards and flat or moderately arched backs, joined by side ribs. In both cases the sound is produced by the vibration of the strings being transmitted into the soundbox via the bridge.

The pitch produced by a string depends not only on its length but also on its thickness, weight and tension. In most instruments it is impractical to vary only the length of the strings, as the lower strings would have to be so long as to be unwieldy, so strings of different thicknesses are used: they may then all be of the same length. The tension of the string is also important. Too slack a tension sounds

ABOVE: *Unlike violins, violas and cellos, viols have frets on their fingerboards.*

ABOVE: *The string family (from left to right): two violins, a viola and a cello. The central motif of the stained-glass window is a lyre, a universal symbol of music.*

ABOVE: *A cello section performing in a modern symphony orchestra.*

there was no clear demarcation between the body and the neck. Examples of such instruments are the mandora and the rebec.

The mandora evolved into the mandolin, while the rebec has survived in the form of the *lyra* of modern Greece and Crete and the Bulgarian *gadulka*. Used as a folk instrument to accompany songs and dances, the traditional *lyra* or *gadulka* has three gut strings that are played with a horsehair bow. It is held vertically while it is played, with the lower end tucked into the player's belt when standing, or held on the hip when seated.

feeble, while too thick a string is hard to get vibrating and restricts the higher harmonics. Low strings are usually wound with a fine wire on a moderate core to allow them to be held under sufficient tension without excessive mass or stiffness.

Shape of stringed instruments

Although stringed instruments come in various shapes and sizes, many have waisted bodies that allow both freedom for the bow and a more complex vibration. Stringed instruments were, however, waisted many centuries before the advent of the bow, and instruments so shaped appear in Babylonian sculptures. The shape may have been used not only for musical effect but perhaps because it had some symbolic or ritual association with the female form.

Early stringed instruments were usually carved from a solid block of wood that tapered in such a way that

RIGHT: *This painting by Jean-Baptiste Mauzaisse (1784–1844) depicts the daughters of the Duke of Orleans being given a harp lesson by their tutor Mme de Genlis. The young musicians are playing pedal harps.*

Violin

The true mission of the violin is to imitate the accents of the human voice, a noble mission that has earned for the violin the glory of being called the king of instruments.

CHARLES-AUGUSTE DE BÉRIOT (1802–70)

The violin is the lead voice and most numerous instrument of the modern orchestra. The average orchestra has about 35 violins, which are divided into two sections – first and second. The violin's four strings give the instrument a range of over four octaves, including all the semitones and many microtones. Its extraordinary musical versatility, coupled with its emotional appeal and agility, makes possible – depending on the skill of the player – an expression of moods ranging from the tender lyrical music of Mozart to the dramatic tones of Wagner.

Origin

Although no one knows who invented the violin, some of the earliest instruments were made by Giovan Giacoba dalla Corna and Zanetto Montichiaro, both of whom are named in Giovanni Lanfranco's *Scintille di Musica* (1533). The first "famous" violin maker, however, was Andrea Amati (1525–1611), who was born in Cremona and became the founder of the Cremonese school of violin-making.

ABOVE: The scroll and pegs of a violin.

Although the violin family (violin, viola and cello) has been the mainstay of the symphony orchestra since its rise in the 17th century, the three-stringed violin had been in existence since the early 1500s. It was certainly known in 1508, for it appears in a wall painting of that date in the Sala del Tesoro at the Palazzo di Ludovico il Moro in Ferrara. Twenty or so years later, Gaudenzio

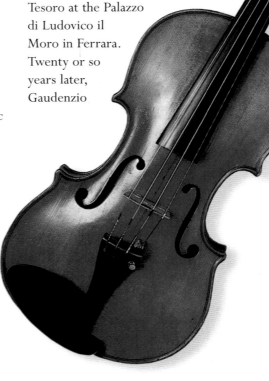

LEFT: The violin is the lead instrument in the orchestra. This one was made by Anton Kreutzinger in 20th-century Germany.

Ferrari depicted the instrument in *The Madonna of the Orange Trees*, painted for the church of San Cristoforo in Vercelli. The same artist included violins in his fresco in the cupola of Saronno Cathedral in 1535.

These early three-stringed violins were an amalgam of two other instruments that were well known at this time – the fiddle and the rebec. The new instrument combined the sonority and playing potential of the former with the simplicity of the latter.

Construction

Although the violin appears to be of simple construction, it is in fact made of over 80 separate parts. The soundboard is generally made of European spruce and the back and the ribs are made of maple. Maple is also used for the neck, pegbox and scroll, while the fingerboard, which runs along the neck and extends over the soundboard towards the bridge, is generally made of ebony.

Originally, all four strings were made of gut. However, from about 1700, to improve the tone, the G string was wound with silver wire. Modern instruments still have the G, D and A strings made in this fashion, while the E string is generally constructed of steel.

The mid 18th century saw some major modifications in the construction of the violin. The emergence of purpose-built concert halls and the resultant larger audiences created a demand for instruments capable of producing greater volume and brilliance of tone. To achieve this, the neck and fingerboard were

ABOVE: *This violin was made by the Italian craftsman Giuseppe Guarneri (1666–1739) in about 1695. Guarneri was the younger son of Andrea Guarneri, who had served as an apprentice to Nicola Amati and began the second great dynasty of Cremonese violin makers.*

lengthened, the bridge was made higher, the soundpost was thickened and the soundboard was made thinner.

Another modification was that the number of nails attaching the neck was reduced from four to three. The neck had to be nailed, as glue would have adversely affected the tone. Modern violins have the neck mortised into the upper block so that nails are no longer needed.

Key features

TYPE: stringed

TUNING: *g, d', a', e"*

NOTABLE PLAYERS OF THE VIOLIN: Niccolò Paganini, Joseph Joachim, Eugène Ysaÿe, Jascha Heifetz, David Oistrakh, Yehudi Menuhin, Isaac Stern, Itzhak Perlman, Kyung-Wha Chung, Nigel Kennedy, Anne-Sophie Mutter.

RIGHT AND BELOW: *A collection of modern violins. These instruments were made in the early 1990s by David Lipkin and Haim Algranati, London.*

ABOVE: *The Bavarian village of Mittenwald has been a centre of violin-making since 1684 when Matthias Klotz, who was born in the village, returned from Cremona. Johann Reiter, a craftsman of Mittenwald, is seen here working in his shop.*

ABOVE: *A depiction of a violinist on a Swedish-made carpet designed by Per Nilsson in 1781.*

RIGHT: *A romantic painting (1893) by Edgar Bundy depicting the violin maker Antonio Stradivari in his workshop. After the death of Nicola Amati in 1684, Stradivari became recognizably superior to all his competitors, and his fame began to spread beyond Cremona to the rest of Europe.*

The violin outside Italy

By about 1550, four strings had become standard and schools of violin-making had been established in Venice, Cremona and Brescia. The makers not only catered for Italian musicians, but also exported instruments to England, France, the Low Countries and Germany. Charles IX of France bought 12 violins from Andrea Amati of Cremona, while the English were such avid customers that they were accused of "dispeopling" Italy of violins. Even in the 16th century, large sums were being paid for fine violins; one sold by Gasparo da Salo of Brescia in 1588 fetched over four times his housemaid's annual wage.

Music for the violin

At first, the violin was used only for doubling the voice and to accompany dancing. For the former purpose, the violinist used the vocal score, while dance musicians played from memory, so no music for the violin was published until the end of the 16th century. The first music known to have been published specifically for the violin was the *Balet Comique de la Royne*, which was devised for the French court by Balthazar de Beaujoyeulx in 1582. It included two dances that were scored for ten violins in four parts. This royal patronage was a breakthrough indeed, for up to this time the violin had been looked down upon, with "virtuous people" preferring the viol, which produced

ABOVE: *Known as the* Emile Sauret *(because it was once owned by that French violinist), this Stradivari violin was made in 1683.*

greater resonance but less volume. The social status of the violin was further enhanced in 1626 when the ensemble known as the *Vingt-quatre Violons du Roi* was founded at the court of Louis XIII.

Stradivari

Without doubt, the greatest of all violin makers was Antonio Stradivari (1644–1737). Descended from an old Cremonese family, young Antonio was first apprenticed to a wood-carver. However, he soon became associated with Nicola Amati (1596–1684), the grandson of Andrea and the finest maker of the Amati family, who taught him the art of violin-making. Stradivari's earliest surviving violin is dated 1666. With the death of his master, Stradivari's fame began to spread and he soon became recognized as the finest violin maker of his day.

Stradivari's highest pinnacle was reached in 1715 when his now well-known, orange-brown coloured varnish, which dried to a light delicate elastic skin, began to appear. Although varnish cannot improve a violin's tone, it can affect it adversely. A hard varnish causes an instrument to produce a hard

ABOVE: The Japanese violinist Kyoko Takezawa playing a Stradivari violin in Munich in 1993.

ABOVE: Two violins made by the two greatest Cremonese violin makers. On the left is the back and front view of Stradivari's Alard which was made in 1715 and is considered to be the finest Stradivari in existence. On the right is Guarneri's del Gesù.

sound, with little or no tone-colour. A thick oily varnish, on the other hand, inhibits the wood's vibrations and a varnish that is applied badly may well prevent the best tones from being realized. Sadly, the recipe for Stradivari's varnish is now lost.

Decline of Italian violin-making

Despite the fact that the violin had become the backbone of the emergent orchestras and operas of Europe by the 18th century, this period coincided with a general decline in violin-making in Italy. By the end of the century, France had become the centre of excellence in violin-making. One of the greatest French makers was Nicolas Lupot (1788–1824) who, taking Stradivari as his model, linked French and Italian workmanship. Another French violin maker was François Tourte (1747–1835) who revolutionized and standardized the design of the bow.

ABOVE: Nigel Kennedy (born 1957) is one of England's most controversial violinists, and is shown here playing a Stradivari violin. His intense concentration, vitality and all-or-nothing approach make him one of the most likeable musicians on the stage today.

ABOVE: This 19th-century photograph shows a Hardanger fiddle being played held against the chest. Despite its name, it is a violin and today, with the addition of a chinrest, the instrument is played in the manner of orchestral violinists.

Playing techniques

Although the violin is basically the same as it was 300 years ago, playing techniques have improved, allowing new types of music to be written. Before the invention of the chinrest – by Louis Spohr in about 1820 – the violin was played in several different ways. It was held either at the chest, at the shoulder, to the right or left of the neck, or, in the case of folk music, cradled against the left upper arm.

By the late 18th century, performance styles had changed so much that the violin needed strengthening. Heavier strings and tighter string tension were needed to produce the stronger sound required to fill the new larger concert halls.

Vibrato

One of the characteristics of modern violin-playing is vibrato. Created by a controlled rocking of the finger that is stopping the string, vibrato adds intensity to the tone. In the 18th and 19th centuries it was considered solely as ornamentation. Such is its universal acceptance, however, that whereas pre-20th-century music was marked where vibrato was required, today it is marked where it is not required. The use of vibrato seems to have become fashionable in the 1930s, due to the influence of performers such as Fritz Kreisler and Jascha Heifetz (1901–87). Some players use it all the time, and some, it is said, use it to cover up bad intonation.

Jazz violin

One of the first great jazz violinists was Eddie South (1904–62), a classically trained black musician who had already formed a popular dance band in Chicago when he toured Europe and discovered gypsy fiddling in Bucharest. He arrived back on the Chicago jazz scene in the late 1920s. South worked with the guitarist Django Reinhardt,

ABOVE: Jascha Heifetz, seen here in 1929, is remembered for his hard sound that could melt unexpectedly into the sweetest, most effortless legato. His nimble left hand and flawless bowing technique astonished all who heard him.

and his version of *Eddie's Blues* (recorded in 1937) is regarded as one of the finest of its genre; South's piteous blue slides and scoops were ably invigorated by Reinhardt's potent

ABOVE: The violin can be held in several different ways — under the chin or resting against the jaw, as shown here, or held against the chest.

guitar. Reinhardt also had a famous partnership with Stéphane Grappelli (1908–97), whose jazz violin style had been inspired by South: the two played together as principal soloists in the Quintet of the Hot Club of France from 1934–39.

Jazz is also a medium in which the electric violin is used. The electric violin has no soundbox and has a solid body, with a set of pick-ups that transmit the sound to an amplifier. It is capable of producing many new sonorities, and various avant-garde jazz players and composers have experimented with the instrument. One of the foremost electric violinists is Jean-Luc Ponty (born 1942) who, as well as working with musicians such as Frank Zappa, has produced hitherto unheard tones, some of which blare out like an electrified jazz horn.

Folk violin

The violin is used in folk music almost all over the world. Folk violinists do not follow the conventions of orchestral violinists, in that the instrument is not always held to

the chin. Country band fiddlers also often perform very skilled acrobatics with their instrument, such as playing it upside down, backwards, behind their back or even under their legs. In North American folk dance music, the violin is held against the chest or even the waist, while in North Africa the performer plays seated on the ground

LEFT: This musician is standing outside the Geigenbau, a stringed instrument museum in the southern Bavarian village of Mittenwald. Today it is a technical school, and a dozen artisans still carry on the long tradition of violin-making in the village.

with the instrument resting upright against the left knee.

Variations on the traditional violin include the single-fret *mazanki* of the Wielkopolska region of Poland. Carved out of one piece of wood, the *mazanki* is usually played in ensemble with the *dudy*, a form of bagpipe. The Hardanger fiddle, or *Hardingfele*, of western and southern Norway, was invented in about 1650, and was improved during the 18th century by Trond Isaksen (1712–72). The instrument, which includes four sympathetic strings placed below the fingerboard and playing strings, is still played today.

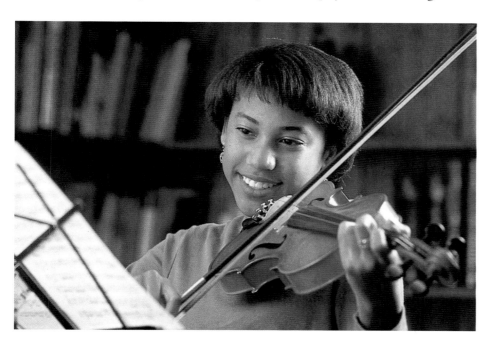

ABOVE: The violin is an extremely popular instrument among young people. Many students will learn the violin at school and carry on playing into adulthood.

ABOVE: Electric violins come in various sizes, including this MIDI of 1999.

Viola

The viola is a philosopher, sad and helpful; always ready to come to the aid of others, but reluctant to call attention to himself.

ALBERT LAVIGNAC (1846–1916)

The viola is the alto of the string section, and is pitched a fifth below the violin, whose fingering and bowing technique it shares. Fortunately, not many people share Wagner's view that it is "commonly played by infirm violinists or by decrepit wind players who were at one time acquainted with the violin". It came into being in northern Italy in the early 16th century and, by 1535, had become established as one of the three principal members of the new violin family. Known as the "instrument of the middle", the viola, with its dark, warm and rich tone, was used for both the alto and tenor registers. The strings were originally made of gut, but modern violas have

> ## Key features
>
> **TYPE:** stringed
>
> **TUNING:** *c, g, d', a'*
>
> **NOTABLE PLAYERS OF THE VIOLA:** Victor Lalo, Lionel Tertis, Paul Hindemith, William Primrose, Yuri Bashmet.

strings that are made of wire wound over gut or metal cores.

The main problem with the original viola was its size; some of the early models were so large that they could barely be played on the arm. The huge Andrea Amati tenor viola, for instance, had a body length of 47cm/19in. This problem was aggravated in the 19th century when some makers attempted to improve the viola's acoustics by making the body even longer. These improvements could only be effective if players had sufficiently long arms.

The perfecting of the Tourte bow, around 1785, opened a new era in string-playing. During the early 19th century the viola went through various alterations to increase string tension and carrying power, modifications that

LEFT: The viola is slightly larger than the violin, and is pitched a fifth lower.

involved the introduction of heavier strings and the lengthening of the neck.

Repertoire

Before 1740 there were no known outstanding violists and consequently, virtually no repertoire for the instrument. Although composers such as Bach, Handel and Vivaldi had given the viola important parts in fugues and concertos, it was not until the late 18th century that it began to be treated as a solo instrument.

One of the first composers to write a major part for the viola was Mozart, who, in his 1779 *Sinfonia Concertante* (K364), treated the viola and violin as equal partners. Paganini played the viola as well as the violin, and wrote caprices for the instrument. In the 20th century, mainly through the presence of outstanding players such as Lionel Tertis and Paul Hindemith, more solo viola works were written, including concertos by Walton, Bartók and the American composer

ABOVE: The composer Paul Hindemith (1895–1963) was an outstanding viola player. He had the distinction of being the first to play Walton's Viola Concerto in 1929.

Quincy Porter (1897–1967). Hindemith himself also wrote a number of works for the viola, including four concertos, four pieces for viola and piano, and two for unaccompanied viola.

Modern viola

Today's violas owe much to the work of the English viola virtuoso Lionel Tertis (1876–1975) who, in the 1940s, created an instrument that, although combining the fullness, depth and beauty of tone of a "full-size" viola, was still manageable by the player. More recently, Carleen Hutchins (born 1911), of the American Catgut Acoustical Society, has designed and built a whole new family of eight instruments acoustically scaled to the violin. Her viola, which

ABOVE: The viola section of the London Symphony Orchestra.

is rescaled to a body measurement of about 53cm/21in, has a spike and is played between the knees like a cello.

Viola d'amore

An instrument related to the viola, the viola d'amore was popular during the late 17th and 18th centuries. It is unfretted with 14 strings – seven playing and seven sympathetic strings tuned an octave higher. Although it fell out of use during the 19th century, it was revived in the 20th century by composers such as Janáček, who used it in his opera *Kátya Kabanová* (1921) and Prokofiev, who included it in the score of the ballet *Romeo and Juliet* (1935).

LEFT: One of the builders of the viola d'amore was Jacob Rauch who made this one in 1718.

BELOW: Despite its name, the viola da gamba is actually a viol. Unlike the viola, the viola da gamba has frets and is played between the knees like a cello.

Harold in Italy

One of the most important 19th-century works for the viola was Berlioz's *Harold en Italie*, a symphony with viola obbligato, written in 1834. Although it had been commissioned by Paganini, who had just acquired a Stradivari viola, when he saw the composition he declined to play it, complaining that it did not give him enough work to do, or adequately display his talents as a virtuoso.

Cello

The cello is like a beautiful woman who has not grown older but younger with time, more slender, more subtle and more graceful.

PABLO CASALS (1876–1973)

The violoncello, commonly referred to by its abbreviated name in English and German, is the bass instrument of the violin family, sounding an octave below the viola. The instrument originated in the 16th century. One of the earliest makers was Andrea Amati of Cremona, who built his *King Amati* in 1572.

One of the disadvantages of the original cello was its size. Early cellos were considerably larger than those of today, some having a body as long as 80cm/32in. This large size made it difficult to play rapid passages and so, in about 1660, experiments began in Bologna to create a smaller cello. At some time between 1707 and 1710 Stradivari decided on a length of about 75cm/30in, a length that has been standard ever since.

It took some time for the cello to become fully accepted, and it was not

RIGHT: A view of a cello player's bow action and fingering technique. This performer is using the modern overhand bow grip with his right hand, while the third finger of his left hand has reached a high note on the top A string.

until the latter half of the 17th century that composers began to score for it regularly. One of the earliest composers for the instrument was the Bolognese cellist Domenico Gabrieli (c.1655–90) who, in 1684, published his *Balletti, gighe, correnti, sarabande, a due violini e violoncello con basso continuo*.

Improvements

In the 18th century various improvements to the cello were carried out, including lengthening and thinning the neck and fingerboard, raising the bridge and introducing thinner and tauter strings, an innovation that produced a clearer and more responsive tone.

There were also improvements to the bow. Until the second half of the 18th century, cello bows were either straight or convex – like those of the viol and violin – and were gripped in the fist,

LEFT: The cello is a large instrument, and since it is supported by a spike and not the left hand, the strings can be stopped with the thumb as well as the fingers.

Key features

TYPE: stringed

TUNING: *C, G, d, a*

NOTABLE PLAYERS OF THE CELLO: Giuseppe Jacchini, Luigi Boccherini, Alfredo Piatti, Karl Davidov, Pablo Casals, Paul Tortelier, Mstislav Rostropovich, Jacqueline du Pré.

ABOVE: A Romanian child playing a gardon by plucking the strings immediately after he has hit them with a stick.

RIGHT: The Portuguese cellist Guilhermina Suggia (1885–1950) played a Stradivari. She is remembered for her grace and style.

Cello music

While it has never been as well provided for as the violin, some notable 20th-century works have been composed for the cello, including Elgar's Cello Concerto (1919), Kodály's Sonata for Cello and Piano, Op. 4 (1910), Webern's *Drei Stücke* (1914), Villa-Lobos's *Bachianas Brasileiras* (1916), part of which is written for eight or more cellos, Britten's Cello Symphony (1963) and Mauricio Kagel's *Match* (1964), in which the two cello soloists dress as table-tennis players and perform against each other.

with the palm facing upward, as for the viol, or downward. François Tourte allowed cello players greater control when he introduced his concave bow of pernambuco wood in the 1780s, and fixed it at a length of 72cm/29in, with the playing hair between 60cm/24in and 62cm/25in.

Method of play

Early cellists either sat with their instrument resting on the floor between their legs, or stood with it leaning against their body. Sometimes it was played resting on a stool, or even in a horizontal position. By 1700, it was usual for the player to place his cello between his knees and support it with his calves. This high posture permitted the player to draw the neck back towards him, so that the left hand could approach the strings from the side, instead of from behind, thereby making the entire compass of the instrument more accessible.

In the 17th century cellos were also played in religious processions, especially in northern Italy. The peripatetic cellists cut a hole in the back of their instrument through which a strap was passed, which was

hung around the player's neck, leaving him free to play with both hands – not an easy task.

Gardon

Originating from the eastern Carpathians, the gardon is a folk instrument similar to the cello, and is played as a rhythm instrument by Romanian gypsies. It used to be made out of a single block of wood, but the modern gardon has a body like that of the cello. It has three or four strings, all tuned to *d*. The player, who either sits or stands, hits the strings with a wooden stick or may slap the fingerboard. The strings may also be plucked.

ABOVE: This painting of 1753 vividly shows the old style of playing the cello with the instrument grasped between the legs – there is no spike. The bowing technique shows the hand under the bow rather than over it, unlike the technique favoured by modern cellists.

Double Bass

A composition without a bass
would be full of confusion and dissonance.

GIOSEFFO ZARLINO (1517–90)

The double bass is the largest and lowest-pitched stringed instrument of the orchestra. As well as being indispensable in the symphony orchestra – the average orchestra has eight – the double bass is also an essential member of jazz and dance bands, where its *pizzicato*-playing provides the rhythmical bass line. Today the bass generally has four strings, tuned in fourths, but this has not always been the case. During the 17th century five-string basses were used in Austria and Germany and in the early 18th century three-string basses were normal.

Size

The double bass has always been made in a number of sizes. The full-size instrument was used in the early Baroque period, but with the development of the overwound gut

Key features

TYPE: stringed

TUNING: *E', A', D, G*

NOTABLE PLAYERS OF THE DOUBLE BASS: Josef Kämpfer, Giovanni Bottesini, Sergey Koussevitzky, Charles Mingus, Ludwig Streicher, Gary Karr, Barry Guy.

RIGHT: On the double bass the tuning pegs jut out at the back. Because of the high tension of the strings, a cog wheel mechanism is used for tuning.

ABOVE: A double bass player.

string, makers were able to reduce it to more manageable dimensions. The modern orchestra generally uses a three-quarter size instrument, with a body length of about 115cm/45in, and all-steel strings are commonly used. Jazz and dance bands also use the three-quarter size, although they sometimes play the "piccolo bass", which is fitted with thin strings and tuned an octave higher than the standard bass. In the 17th century half-size basses were carried in processions, suspended by a strap over the shoulder. At the other extreme, some gigantic basses have been built. These include Vuillaume's *octobasse*, which was built in 1849. Over 4m/13ft high and tuned an octave below the conventional bass, it was so big that it required two people to play it and the strings could only be stopped by operating a system of levers and pedals. Even larger was Paul de Wit's bass, 4.8m/16ft high, which he built for the 1889 Cincinnati Music Festival. One of the largest double basses built in Britain – if not the largest ever – was that constructed by Mr Martin, the landlord of the Blackamoor Lady in Leicester. Martin's instrument was so big that a hole had to be cut in his ceiling

ABOVE: Vuillaume's octobasse (1849) was so big that the bow had to be held in place by a kind of oarlock.

ABOVE: Double bass strings are very long, so they vibrate well — the instrument is highly suited to playing pizzicato.

through which the neck protruded, and it could only be tuned by going upstairs into the room above.

Virtuosi

Domenico Dragonetti (1763–1846), a Venetian, was considered the world's finest bass player of his time. He was a great friend and admirer of Beethoven and wrote several concertos and other pieces for the instrument. He freed it from doubling the cello part and assured its permanent place in the orchestra by pushing the playing technique to new heights. Such was Dragonetti's mastery over his instrument that once, while staying at a monastery, he stood in the corridor outside his room during the night and imitated a storm with his bass. The next day the main topic of the monks' conversation was the "thunderstorm" of the previous night.

Giovanni Bottesini (1822–89) extended the range of the double bass even further than Dragonetti, and was known in his day as the "Paganini of the double bass", particularly for his use of high harmonics. He toured Europe, Russia and the United States as a double bass soloist, wrote an important book on the instrument and composed a large number of works for it. A friend of Verdi, he conducted the first performance of Verdi's opera *Aida* in Cairo in 1871.

Bowing techniques

Methods of bowing for the double bass vary in different countries. Most players in Europe use the Bottesini, or "French" bow, which is shaped like a shorter, heavier cello bow and held overhand as for the cello. In central and eastern Europe, however, players prefer the "German" bow designed by Franz Simandl (1840–1912), which is derived from the old Dragonetti bow. Used underhand like a viol bow, it is also known as the "meat saw".

Bass music

It was only in the 19th century that composers started to write distinctive double bass parts. Before this time the bass player shared the cello part, usually playing an octave below the cello. By the early 19th century the bass was becoming popular as a solo instrument and composers were writing more exposed passages for the instrument, such as that in Schubert's "Trout" Quintet of 1819. In Saint-Saëns's *Le Carnaval des Animaux* (1886), the elephant is represented by the double bass. Other composers for the double bass include Hindemith, Prokofiev and Darius Milhaud.

ABOVE: This double bass player is using the German technique, whereby the bow is held from underneath — similar to viol technique.

Harp

His harp, the sole companion of his way.

JAMES BEATTIE (1735–1803), "THE MINSTREL"

One of the largest of all orchestral instruments, the modern harp has 46 strings with a compass of six and a half octaves. It is played tilted back against the player's right shoulder and usually has double-action pedals, which allow the player to raise the pitch of the strings by either a semitone or a tone. The harp is unique in that the strings run perpendicular to the resonator, whereas in all other stringed instruments the strings run parallel. The strings are plucked with the fingers, as was the case with early harps, although by 2000 BC the plectrum had been introduced.

The modern frame harp is descended from two basic types: the bow or arched harp, and the angular harp.

Bow or arched harp

The earliest form of harp is thought to have developed from the hunter's bow. Bow harps first appeared in western Asia in about 3000 BC, where they were played in processions and at

LEFT: A beautifully decorated modern pedal harp made by Leffler of Germany.

banquets. They had a resonator at the base from which the strings were attached to a curved neck. Many of these harps, which were just over 1m/3ft long, were decorated with a bull's head motif.

The first Egyptian harps of which we know date from the Fourth Dynasty (2625–2500 BC). They were used alone to accompany singing as well as in larger bands, and varied in size from the hand-held shoulder harp, usually played by women, to the larger instruments that were played by men. One of these, over 2m/6ft in height, is seen on a wall painting in the tomb of Rameses III (c.1150 BC). Played with the resonator resting on the floor, this instrument is decorated with a carved human head. Today the arched harp survives mainly in Africa and East Asia.

Angular harp

The earliest evidence of angular harps is to be found in three marble statuettes of seated musicians which date from about 2000 BC. Usually played by women, these instruments were in the shape of an equilateral triangle with each side some 55cm/21½in long. The strings were attached to the neck, forming a 60° angle with the resonator that rested on the player's right thigh.

Although the angular harp had been introduced into Egypt by about 1500 BC, it was several centuries

LEFT: This Egyptian mural from the tomb of Rameses III at Thebes (c.1150 BC) shows a harp with nine strings and a carved human face at the base of the resonator.

LEFT: An ancient Egyptian musician playing an arched harp. Played with the resonator resting on the floor, this six-stringed instrument is typically decorated with a carved human head.

Western Europe

The harp was known in western Europe by the 7th century. An 8th-century Anglo-Saxon manuscript depicts a frame harp, as does the 9th-century Utrecht Psalter. There is also a reference to the harp in Wace's 12th-century French poem, *Roman de Brut*. In the frame harp, the third side of the triangle, left open in the angular harp, is closed by the piece known as the pillar, so that the strings are enclosed within a frame. In early European harps, the pillar was usually curved.

before it gained full acceptance. It was played in an upright position, with the resonator held against the body and the neck resting in the player's lap.

Egyptian harpists evolved highly developed playing techniques, such as using the flat of the hand to dampen the strings. Another innovation was the sounding of stopped as well as open strings.

In Greece the harp never achieved the popularity of the lyre and was denounced by Plato as a "dreamy" instrument that was usually played only by women. The angular harp became popular in Imperial Rome where it was often played (again by women) in processions, sacrificial ceremonies and at the religious rites associated with the cult of Isis, which the Romans had adopted from the Egyptians.

ABOVE: This illustration of a harp player, entitled Gabinetto Armonico, *was drawn by Bonanni in the 18th century.*

RIGHT: A late 13th-century French illustration showing King David playing the harp.

Irish harp

The earliest evidence of the Irish harp, with its slender neck, pillar and resonator, is seen on relief carvings on 9th-century stone crosses. The instrument, which had a pronounced outward curve of the pillar, from which a low neck projected, was played held against the player's left shoulder. The harpist plucked the metal strings of the upper register with the long fingernails of his left hand. Early instruments were about 60cm/24in high and had up to 30 strings, but by the 16th century they had become larger and boasted up to 43 strings. Unlike earlier harps played with both hands, the new type was held against the body with one hand and played with the other. The Irish harp virtually died out in the late 18th century.

BELOW: A wooden Irish, or Celtic, harp. It has 22 strings with a flat soundboard on a round-backed resonator. The strings are tuned by means of pegs.

ABOVE: An Irish, or Celtic, harp decorated with gilt vine. This harp differed from other harps in that the strings were played with the fingernails instead of the fingertips.

Welsh harp

Known as the *telyn*, the Welsh harp is mentioned in poetry from the 10th century. Such was its importance that it was said to be one of the three indispensable possessions of a freeman. Unlike its Irish relation, the Welsh harp's strings, 31 or 34 in number, were made of horsehair or gut.

In the late 17th century the traditional Welsh harp was superseded by the triple harp, a chromatic instrument capable of producing all the notes in every key, and this remained the standard bardic instrument until the 19th century. Its diatonic strings were in the two outer rows, tuned in unison, allowing repeated notes to be played quickly using alternate hands. The strings in the inner row were tuned to the semitones. Held at the shoulder, the left hand generally played the treble and the right the bass strings.

Modern harp

An alternative to the chromatic harp was the hook harp, in which the pitch was raised a semitone by a series of U-shaped hooks set in the neck. The drawback with this system was that it was manually operated, so the player temporarily lost the use of one hand when tuning each string. This inconvenience was remedied in about 1720 by the invention of the pedal harp by Jakob Hochbrucker of Donauwörth and Johann Vetter of Nuremberg. The first pedal harps had five pedals that were connected to the hooks by wires passing through the hollow pillar. By depressing one of the pedals, all the strings of one note were raised by a semitone. The number of

ABOVE: An early 19th-century pedal harp player.

ABOVE: *Detail of the top area of a modern harp, showing the tuning pegs and chromatic shift mechanisms.*

pedals was eventually increased to seven – one for each note of the diatonic scale, and this has remained the number in common use today.

Refinements to the system – replacing hooks with levers or forks – were made by the French makers Cousineau and Erard in the late 18th century. Erard created the double-action harp, with pedals that can be set in two positions to raise the pitch of each string by either a semitone or a whole tone. The harp was considered

ABOVE: *A close-up view of three harp pedals.*

to be a suitable instrument for ladies to play, and many were sold for domestic use during the 18th and 19th centuries.

One of the more notable harp makers of the 20th century is Victor Salvi (born 1921), who made his first harp in 1954. Seeking traditional Italian carving and veneering skills, Salvi moved from New York to Genoa, Italy, where he began producing harps such as the *Orchestra*. Salvi's innovations include a stainless steel linking system and nylon bearings, eliminating the need for lubrication. By the 1970s Salvi harps were available in a number of different sizes, ranging from the 164cm/65in high *Angelica* to the 188.5cm/74in high *Electra*.

Repertoire

The first symphony to include a part for the harp was Berlioz's *Symphonie Fantastique* (1830). Before this it had mainly been used orchestrally for special effects, as in the operas of Handel and Gluck. An exception was Mozart's Concerto for Flute and Harp, which he wrote in 1778 as one of a series of works commissioned by a wealthy flautist.

At the end of Wagner's *Das Rheingold*, the gods enter Valhalla accompanied by an orchestra including six harps. Both Debussy and Ravel wrote chamber music for the instrument, each having been commissioned by rival harp makers. Following the folk tradition, the modern harp is sometimes used to accompany voices, as in Benjamin Britten's 1942 *Ceremony of Carols* as well as works by Falla and Webern.

ABOVE: *Although not all musical works include a part for the harp, the modern harpist is a key member of most large symphony orchestras.*

Electric harp

The first to use an amplified harp was the American harpist Lloyd Lindroth, who introduced it in 1964. He also later modified his harp to include a "wah-wah" pedal that "bent" the harp tone.

Key features

TYPE: stringed

PITCH: concert

NOTABLE PLAYERS OF THE HARP: Turlough Carolan, Nicholas Bochsa, Elias Parrish Alvars, Sidonie Goossens, Marisa Robles.

Guitar

A guitar has moonlight in it.

JAMES M. CAIN (1892–1977)

The guitar's wide appeal as a folk instrument led to its current pre-eminent role in rock and pop music. The instrument has a long history and, although as a classical instrument it has hardly figured in the orchestra, its solo repertoire is extensive.

Gittern

The modern guitar is a descendant of the gittern, a small lute-like instrument that came to Europe via Moorish Spain in the second half of the 13th century. The gittern, which had four gut strings, was popular not only among minstrels but also with the aristocracy. During the 15th century, the instrument increased in length and the number of strings changed to three courses of two, tuned to *D*, *G* and *B*, with a single chanterelle tuned to *E*. The second string of each pair doubled at the octave.

Vihuela

In Spain the gittern became transformed into the vihuela, a flat instrument curved in at the sides, with five pairs of strings and a single chanterelle. Although it was rarely found outside Spain, Henry VIII of England was known to have had four "Spanish vialles". These possibly came into his possession though his marriage to his first wife Catherine, daughter of

BELOW: The classical guitar, made famous by Andrés Segovia, a great guitarist of the 20th century.

Ferdinand of Aragon. The vihuela was an instrument of courtly society, whereas the smaller, four-course guitar was used for more popular music, and by the end of the 16th century was famous all over Europe. By the mid 16th century music was being especially written for the guitar, and in 1586 Juan Carlos Amat brought out the first edition of his tutor, *Guitarra Española*. Within 100 years the guitar had become the instrument of choice even in Spain, and the days of the vihuela were numbered.

Renaissance guitar

The Renaissance four-course guitar appeared during the early 15th century. Played with a quill plectrum,

the strings were strung over gut frets that were tied around the neck, and passed over a movable bridge before terminating at a fixed frontal string holder. It was a much smaller instrument than we know today, combining the small size of the gittern with the body shape of the much larger vihuela. In the late 17th century a fifth course of strings was added below the other four.

Modern guitar

The playing technique was simplified by removing one string of each pair, and the modern six-string guitar, which has a wooden resonating chamber with incurved sidewalls and a flat back, began to make its appearance in the 18th century. Early instruments were much narrower and more elongated than

ABOVE: This 17th-century painting by Vermeer shows a girl playing a five-course guitar made by Vaboam, whose trademark ornamental rose sound-hole can be seen.

RIGHT: A four-stringed gittern carved with hunting scenes, grotesques and the arms of Queen Elizabeth I.

Key features

TYPE: stringed

PITCH: varies according to type of instrument

NOTABLE PLAYERS OF THE GUITAR: Niccolò Paganini, Francisco Tarrega, Andrés Segovia, Julian Bream, John Williams, Jimi Hendrix.

those of today. Eminent makers included José Pages of Cadiz, René François Lacote of Paris and the London-based Lewis Panormo.

In the 19th century the body was broadened and the internal bracing changed to a fan shape. Fixed metal frets were fitted to the neck and the bridge was raised. These innovations were largely the work of the Spanish guitar maker Antonio Torres Jurado (1817–92), who also standardized the

ABOVE: Chuck Berry was an early rock 'n' roll singer who helped promote the popularity of the guitar. Many young people purchased a guitar to imitate their idols.

ABOVE: The guitar is an ideal instrument for street buskers. This unusual group from Santa Monica, California, consists of two guitars and a balalaika.

string length to 65cm/26in. Metal screws replaced the wooden tuning pegs and, during the 20th century, further modifications were made, including lengthening the fingerboard down to the sound-hole.

The guitar in rock music

Today the guitar is most widely used by popular music bands. The electric guitar, using pick-ups to amplify the sounds of the strings, was developed in the 1930s and the solid-body guitar was invented by Les Paul in the 1940s. As an aid to rock musicians, transposition is facilitated by a *capo tasto* that is fitted over the fretboard, stopping all the strings simultaneously. Modern electric guitars are strung with heavy metal strings and played with a plectrum.

ABOVE RIGHT: *The* tres, *indigenous to Cuba and the Dominican Republic, has three double courses of strings. It is often used to accompany dance.*

MIDDLE RIGHT: *The electric guitar is always played with a plectrum. The vibrations of the strings are picked up electronically so there are no sound-holes.*

RIGHT: *The bass guitar has four thick steel strings and is made in many varied shapes. It is mainly used in rock and dance bands.*

LEFT: *The acoustic guitar, still the instrument of choice for folk and classical players.*

BELOW: *The 12-string guitar has six double courses of strings. It often has gut strings for a softer tone.*

Hawaiian guitar

A modification of the Spanish guitar, the Hawaiian guitar was introduced into the islands in the 1830s. It is believed that one Joseph Kekuku was the first person to place the guitar across his knees, in the manner of a fretted folk zither, and run a comb along the strings to produce the

BELOW: The Hawaiian guitar, played across the player's knees, is best known for the glissando effect achieved by running a steel bar along its strings.

glissandos for which modern Hawaiian music has become known.

In the early 20th century the Hawaiian guitar became popular in the United States and makers began to market models for which a steel bar was sold as an accessory for slide playing – hence the American term "steel guitar".

Outside Hawaii, the use of the steel guitar is now almost solely restricted to country music bands, where the doleful sound is a feature of many songs about lost love. The player holds the steel bar in one hand, while the fingers of the other wear plectra that are used to pluck the strings. In the 1950s, pedals and knee levers were introduced as an aid to rapid alteration in tuning.

Dobro

The dobro is a guitar that has one or more metal resonator discs inside the body under the bridge. It was first produced by the National String Instrument Corporation of Los Angeles in 1925 to a design by John Dopyera, the son of a Czech violin maker. Three years later Dopyera left the company to set up – with two of his brothers – the Dobro Corporation. The idea for the resonator discs came from the banjo, which sometimes had a metal resonator in its back. The dobro was originally developed in response to the growing demand for a guitar that would produce a greater volume than the conventional instrument. Although occasionally used by rock musicians, the dobro is mainly used in country and bluegrass music, where it is often played, Hawaiian-style, across the knees.

The name "Dobro" was formed by eliding the first syllables of Dopyera

ABOVE: This 19th-century painting, The Concert by Vincente Palmaroli, shows a Spanish woman playing her guitar to a small audience at home.

Brothers – though it also, helpfully, means "good" in Czech.

Ukulele

In 1879 Portuguese sailors introduced their *machete de braca*, a cross between a guitar and a mandolin, into Hawaii, where it was transformed into the ukulele, a word meaning "leaping flea". For

ABOVE, FROM MIDDLE TO BOTTOM: The dobro is an acoustic guitar with metal resonator discs inside the body which add volume to the sound. It is used by rock musicians – most famously by Mark Knopfler of Dire Straits – and country and bluegrass singers.

The ukulele was advertised in 1916 as the most popular instrument of the day, its popularity being mainly due to its small size, light weight and low cost.

ABOVE: Two mandolins – English (top) and an Italian copy, both played by plucking the strings.

about 30 years the instrument remained relatively unknown outside the islands; its introduction to American popular music came in 1915 at the San Francisco Panama Pacific Exposition, where a group of Hawaiian performers enthralled the crowds with their music and in so doing created a new musical vogue.

The instrument reached a peak of popularity in the 1930s and '40s, in Britain mainly due to the music-hall artist George Formby, and in the United States due to the television

ABOVE: *In Hawaii a small type of guitar is used to accompany the joyful vocal groups that are a feature of these wonderful islands.*

star Arthur Godfrey. Its music is usually written in tablature — representing the player's finger positions rather than pitch.

Guitarillo

The Bolivian guitarillo has five double courses of gut strings and six frets. The instruments are often played in pairs by the Chipaya people to accompany

the *waynus de cordero* and *tonadas del cordero* (songs in praise of sheep and cattle) at the *k'illpa* festival.

BELOW, FROM TOP TO BOTTOM: *A Gibson Stereo electric guitar and an Epiphone mandolin with four double courses of strings, usually plucked with a plectrum.*

ABOVE: *A guitarist in Buenos Aires playing with the aid of a* capo tasto. *Fitted over the fretboard, this device enables different keys to be played with the same chord positions.*

Fiddles

They hadde menstrales of moch honours,
Fydelers, sytolyrs, and trompours.

THOMAS CHESTRE, "SIR LAUNFAL" (C.1400)

The first fiddles were almost as tall as their standing players. Held vertically, they had three strings and a round pegbox. Although all fiddles were generally made from a single block of wood, hollowed out and covered with a wooden soundboard, there were regional variations in shape. Three strings continued to be the norm until well into the 13th century, when five strings became general. Although gut was the usual material for strings, silk was sometimes used, and from the 13th century metal strings began to appear.

There were two distinct methods of playing the fiddle. In areas of Islamic influence it was held upright with the lower end resting against the player's knees or on the floor. The bow was held palm-up. In all other areas it was held approximately horizontally,

BELOW: The Cretan lyra *is a short-necked fiddle with three gut or wire strings. The bow was once fitted with small bells to give rhythmic accompaniment.*

sometimes supported across the chest with a strap, or vertically with the lower end against the player's chest or shoulder and the pegbox pointing down to the ground.

Kit

Used mainly by French dancing masters from the 16th to the 19th centuries, the kit was a small unfretted fiddle that was made in a great variety of shapes. When not in use the instrument was kept in a pocket in the teacher's coat-tails, a practice that gave it its nickname "pocket violin". The kit was made in four main forms: rebec,

ABOVE: A woodcut from Agricola's Musica Instrumentalis Deudsch *(1529) showing four fretted viol-type fiddles: bass, tenor, alto and descant. Each instrument has not only a round sound-hole in the centre of the resonating box, but also two f-holes by the neck.*

ABOVE: This 19th-century watercolour by Per Nordquist shows a man playing the nyckelharpa or keyed fiddle.

mandora, viola and violin – the last being the most common. Its name may be derived from the Greek kithara, or may be a reference to its diminutive size, like the kitten of the violin family.

Nyckelharpa

Used throughout Scandinavia for popular dance, festive and folk music, the nyckelharpa is a keyed fiddle. Fifteenth-century nyckelharpan had between seven and 12 wooden keys and from three to six strings, some of which were drones. The oldest surviving nyckelharpan date from the 16th century and are of two types. One has an elongated body in the shape of a figure eight, with a flat bottom and flat soundboard. The

LEFT: This 15th-century fresco by Fra Angelico at San Marco, Florence, depicts an angel playing a pear-shaped rebec.

century, when it was the recognized instrument of professional minstrels attached to noble households, and was played at courtly feasts and dances.

By the mid 16th century the rebec had been relegated to street musicians as people took up the increasingly popular violin. Indeed, such was the pejorative feeling against the rebec that in 1682 the French forbade musicians to exercise their trade unless they had served a six-year apprenticeship and had passed an examination; those who failed the examination were permitted to play only the rebec.

ABOVE: The rebec was introduced into Spain by the Arab invaders and, after undergoing various modifications, it evolved into the pear-shaped instrument of the early 11th century, which was played held propped against the shoulder.

second type is pear-shaped and the soundboard and neck are made in a single piece. More recently, the shape of this type has come to resemble that of the violin family.

Rebec

An adaptation of the Byzantine lyre and the Islamic two-stringed rabab, the rebec was a plucked lute that dates back to at least the 8th century. The rebec was a bowed string instrument with a vaulted back, carved from one piece of wood that tapered in such a way that there was no clear demarcation between the body and the neck. At first the instrument had only two strings – tuned a fifth apart – with a compass of ten tones. However, by the 15th century it had anything from one to five strings, the average being three.

Although as early as the 13th century both the French and English courts employed rebec players, the heyday of the instrument was during the 15th

ABOVE: When the bow reached Europe it was applied to instruments that had hitherto been plucked. For the first time, instruments such as this guitar-shaped fiddle were bowed, thus allowing them to produce a sustained sound.

Lyre

The lyre is welcome at the feasts of Jupiter.

HORACE (65–8 BC), "ODES"

The lyre is distinct from the harp in that its strings are attached to a yoke that lies in the same plane as the soundboard. There are two types of lyre: the box lyre, in which the resonator is a built-up wooden box, and the bowl type, which has a natural or artificially hollowed-out bowl as the resonator.

Origins

The lyre was played in Sumeria, since a representation of a lyre, standing higher than the seated player, has been found on a seal of about 3000 BC. Such lyres were asymmetrical, with the longer arm held away from the player. Plucked with the fingers of both hands, they had from eight to 12 strings that were fastened in a bunch on the lower left of the resonator before fanning out to the crossbar. Tuning was achieved by winding each string around a small rod tangential to the crossbar. Many lyres were carved with a bull's head and sometimes the strings emerged from a bull's body, perhaps giving a quasi-

divine voice to the instrument. From Mesopotamia, the lyre passed on to Syria and Israel. The Hebrew lyre, or *kinnor*, had strings of sheep gut and

LEFT: The main type of lyre used in ancient Greece was the kithara. It had a wooden resonator and a row of gut strings attached to a bridge and crossbar, but no examples have survived. The words "guitar" and "zither" probably derive from "kithara".

was probably the "harp" of King David. The Hebrews had two methods of playing the lyre. For the dance, a plectrum was used, while for accompanying the voice, the strings were plucked with the fingers. The Israelites used the lyre only to express joy; it was considered a sacred instrument and was never used for sad music. When the Jews were in exile they suspended their "harps" on the willows, unable to "sing the Lord's song in a strange land".

Egypt and Greece

Around 1360 BC huge lyres appeared in Egypt, often decorated with a duck's head as a sign that they were associated with the god Amun. They were played with a long plectrum held in the right hand; all the strings, which varied in number from 7–15, were struck with a sweeping movement, while the left hand dampened those that were not wanted.

Lyres appeared in Crete by about 1800 BC, from where they passed to the Greek

RIGHT: An artist's impression of some of the instruments used by the ancient Egyptians and Hebrews. The blue instrument in the centre of the picture is an Egyptian lyre.

ABOVE: A Roman woman using a plectrum on a form of lyre.

and louder, with a wooden sound-chest and arms. Held at a tilt, the kithara was the primary instrument of Greek classical drama, contests and official cults.

Rome

From Greece the lyre migrated to Etruria, where tomb paintings of the 5th century BC show instruments with six or seven strings, a heavy bridge and a small body with long arms. Although the lyre was known to the Romans from this time, it did not play an important part in the city-state's musical life. In Roman art, Orpheus was often depicted playing his lyre to pacify lions. In the early days of Christianity, this subject was replaced by that of Christ with a flock of sheep, signifying the "Good Shepherd".

mainland, assuming a horseshoe shape. The Greeks originally made their resonators out of tortoiseshell. Later other materials were used, but were made to resemble tortoiseshell. In Greece the lyre evolved into the more sophisticated kithara, which was larger

ABOVE: The 19th-century Italian mezzo-soprano Sofia Scalchi in Gluck's opera, Orpheus, *holding a replica of a Greek lyre.*

ABOVE: This painting by Madjera (c.1900) shows a Roman muse playing the lyre.

Medieval lyre

A six-stringed lyre was the main stringed instrument of northern Europe between the 5th and 7th centuries. Substantial remains of a lyre were discovered in the excavation of the Sutton Hoo ship burial, dating from before AD 625. Early medieval lyres were usually made from a hollowed block of oak, 3–4cm/1¼–1⅓in thick, to which a thin

ABOVE: *This painting by John Strundwick shows an angel playing a* rotte, *a medieval type of lyre. In its early form it was plucked, but by the 11th century it was bowed.*

ABOVE: *An early 19th-century painting of Elizabeth O'Neil as Melpomene the Tragic Muse leaning on a lyre. This is a medieval lyre with tuning pegs on the crossbar, rather than the Greek method of rings and rods.*

soundboard of maple or other fine-grained wood was attached. Ranging in length from 40cm/16in to 80cm/32in, these were an improvement on the classical lyre, in that the tuning was now achieved by pegs inserted into the top, as opposed to the rings and rods used previously. The lower ends of the strings, which numbered five, six or seven, were secured to a short projection at the bottom of the resonator. The lyre was held in front of the body, resting on the player's knee, and the strings were played with a plectrum.

Bowed lyre

By the 11th century, the four-stringed bowed lyre, or *rotte*, had evolved. Instruments that are bowed require strings to be under a greater tension than plucked ones, so the frame of the lyre had to be strengthened. The former yoke was enlarged and the open arc considerably diminished, ultimately becoming little more than a hand-hole. Of the four strings, only one was played, the others acting as drones. Bowed lyres were generally played resting against the player's chest, shoulder or, as a sign of the fiddle to come, the chin. They were also played supported by the left arm in an upward slanting position, resting on the player's right thigh.

During the early Middle Ages a "figure-of-eight" lyre evolved in central Europe; it was three times longer than it was wide, but was doomed to failure as it was not able to withstand the strain imposed upon it by the bow.

LEFT: *Lyres were introduced to Ethiopia from Egypt at a very early date. They have survived to the present day almost unchanged, as can be seen from this Eritrean box lyre.*

ABOVE: A 16th-century Italian depiction of a lyre, the shape of which has come to serve as a universal symbol for music in Western civilization.

crwth was played in the violin position. In addition to the four playing strings it had two drone strings, which were set individually to the left of the fingerboard. Its unique feature was the bridge, which had two feet: a short one that rested on the soundboard and a longer one that passed through one of the small circular sound-holes and rested on the back of the body, thus serving as a soundpost to transmit the vibrations to the back.

African lyre

Forms of lyre are still played (mainly as a solo instrument to accompany the player's singing) in parts of Africa such as Ethiopia, the Sudan, Kenya and Zaire. Some have a wooden resonating bowl covered with lizard skin. In the absence of a bridge, the plucked strings create a buzzing sound when they hit the soundtable. In Kenya, where it is viewed as a ritual object with healing powers, the lyre is played at weddings, both as an entertainment and as a blessing. In Buganda it sometimes appears in consort with flute, drum and tube fiddle.

BELOW: The crwth is a form of Welsh lyre. Unlike its ancestors, the crwth has sound-holes in the resonator.

Although the plectrum-played lyre died out in the early Middle Ages, the bowed version survived into the 15th century, by which time it had been replaced almost everywhere by the fiddle. It did survive, however, in parts of Wales and East Africa.

Crwth

In Wales the lyre lived on in the form of the crwth, which is about 60cm/24in long, 30cm/12in wide and 6cm/2½in deep, the body, arms and crossbar all being made in one piece. Still in use in the 19th century, the

Lute

The lute is the most perfect of all instruments.

GIOVANNI LANFRANCO (1490–1545), "SCINTILLE DI MUSICA"

The lute is believed to have originated in Mesopotamia; the earliest depiction of a primitive lute-like instrument, which may have either two or three strings, appears on a terracotta plaque dating from the 17th century BC, now housed in Baghdad Museum. Always played by men, the prototype lute had a small ovoid body and a long fretted neck.

Africa and Asia

The instrument soon reached Egypt where, interestingly, it was played by women. Some of these two-stringed lutes were made with a tortoiseshell body and an animal-hide belly with six sound-holes. Sometimes the end of the neck, which was about 32cm/12¾in long, was carved with the head of a goose or falcon. Played with a plectrum, contemporary paintings show lutes with ovoid bodies and fretted necks that penetrate the whole length of the body. The strings

BELOW: An Italian lute built in about 1600 by Magno Tieffenbrucher of Venice, showing the sharp angle between the pegbox and neck.

were fastened underneath the belly, through which they issued through a hole and were secured by tuning pegs at the upper end of the neck. Over 3000 years later this type of lute still survives in north-western Africa.

The long-necked lute appeared in Greece in the 4th century BC, whence it travelled to Etruria and Rome, although it never achieved popularity in any of these areas. In the 5th century AD long-necked lutes were being played in Byzantium and Libya, but did not reach India until the 10th century.

Ud

The Western lute is directly descended from the Arab ud, a short-necked instrument with four strings, played with a plectrum. The ud first appeared in Mecca during the 6th century. Tuned in fourths, the instrument was improved when a fifth string course – and subsequently a sixth – was added. Although the ud was introduced into Europe by the Moors during their occupation of Spain (711–1492), it did not appear in other parts of Europe until the 13th century.

ABOVE: The lute has survived in various forms. In Morocco, because of the country's strong historic links with the Arab world, the instrument of choice is the ud.

BELOW: The saz *is a long-necked fretted lute originating from Iran and Turkey. It has eight to ten metal strings.*

LEFT: The kora *is a long-necked, 21-stringed, plucked lute-like instrument found in Senegal and neighbouring countries.*

RIGHT: The ud is the principal instrument of the Arab world. Its name means "wood" and "tortoise", referring to the material from which it is made, or to its shape.

Structure of the lute

The medieval lute was characterized by its vaulted body and flat soundboard. The body was constructed from a number of separate ribs, usually of maple or sycamore, shaped, bent and glued together. The strings were laid along the distinct neck and the fingerboard, which was tied with four gut frets. By 1480 the frets were being made of fixed metal, and over the years their number was increased to ten. One of the most notable features of the lute is the pegbox, which is placed

Lute music

The first half of the 16th century was the golden age for lute music, with more than 400 pieces being published all over Europe. The first music specifically written for the lute was Spinaccino's *Ricercai*, composed in 1507. Much lute music developed an international character that reflected the travels of the great lutenists of the day, such as Francesco Canova da Milano (1497–1543), Alberto da Ripe and the Hungarian Bakfark.

almost at a right angle to the neck. The lute's strings are arranged in paired courses. At first, European lutes had four courses of strings, but during the 15th century a fifth course was added and, in about 1600, a sixth. By 1630, ten and even 12 courses were common. Metal strings were a German invention and first appeared in Nuremberg in 1414.

ABOVE: A 15th-century illumination showing a lute player and two men playing the anvil as a percussion instrument.

ABOVE: This early 16th-century Italian lute has five courses of strings and ten frets.

By the beginning of the 16th century the lute had attained its perfection of form. In spite of the great size of its resonance cavity, it was remarkably light, since the ribs that made up the swelling, pear-shaped body were extremely thin. The strings were tied to the bridge, which was glued to the soundboard. The bent-back pegbox was also made as light as possible. The most famous lute-making centre at this time was in Bologna, the workshop of Laux Maler (1518–52) being one of the finest. Other craftsmen worked in Venice and Padua, and, although working in Italy, nearly all were German.

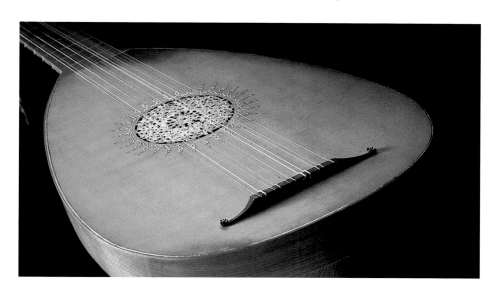

ABOVE: The lute is instantly recognizable by its characteristic swelling pear-shaped body and flat belly. This lute has six courses of strings, five of which are paired.

Playing methods

The medieval lute was a melodic instrument that was played with a quill plectrum. It played one line of music, with chords at cadences and phrase endings. During the 15th century, however, it began to be played with the fingertips, a development that allowed for the playing of several parts at once. The substitution of fingers for plectrum-plucking is a sign that the lute was becoming a solo instrument with a polyphonic style of playing.

Notwithstanding its popularity, the lute was in a sense the most inefficient musical instrument ever conceived; the bulbous form of its large body made it difficult to keep in position. This was such a problem that it was not unknown for the little finger of the left hand to be "glued" to the soundboard, thereby immobilizing the entire hand. The lute was also difficult to tune and the strings were often breaking. Indeed, in 1713, it was said that an 80-year-old lutenist had spent 60 of his years just tuning his instrument.

Theorbo

Believed to have been invented by the Florentine Antonio Naldi in the late 16th century, the theorbo was longer

ABOVE: *The theorbo is still occasionally seen today and one musician who has revived the instrument is Paula Chateauneuf, who is seen here performing in 1993.*

ABOVE: *Longer than the lute, the theorbo has a separate nut and pegbox for the unstopped bass strings. When the theorbo was introduced into England (1605) it was confiscated by the customs who, remembering the recent activities of Guy Fawkes, believed it to be a device to kill the king.*

than the conventional lute and had a separate nut and pegbox for its set of unstopped bass strings, which were known as diapasons. It was popular during the 17th and 18th centuries both as a solo instrument and as an accompaniment to singing.

Archlute

During the 16th century, in response to the lutenists' requirements for additional bass strings, a new series of bass lutes came into being. They were characterized by their open bass strings secured to a separate pegbox as with the theorbo, as opposed to the conventional lute whose bass strings were always stopped. The archlute resembled a smaller version of the theorbo, but had 13 or 14 double string courses, whereas the theorbo had single courses. Used both for solos and accompaniment during the 17th

ABOVE: *An engraving from Bonanni's* Gabinetto Armonico *of 1723 depicting an archlute player.*

and early 18th centuries, the archlute was plucked using the fingernails of the right hand. One of the last composers to write for the archlute was Handel, who gave it a part in his oratorio *Athalia* in 1733.

Balalaika

A descendant of the 16th-century *dombra*, the balalaika is a lute-like folk instrument of northern and central Russia. It has a triangular

BELOW: *Today the balalaika is internationally known, in no small part due to the tours in the 1960s and '70s of the former Red Army Ensemble, and its prominence in the score for the film* Dr Zhivago.

body, a long neck with four or five movable frets, three rib-fastened gut strings and a simple pegdisc. It has a flat back and a thin, slightly arched soundboard made from four strips of spruce into which the small sound-hole is cut. In the later years of the 19th century the St Petersburg musician Vassil Vassilyevitch Andreyev (1861–1918) designed balalaikas in six sizes, each with three strings. Andreyev's work transformed the balalaika from the realms of folk music into a popular instrument used in bands and orchestras.

ABOVE: The balalaika is often used to accompany the hectic folk-dancing for which the Russians are famed.

plantations the banjo slowly moved north, where it became a feature of black-faced minstrel shows. Through the influence of white banjoists in these shows, such as Joel Sweeney (c.1810–60) and Dan Emmet (1815–1904), the composer of *I Wish I Was in Dixie*, the banjo was rapidly introduced to American white urban culture, where it was increasingly played as a parlour instrument in the 19th century. It was exported to Britain and taken up by music hall entertainers and jazz bands. It has occasionally been used in 20th-century orchestral music, such as Kurt Weill's *Mahagonny* (1927) and Gershwin's *Porgy and Bess* (1935).

The modern banjo has five steel strings, although "classical" banjo players still use gut strings. The fifth of these – the "thumb string" – is short and is secured by a peg in the side of the neck at the level of the fifth fret. It is tuned to *G* and plays only that note, usually being sounded between beats.

BELOW: The modern banjo's tambourine-shaped body consists of a plastic membrane stretched over a circular frame, tightened by screws.

ABOVE: Side and front views of a balalaika, showing the distinctive triangular ribbed shape of the body. The balalaika has only three strings, and comes in a variety of sizes.

Banjo

A long-necked lute-type instrument, the banjo originated in West Africa and was introduced into North America by African slaves as early as the 17th century. From the southern

Banjo key features

TYPE: stringed

TUNING: *g', c, g, b, d'*

NOTABLE PLAYERS OF THE BANJO: Pete Seeger, Earl Scruggs.

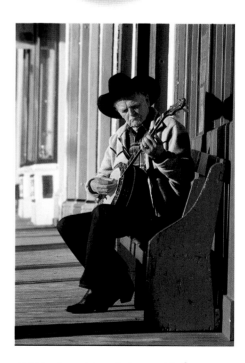

ABOVE: A musician sitting on his front porch in Nevada playing the banjo. The banjo became a popular instrument in the southern states of America.

Cittern

A citole in hir right hand hadde she.

GEOFFREY CHAUCER (C. 1340–1400), "THE KNIGHT'S TALE"

The cittern evolved from the citole, a plucked lute-like instrument played by 13th-century French troubadours. Made from a single piece of wood, the citole had a flat, pear-shaped body and a short neck, and was usually fitted with three single brass or steel strings that passed from a flat pegdisc to a frontal string-holder.

Shape of the citole

In different parts of Europe the citole assumed various shapes, all of which had a protuberance at the bottom to which the strings were attached. The Italian style was a "spade-fiddle" shape, with the shoulders swept upwards to form points. In France, the shoulders developed into wings and the oval sides became either straight or slightly waisted. The English and Germans preferred a citole of a "holly-leaf" shape with the

RIGHT: The flat-backed cittern was the most important plectrum-plucked instrument of the Renaissance, and its popularity is attested by numerous literary references.

ABOVE: This finely carved cittern is said to have been made by the great Italian stringed instrument maker Antonio Stradivari in 1700.

sides forming points at the intersections of concave curves.

During the 15th century a bridge was added to raise the strings off the soundboard, the pegdisc became a pegbox and the neck was fitted with 12 or more brass frets. The quill was abandoned and the four courses of strings began to be plucked with the fingers. The citole seems to have lasted longest in Spain, but by the early 16th

century it had become universally transformed into the cittern.

Early cittern

A characteristic of the cittern, which was very popular in the 16th and 17th centuries, was its unusual neck, which was half cut away from behind the fingerboard on the bass side. The resulting overlap formed a "channel", which facilitated very rapid shifts to and from the high positions that were so often required in the instrument's solo repertory.

Modifications

During its early years the cittern underwent many modifications, including increasing the number of courses of strings from five to 12. In 16th-century France and northern Europe the cittern eventually became standardized as a four-course instrument, with the top two courses of strings doubled and the other two trebled.

Towards the end of the 16th century a larger cittern with extra bass strings appeared. Called the *ceterone*, it was developed as a continuo instrument, its extra strings being secured to a separate pegbox, much like the theorbo. In the early 17th century a small English version of the cittern appeared. One person who enjoyed

ABOVE: This 18th-century engraving shows a trio of musicians, with one playing a bass cittern. It had seven courses of single strings and a set of five extra bass strings that were fixed to a separate pegboard.

ABOVE: This early 17th-century painting by Wouter Pietersz Crabeth shows a cittern (left) being played in company with a lute and flute.

ABOVE, FROM LEFT TO RIGHT: Back and front views of a bell cittern, which became popular in Germany in the 17th century. The Neapolitan mandolin is distinguished from other lute-type instruments by the pronounced increase in depth of vaulting at the body's lower end.

playing the *Englisches Zitterlein* was J. S. Bach's grandfather Veit, who, it is said, played it while working in his mill.

Demise of the cittern

By the mid 17th century in England and France, the cittern had degenerated into a barbershop instrument and was fast losing out to the increasingly popular guitar. By the mid 19th century the guitar had completely taken over and, apart from a few pockets in rural areas of Germany and Switzerland, the cittern had died out by the beginning of the 20th century.

Archcittern

During the 17th century Italian and French builders began to make larger citterns with two pegboxes. These archcitterns had from five to seven melody gut strings and six or seven off-board strings on the lines of the theorbo. Popular in the 18th century, they were about 1m/3ft long, and reportedly as loud as a harpsichord.

Hurdy-gurdy

*One of the street musicians was an old lady who played upon a hurdy-gurdy.
She had been about the streets of London for upwards of forty years, and being blind,
had had during that period four guides, and worn out three instruments.*

HENRY MAYHEW (1812–87), "LONDON LABOUR AND THE LONDON POOR"

Originally known as the organistrum, the hurdy-gurdy is a kind of mechanical violin able to sound two or more notes simultaneously while producing a continuous drone. Although it was built for use in churches and monastery schools to teach music and provide correct intonation for singers, by the end of the 13th century it had lost its ecclesiastical position to the newly developed portative organ.

Known from at least the 10th century, these early instruments, which had three strings, were up to 2m/6ft long. To play, they were set horizontally across two players' laps. One turned a handle to rotate the wheel that set the strings into vibration, while the other operated the keys that determined the pitch. For singers, the advantage of the organistrum over other conventional stringed instruments was that the stopping mechanism ensured an exact, invariable pitch, while the disadvantage was that only slow playing was possible.

Evolution

By 1300, the organistrum had become much smaller and was played by one musician. It now had a higher pitch, a range of over an octave, and could be played much faster than before. It became fully established as a minstrel instrument and was played suspended by a strap around the neck, in particular by blind musicians and beggars. Its use as a beggar's

BELOW: This replica of a six-stringed hurdy-gurdy clearly shows the keys and the handle.

Hurdy-gurdy music

In 18th-century Germany, marches and polonaises were written for the hurdy-gurdy, and in 1786 Haydn wrote five concertos for the instrument. Mozart scored for it in a set of minuets (K601) and four German dances (K602), while Nicolas Chédeville (1705–82) adapted Vivaldi's *Four Seasons* for the instrument. Gaetano Donizetti (1797–1848) included two Savoyard songs with hurdy-gurdy accompaniment in *Linda di Chamounix* (1842) and it is interesting to note that itinerant Savoyards were still playing the instrument in the streets of London and Paris at the end of the 19th century.

instrument continued, for in the 17th century the French were referring to it as an *instrument de truand*, while those still writing in Latin called it the *lyra mendicorum*. Its name also changed in England, the name "hurdy-gurdy" first appearing in 1749. In Italy it was known as the *lira tedesca*, possibly signifying that the instrument had been imported from Germany.

The hurdy-gurdy as a "serious" instrument

In 18th-century France, where it was known as the *symphonie* (a name that could be applied to almost any

ABOVE: A 17th-century hurdy-gurdy player in Georges de la Tour's Le Vielleur.

instrument that could emit two or more tones simultaneously) or the *vielle*, the hurdy-gurdy achieved heights not reached elsewhere when it became accepted as a fashionable court instrument during the vogue for *fêtes champêtres*. The variation favoured by the aristocracy was the *lira organizzata*, an instrument that had two ranks of organ pipes and bellows housed in its body. There were many French virtuosi of the hurdy-gurdy, and many composers wrote music for it. The most notable of them were Henri Baton (died 1728), who redesigned the *vielle*, and his son Charles (died 1754), who composed a number of suites for it and also wrote a history of the instrument in 1741. As with many other things associated with the aristocracy, the popularity of the hurdy-gurdy in France ended with the Revolution.

ABOVE: The neck of this six-stringed German hurdy-gurdy is finely decorated and is carved in the shape of a head.

ABOVE: Detail from Four Musicians, *painted in 1678 by Jacob Toorenvliet, showing a hurdy-gurdy player.*

ABOVE: **The Blind Hurdy-gurdy Player** *by David Vinckboons (1576–1632). Because it was easily portable, the hurdy-gurdy was widely used by travelling minstrels, pilgrims and especially by the blind, who could make a living from it even if they had learnt only a few tunes.*

Zither

It was an Abyssinian maid,
And on her dulcimer she played, Singing of Mount Abora.

SAMUEL TAYLOR COLERIDGE (1772–1834), "KUBLA KHAN"

The term "zither" is generically applied to any stringed instruments not classified as harps, lutes or lyres. It refers to instruments in which the resonator can be detached from the string-bearer without destroying the sound-producing apparatus. Evolved from instruments played over 2000 years ago, there are various forms of the instrument, ranging from the simple ground zither to the more sophisticated folk instruments that are played in southern Germany and Austria.

ABOVE: The harp zither is used by Austrian folk musicians.

Ground and trough zithers

The most primitive of the family is the ground zither, which is nothing more than a string stretched between posts in the ground, set over a bark-covered pit that acts as the resonator. The string is beaten by pieces of wood, and is used to accompany singing mainly to reinforce the rhythm of the music. Evidence of ground zithers has been found in neolithic excavations, and they are still played in parts of Africa and South-east Asia. A development of the ground zither is the trough zither, which is also found in Africa. This is usually plucked and consists of a hollowed-out piece of wood, sometimes elaborately sculpted, with a length of string laced back and forth over it.

Tube and raft zithers

The tube zither, as the name implies, is based on a wooden tube, usually cane. These are found in diverse parts of the world, ranging from New Guinea to eastern Europe. The strings are formed by detaching long fibres from the body of the tube and raising them on bridges. Several tube zithers bound together form a raft zither, which is played in parts of Africa. The Nigerian version has a gourd resonator attached to the underside. Popular in Cameroon, the harp zither has strings made of raffia that run over a tall vertical bridge.

Psaltery

An ancestor of the modern European zither is the psaltery, a development of the Turkish *qanun* that reached Europe in the 11th century. Psalteries were flat boxes of various shapes, ranging from the early square or triangular to the wing shape of the 14th and 15th centuries. They could also have incurved sides and some were even semicircular, and they were often made with finely decorated cases. The psaltery was played with quill plectra or sometimes plucked with the fingers, either resting on the lap or leaning against the chest.

ABOVE: A wood cut, Die Hackbrettspielerin, *by Tobias Stimmer (1539–84). One of a series of nine, it depicts a courtier playing a medieval trapeze-shaped zither.*

ABOVE: Unlike most of the rest of the world, in Iran the zither occupies a pre-eminent place in classical music and is never used in folk music. It is played with two hammers.

Dulcimer

The dulcimer is virtually identical to the psaltery, but is played by striking the strings with small hammers, the instrument resting either on the lap or on a table. It probably originated in Persia, and is still played in modern Iran. The Hungarian version is a large concert instrument called the *cimbalom*, which features in Kodály's opera *Háry János* (1926). The dulcimer is also played in China, where it arrived from the West around 1800. It is called *yang ch'in*, or "foreign zither".

Ch'in

The indigenous Chinese zither is a plucked instrument with seven strings and no bridges, and is one of the oldest instruments in China. As such, it is a symbol of culture and civilization and is often depicted as an attribute of the sage, especially Confucius.

Scandinavian zither

Although unfretted box zithers were in use in Europe from at least the 12th century onwards, fretted zithers seem to have been developed from the 16th century in northern Europe. The concept was probably brought back to Europe by merchants who had travelled in the East.

Alpine zither

Most modern European zithers, which are popular in Austrian and southern German folk music, are board zithers. Laid flat on the knees or on a table, they consist of a shallow wooden box either with two curved sides or one curved and one straight. Usually the body acts as a resonator, although

BELOW: The ukelin is a kind of bowed zither used in North American folk music. It has a system of hoops along the side of the instrument; by threading the bow through different hoops, chords can be played.

sometimes a supplementary resonator is added. The 45 strings, of which five are melodic and the rest accompaniment, run parallel to the body along its entire length.

Several variations of the alpine zither have been invented, and various schools of playing have developed. The most common type today is the

ABOVE: The dulcimer is now restricted to the alpine regions of Austria and Switzerland. It can be played on its own, but is more often accompanied by guitars and accordions.

Salzburg form, with a semicircular projection on one side, which can be played in one of two tunings, the "Munich" or the "Viennese".

ABOVE: The zither has been used as a folk instrument in Scandinavia since the 16th century. In Sweden it is referred to as a långharpa *and in Norway it is a* langspil.

Sitar

The mark of a good sitar player is the ability to improvise extensively without abandoning the laid down set of rules defining the raag.

JAMEELA SIDDIQI

The sitar, a large, fretted, long-necked lute, is the best-known Indian instrument. Prominent in the classical chamber music formerly played at the Muslim and Hindu courts, tradition credits the invention of the sitar to the court poet Amir Khusrav (c.1253–1325). The name is an Urdu transcription of the Persian *sihtar*, or "three-stringed", Persian being the court language of northern India between the 13th and 19th centuries. The *tambura*, a long-necked lute and near relation of the sitar, is recorded in a late 16th-century contemporary account of court musicians in the reign of Akbar.

The sitar took on the outline of its present form as a classical solo instrument in the 18th century, when the use of a gourd for the shell and the adoption of the carvel-built ribs and heavy metal frets and strings became the norm. Usually accompanied by the tabla drums, the sitar has six or seven main strings, four of

RIGHT: The characteristic sound of the sitar is derived from the shimmering echoes of the sympathetic strings and the distinctive rectangular bridge.

which are played by a plectrum, the others being drones. In addition there are anything from 11–19 sympathetic strings, fitted on to a separate bridge. To the long hollow neck are fitted 20 brass frets that can be moved easily to conform to the scale of a particular *raag*. The convex neck allows the player to alter the pitch by pulling the string sideways across the fret, thus creating the sliding *portamento* that is so characteristic of Indian music.

Although several types of sitar are made, the most common is the *tarafdar sitar* (concert sitar), which is made in two main models: the single-gourd and the double-gourd. It is made of wood with a bulging gourd segment and is based on the large sitar of the 19th century, which was standardized to a length of about 122cm/48in. The wood used is usually toonwood (from the Punjab) or teak. The neck is a large

ABOVE: An Indian shop showing a row of sitars displayed for sale.

ABOVE: Sometimes referred to as the glory of all stick zithers, the vina is a type of sitar with its strings passed between two large gourd resonators.

ABOVE: Ravi Shankar (born 1920) is the foremost player of and composer for the sitar.

Ravi Shankar

As well as being one of the world's foremost players of the sitar, Ravi Shankar – who as a young man trained as a dancer as well as a musician – is also a composer for the instrument. He came to world attention in the 1960s when George Harrison of the Beatles was inspired by some of his complex, yet graceful, sitar improvisation. His mesmerizing impromptu performances introduced the West to the sophistication and beauty of Indian music.

hollowed piece of wood, rounded at the back, and about 90cm/36in long and 9cm/3½in wide.

The sitar is always played with a twisted wire plectrum worn on the right index finger. The player sits on the floor with the left leg tucked flat beneath the right and the shell supported in the hollow of the right foot. Some players sit cross-legged with the raised right thigh supporting the neck of the sitar.

Surbahar

The surbahar is a bass sitar that produces a deep, dignified sound. The neck is wider and longer than that of the sitar but its frets are fixed. The soundtable is also much larger, with a diameter of over 40cm/16in. The instrument was invented in about 1820 by the sitar player Glunlam Muhammad of Lucknow.

ABOVE: Played by both men and women, the sitar is India's most popular instrument.

Vina

The name "vina" has become a generic term for stringed instruments in southern India, and the sitar is sometimes described as one. Originally, the vina was a type of stick zither with the fingerboard stretched between two gourds, but it underwent structural changes in the 16th century. The modern instrument is a kind of lute, with a hollow neck attached to a large hollow body and a soundboard made of wood. It has seven strings, three of which are drones, and there are 24 adjustable frets along the neck. It has a softer, sweeter tone than the sitar and is the principal instrument of classical southern Indian music.

ABOVE: Illustration of a vina from Oriental Drawings *(1806) by Charles Emilius Gold.*

Woodwind
❧ and ❧
Brass

Harnessing the Breath

Never let the horns and woodwind out of your sight:
if you can hear them at all, they are too strong.

RICHARD STRAUSS (1864–1949)

Wind instruments can be classed in two main groups: woodwind and brass. Technically known as "aerophones", wind instruments produce sound when the column of air inside them is set into vibration by either a reed or the player's lips. They depend for their tuning on the length of their pipe; the longer the pipe, the deeper the note that is produced.

Transposing instruments

Instruments with a fundamental note other than C are described as "transposing" instruments. This means that their music is written not at the actual pitch produced, but transposed by a specific interval upwards or downwards. The result is that the player can maintain the same fingering (or harmonics, in the case of brass)

ABOVE: *The woodwind section of the BBC Symphony Orchestra rehearsing in London.*

when playing instruments of different pitch. For instance, the B flat trumpet's written part sounds a tone below that which is written – if it is to play in the key of G major its part is written in A major. Other transposing instruments include the F horn and B flat clarinet.

Woodwind

Four distinct families of instruments make up the woodwind section of the modern symphony orchestra: flutes, oboes, clarinets and bassoons. Although today some of these instruments are no longer made entirely of wood, they still keep the appellation "woodwind", and can be divided into two types depending on

the shape of the bore, which is either cylindrical or conical.

Early woodwind instruments, such as the curtal, shawm and racket, were not only difficult to play in tune but also made harsh sounds. As such they were not popular, and in the mid 17th century Lully excluded them from his band. The then leading French woodwind maker, Jean Hotteterre (c.1605–90) and the court musician Michel Danican Philidor (c.1600–59) are credited with the design and production of new-style instruments, including the transverse flute and the three-section recorder. The shawm was redesigned to create the oboe, and the bassoon was a development of the curtal. The new instruments had a

ABOVE: *The woodwind section consists of flutes, oboes, clarinets and bassoons.*

ABOVE: B flat euphoniums are really tenor tubas, and are a major feature of brass and military bands. Although they are not a standard orchestral instrument, they are sometimes used to great effect. Holst, for example, wrote a part for the euphonium in his suite The Planets *(1916).*

Brass

A modern orchestral brass section usually consists of four horns, two trumpets, three trombones and a tuba. Brass instruments — which were originally used in hunting, for military functions or on religious occasions — became regular members of the orchestra in the 18th century, when court orchestras called on the resources of the military bands attached to the same household.

Mouthpiece

The cup mouthpiece can be dated back at least 3000 years, having been found on northern European *lurs*. *Lurs* were bronze conical trumpets built in two or more detachable parts, the smallest of which had the cup mouthpiece cast with it. The Etruscans, whose civilization can be traced back beyond the 8th century BC, were noted bronze workers whose horns and trumpets — which were played with cup mouthpieces — were eventually adopted by the Romans. Etruscan horns in the shape of three-quarters of a circle are seen in tomb murals from the 5th century BC. These were carried in funeral processions on the shoulders of white-robed officials, who held them by a crossbar as they played.

refinement and flexibility that enabled them to co-exist with Lully's violin orchestra, and he accepted them back into his band.

In the 1830s the woodwind instruments were redesigned again, this time by Theobald Boehm, who developed a new system of keys.

ABOVE: Besson & Co. were the foremost manufacturers of brass instruments in the 19th and early 20th centuries. Founded in Paris in about 1838, the firm opened in London in 1851. The makers were inventors and patentees of the "Prototype" system of manufacture, assuring the exact duplication of instruments, as well as marking the birth of modern methods of musical instrument manufacture.

ABOVE: A brass section: horns, euphonium, trumpets, trombones, tubas (and saxophones).

ABOVE: The modern trombone mouthpiece is deeper than its medieval counterpart.

Flute

The flute has now achieved such perfection and evenness of tone that no further improvement remains to be desired.

HECTOR BERLIOZ (1803–69)

Except for percussion, the flute is arguably the oldest musical instrument known, and ancient examples have been found all over the world, apart from Australia and New Zealand. Unlike the modern side-blown (cross or transverse) instrument, early flutes were end-blown (vertical) and were made of animal bones, such as a reindeer horn or sheep's tibia, pierced with a blow-hole and several finger-holes. The flute has been used as a decoy instrument throughout history, from the Pied Piper of medieval central European folklore to bird-catchers of the 20th century.

BELOW: *The modern flute follows the improved design devised by the Bavarian goldsmith and musician Theobald Boehm in the 1830s.*

Boehm's system used larger holes than hitherto; he also changed all the closed keys into open keys and cut the holes within easier control of the fingers. In 1847 he brought out an improved metal flute with 15 holes and 23 levers and keys. This system was so successful that it was adapted for the oboe, clarinet and bassoon.

Ancient Egypt

A 5000-year-old Egyptian palette from Hierakonpolis has been found that depicts a fox playing a flute, accompanying a dancing ibex and a giraffe. Egyptian flutes predating the pharaonic dynasties were made of cane or metal. Known as *m'ats*, and dating back to at least 2000 BC, they were 90–100cm/36–39in long. These early forms of flute had from two to six finger-holes and were played by being blown across the sharp top end of the tube. A descendant of the *m'at*, known as the *n'ay*, is still played today in some Islamic countries.

Early transverse flute

The transverse flute has been known in Etruria and Greece since at least the 4th century BC, since it is found depicted on Etruscan tombs and urns of that period as well as in contemporary Greek art. An early reference to the instrument and its method of playing appears in Apuleius's *Metamorphosis*, written in the 2nd century AD, which describes "tibia players who have their oblique instruments extended towards the right ear".

Western Europe

The earliest unambiguous reference to the use of the transverse flute in western Europe occurs in the mid 12th-century *Hortus deliciarum* of the Abbess Herrad of Landsberg. During the 14th century the flute spread to most parts of Europe, especially Spain, France and Flanders. The first extant

ABOVE: *This painting by Dirck de Quade van Ravesteyn (c.1612) shows a woman playing a keyless cylindrical flute.*

written reference to the instrument in England – "… and many flowte and lyltyng horn …" – appears in Chaucer's *House of Fame*, written from 1378–80.

Although the main material used for making flutes was boxwood, some were made of other materials such as silver, and it is possible that the *flute traversaine* mentioned in the inventory of the Duke of Anjou's property in 1360 was made of this metal rather than wood. Henry VIII had three flutes made of glass, a material that was still being used by certain French makers in the early 1800s.

As international trade grew in the 19th century, flutes began to be made of harder woods, such as South American granadilla, pallisando or rosewood, and ebony from Africa. From the 1840s artificial materials were sometimes used, such as ebonite, a substance that is still popular today for instruments intended for beginners and schoolchildren. Wood is now rarely used, as silver and even denser metals, such as gold or platinum alloys, are considered to enable the player to produce a more expressive tone.

ABOVE: *The newly fashionable one-keyed Baroque flute became a firm favourite with both professionals and amateurs, so much so that it was fashioned in the form of walking sticks. In mid 18th-century Dublin these were referred to as* German Canes. *Twenty years later Parisians were still able to buy* flûtes en forme de canne.

ABOVE: *This 1759 portrait by Gainsborough shows William Wollaston holding a one-keyed four-sectioned flute.*

ABOVE: *A depiction of a transverse flute of the early 18th century.*

The flute in the orchestra

The transverse flute is believed to have been used for the first time in the orchestra in 1681, in one of Lully's ballets for the French court. By 1691 the flute had entered the French Royal Chapel band, and over the next 50 years, coupled with the advent of public concerts in France, Germany and England, it became an indispensable member of the orchestra.

In 1702 Michel de la Barre gave the world his *Pièces pour la flûte traversière avec la basse-continue* – the first music for solo flute ever published. In 1717 the instrument received a seal of approval when J. S. Bach scored specifically for the *flauto traverso*. Hitherto he had preferred the recorder, whose dulcet tones compared favourably with the shrill sound of the flute. As well as Bach, Handel was also a prolific composer for the instrument. Handel's set of 12 *Sonates pour une traversière, un violon ou hautbois avec basse-continue* (1730) still occupies a central place in the repertoire of many modern flautists. By the end of the 18th century the position of the transverse flute was secure, and it had completely replaced the recorder in the orchestra.

Boehm flute

Always a difficult instrument to master, many people have tried to improve the mechanics of the flute. One of its more important modifiers was Theobald Boehm (1794–1881), a flautist from Munich, who in the 1830s introduced a large-holed instrument that overcame the acoustic deficiencies inherent in earlier flutes. Boehm's changes were revolutionary inasmuch as they changed the hitherto closed keys into open keys controlled by rings. By 1847 he had increased the size of the tone-holes so much that they had to be closed by padded covers, worked by keys that both operated independently and interacted with others, and it is this type of flute that is played today.

ABOVE: The flute section of a youth band.

BELOW: The alto flute, a fourth lower than the concert flute, was invented by Theobald Boehm in the 1890s. It is a larger version of the standard flute, measuring 87cm/34in, and is specially adapted to allow the player to reach the more widely spaced holes.

The alto flute was said to be Boehm's favourite instrument due to its distinctive "song style"; it produces an unmistakable, full tone with a haunting sound in all registers, and is used to beautiful effect in three famous works composed between 1912 and 1916: Ravel's Daphnis et Chloé (1912), Stravinsky's The Rite of Spring (1913) and Holst's The Planets (1916). More recently, the alto flute has been used in Britten's works for the stage, in compositions by Boulez and Stockhausen, and in music composed for television.

LEFT: The bass flute is pitched an octave below the flute. Its tubing is 130cm/51in long, and it is bent back on itself near the mouthpiece to make it more manageable.

Fife

Smaller than the flute, the fife has a narrower bore and hence a louder and shriller sound. Played to accompany marching and for giving signals during battle, the fife was used in the British army until the 1890s. Fife and drum corps continue to thrive in the United States, performing early American martial music.

Alto and bass flutes

Pitched in G and a fourth lower than the concert flute, the alto flute was developed in the 1890s. It proved popular in France, where its slightly melancholic, haunting tone was used to the full by Ravel in *Daphnis et Chloé* (1912) and by Stravinsky in *The Rite of Spring* (1913). The bass – or double bass – flute in C, pitched an octave below the standard flute, is now rarely found.

Piccolo

Pitched in C and an octave higher than and half the size of the concert flute, the piccolo evolved early in the 19th century. One of the first composers to write regularly for the piccolo was Beethoven, who used it in his Fifth and Sixth Symphonies.

BELOW: The piccolo is pitched an octave higher than the flute. Perhaps the first composer to use the piccolo to its full potential was Tchaikovsky.

RIGHT: The well-known 1866 painting by Edouard Manet, entitled Le Fifre *("The Piper").*

Recorder

*Did buy a recorder, which I do intend to learn to play on, the sound
of it being, of all sounds in the world, most pleasing to me.*

SAMUEL PEPYS (1633–1703)

The recorder is a relatively simple instrument and can be traced back about a thousand years, for what looks like a duct flute with a tapering bore appears in an 11th-century French miniature. It is possible, therefore, that the Normans introduced the instrument to England, the only country, incidentally, where the instrument is called a "recorder" – mainland Europe preferring such terms as *flûte à bec* or *Schnabelflöte*. In England the name goes back to at least 1388, when the recorder is mentioned in the household accounts of the Earl of Derby, who later became Henry IV.

The recorder is relatively simple to play and was one of the most popular instruments of European Renaissance and Baroque music. A type of whistle flute with a wide tapering bore, it was originally made of a single piece of boxwood or ivory with a beaked mouthpiece. French 17th-century makers improved its construction,

*ABOVE, FROM LEFT TO RIGHT:
Three modern recorders of varying pitches –
tenor, treble and descant.*

making it in three sections. Twentieth-century examples are made from many kinds of wood, or from plastic.

Early types of recorder
Until 1470, the recorder had six equidistant finger-holes and a thumb-hole. In Italy, in or about that year, an extra hole was added. Although Italian recorders continued to be built with a wide bore, in northern countries it was somewhat narrower. The two types can be clearly seen in two pictures: Caravaggio's *Lute Player* includes a wide-bore instrument in the composition, while Dürer's *The Men's*

Bath depicts a recorder with an extremely narrow bore. Another early illustration of the instrument is a woodcut of four recorders published in Sebastian Virdung's *Musica getutscht und ausgezogen* in 1511. The earliest known extant recorder was found under a 15th-century house in Dordrecht, and is presumed to be at least as old as the house.

The Renaissance recorder was built for playing in consort rather than as a solo instrument. Henry VIII was a recorder player and had many cased sets of between four and nine instruments. These would have been made together and tuned to match each other. Samuel Pepys and his wife

ABOVE: During the 16th and 17th centuries recorders were played in consorts of various sizes. This picture shows the very large, bassoon-like bass recorder.

Recorder music

The renewed popularity of the recorder in the 20th century led composers such as Benjamin Britten (*Noyes Fludde* and *A Midsummer Night's Dream*) and Hans Ulrich Staeps (*Sieben Flötentänze*) to score for the instrument.

ABOVE, FROM LEFT TO RIGHT: A selection of recorder-type instruments – one-keyed flute, bass recorder, double flagolet and boxwood recorder.

both played the flageolet, but he heard the recorder played at the theatre in 1668 and thought it superior.

In late 16th-century Germany recorder-like instruments, turned on a lathe, were known as *Kolomen*, while in France, by the mid 18th century, the recorder was known as the *flûte à neuf trous*. The ninth hole to which this name refers was an alternative hole for the little finger used by left-handed players of the one-piece instrument; the unused hole on the other side was sealed with a plug of wood or wax.

The recorder in the orchestra

By the 16th century recorders were being made in five different sizes: descant, treble, tenor, bass and contrabass, the latter between 2.5m/8ft and 2.8m/9ft long. In the 16th and 17th centuries they were widely played by groups of amateurs, but by the 18th century the recorder

had become an established part of the orchestra, and both Bach and Handel scored for it, the latter writing a number of sonatas for the *flûte à bec*. Around 1750, however, the recorder – which was known in France as the *flûte d'Angleterre* – was being discarded in favour of the transverse flute, which offered a greater dynamic range and better pitch control. By the 1790s the recorder had totally disappeared from the orchestra.

Twentieth-century revival

Were it not for the revival of interest by Arnold Dolmetsch (1858–1940), the recorder might now be only a museum piece. Dolmetsch pioneered the reconstruction of obsolete instruments, realizing that without them the music that had been written for them could not be heard. He made his first recorder in 1919, and presented a consort of four in a performance in 1926. His son Carl, a recorder virtuoso, made further

improvements that enabled the recorder to play effectively with a modern string orchestra.

The renewed popularity of the instrument led to the development of cheap plastic recorders which are particularly useful in schools, where the recorder is often the first musical instrument taught to children. It was first introduced into schools in the 1930s. In this way, the modern recorder has become widespread in most of Europe and the United States.

LEFT: The bass recorder, unlike its smaller counterparts, is blown via a curved metal mouthpiece called a crook. The bass recorder's sound is deep and resonating.

LEFT: This 17th-century German columnar alto recorder bears the device of two trefoils, with the stems curving to the right beneath the upper grill and on the base.

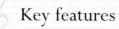

Key features

TYPE: aerophone woodwind

PITCH: C or F

NOTABLE PLAYERS OF THE RECORDER: Franz Brüggen, Rudolf Barthel, Amico Dolci, David Munrow.

RIGHT: Recorders were originally made from one piece of boxwood or ivory, rather than the three-piece instruments common today. Here we see a one-keyed flute and a boxwood recorder.

Oboe

The inimitable, charming sweet tone of the oboe.

JOHN BANISTER (1630–79)

The English word "oboe" is a phonetic rendering of the French *hautbois*, meaning "high wood", which refers to the instrument's tone. It is not known who actually invented the oboe, but it was being played in Paris by 1670 and within ten years had spread to other European cities. It was developed as a woodwind instrument that could provide a tone quality suitable for indoor music, as opposed to the shrill sound of the shawm, which was regarded as fit only for open-air performances. Prototype oboes had two keys, and were first played in the band of Louis XIV's *Grande écurie* in 1657. One of the first compositions actually to specify a line for the oboe was Robert Cambert's opera *Pomone* (1671).

LEFT: The oboe's broad, sweet, plaintive and melancholic tone — which blends in so well with the violins — is an unmistakable feature of the modern symphony orchestra.

The oboe differed from the shawm in that whereas the latter was a one-piece instrument, the oboe was made in three sections connected by tenon-and-socket joints. The oboe's musical superiority over the shawm was assisted by the abolition of the pirouette, the turned wooden component into which the double reed was inserted. Instead, the reed was mounted on a staple clear of the body, facilitating a more delicate control of the reed between the lips. A greater compass was also attained by altering the size and disposition of the finger-holes to allow for a fully chromatic system of fork or cross fingerings through two octaves.

The oboe reached England in 1674, when a band of French musicians was brought over for a performance of John Crowne's masque *Calisto*. One of these instrumentalists was James Paisible (died 1721), who remained in London, entered the king's service, and became the first professional oboist in

ABOVE: An early 18th-century oboe as depicted by Johann Weigel.

England. The oboe soon became popular, and by 1695 the first printed tutor for the two-keyed oboe was published. One of the first to score for it was Henry Purcell (1659–95), who used it in all his larger works, including at least three obbligato parts for solo oboe.

The Horse Grenadiers adopted the instrument in 1678, and by the early 18th century almost every European band and orchestra included a pair of oboes. By the 1750s, players had begun to hold the instrument with the left hand above the right, as is standard today.

Nineteenth-century oboe

During the 19th century the original two keys were increased to eight and a speaker, or octave, key was introduced. This small aperture, which was placed above the finger-holes, greatly facilitated over-blowing, thereby giving the

Key features

TYPE: double-reed woodwind

PITCH: C

NOTABLE PLAYERS OF THE OBOE: Jacques Hotteterre, Giuseppe Sammartini, Johann Christian Fischer, Leon Goossens, Pierre Pierlot, Heinz Holliger.

instrument a wider compass. The two-keyed model was still being made up to the 1820s, with the four-keyed variety becoming popular in the 1830s. At about this time, the French makers began to develop the instrument in ways that differed from the simpler German and Austrian construction.

Frédéric Triébert

The most celebrated of the French oboe makers was Frédéric Triébert (1813–78). His contributions to the development of the oboe included narrowing the instrument's bore, resulting in a much more refined tone. The reed was made narrower and thinner, and the position and size of the finger-holes changed. The firm

ABOVE: A present-day oboe player.

LEFT: The algaita is a type of oboe played in West Africa, made from a single piece of wood covered in leather. The player presses his lips to the disc and uses his cheeks as an air reservoir so that the instrument can be blown continuously.

Oboe music

An obbligato part for the oboe appears in Purcell's *Come Ye Sons of Art* (1694), and during the 18th century it became a leading solo instrument, featuring in concertos by Vivaldi and Albinoni. It was used extensively by Bach and Handel, and was particularly well understood by Mozart, who wrote an Oboe Concerto in C (K314). It was not prominent as a solo instrument in the 19th century, but in the 20th century oboe soloists came into their own with concertos by Richard Strauss, Ralph Vaughan Williams, Gustav Holst and many others. One of the major composers for the oboe is the player Heinz Holliger, whose *Siebengesang* of 1966 has an elaborate oboe part.

of Triébert introduced both the "thumb-plate" and "Conservatoire" systems, which are still in use on modern instruments. After Triébert's death, his erstwhile foreman François Lorée continued to experiment with the instrument, developing a complicated key system known as the "plateau". Today, at least four systems of keywork are in use on the oboe.

RIGHT: The oboe is the principal instrument of the orchestra's woodwind section.

Cor anglais

The cor anglais or English horn, the tenor version of the oboe, is a misnomer, for it is neither English nor a horn, and the origin of its name is a mystery. Played with a curved brass crook that carries the reed, the fingering and keywork of the cor anglais are the same as that for the

ABOVE: *The cor anglais is used only in certain passages of music. This player has his oboe by his side, ready to be taken up when the music no longer calls for the cor anglais, or tenor instrument.*

RIGHT: *The straight cor anglais that is played today is based on Henri Brod's model of 1839. The origin of the name is unknown, but it is known that Haydn referred to the instrument as the* cor anglé *("bent horn").*

oboe. The cor anglais of the mid 18th century was usually curved to a crescent or bent at an angle and covered in black leather. As the holes were of necessity farther apart than those on the conventional oboe, the curve or bend made the instrument both easier to hold and to play. The straight cor anglais that is familiar today, with its characteristic globular bell, is based on Henri Brod's *cor anglais moderne* of 1839. Brod got around the problem of reaching the widely spaced finger-holes by introducing keys with long levers.

Although the cor anglais was mainly used in French military music, both

ABOVE: *The characteristic long curved brass crook that carries the reed of the cor anglais.*

Bach and Purcell included the instrument in their orchestral scores, as have various later composers.

Oboe d'amore

A close relation to the cor anglais is the oboe d'amore, pitched in A. Known since about 1720, the distinctive feature of the oboe d'amore is the bulbous end joint that modifies the timbre by allowing the air to expand before it is forced through a smaller aperture. It was used by J. S. Bach in his *St John Passion* (1723) and about 60 other works, in order to achieve low notes then outside the oboe's range and also because it could cope with sharp keys. Due to the difficulties of playing it in tune, the oboe d'amore did not survive much beyond the 1750s, but it was revived in 1854 when the Belgian instrument maker Victor Mahillon reconstructed one for a performance of one of Bach's works in Brussels. Since then it has rarely been used; the most notable 20th-century work requiring the oboe d'amore is Richard Strauss's *Symphonia domestica* (1904).

Baritone oboe

The earliest baritone oboe known, which was pitched one octave below the regular orchestral oboe, was that made by Charles

RIGHT: *The baritone oboe.*

LEFT: *The oboe d'amore, whose pitch falls between the oboe and the cor anglais, has a narrow bore and a bulbous end joint, resulting in a less strident tone.*

experimentation, Heckel produced his heckelphone – however, it had taken him so long that Wagner had been dead for 20 years before the first one was produced.

Generically allied to the oboe and pitched at baritone range, the heckelphone was built in three sections, with a wide conical bore and bulbous bell, the large diameter of the instrument calling for a powerful double reed like that of a bassoon, which is carried on a curved crook. In 1905 Richard Strauss wrote an important part for the heckelphone in *Salome*, and since then its deep and powerful tone has been used freely as a substitute for the bass oboe.

RIGHT: *This three-keyed fruitwood oboe with fishtail brass keys and trapezoidal covers was made by Andreas Kenisgperger.*

Bizet in the 1740s, which now resides in the Paris Conservatoire de Musique. Bizet solved the problem of the excessive length of tubing by doubling the bore on itself and carrying the mouthpiece on a crook. He was also able to reduce the distance between the adjacent finger-holes by boring them obliquely through thickenings in the tube wall. Although Delius scored parts for the baritone oboe, today it is virtually a museum piece.

Heckelphone

In 1884 Richard Wagner asked the maker Wilhelm Heckel of Biebrich for a baritone double-reed instrument that would combine the character of the oboe with the soft but powerful tone of the alphorn. After much

ABOVE: *The oboe section of the London Symphony Orchestra.*

Clarinet

The many-keyed clarinet, which can sound so ghostly in the deep chalumeau register but higher up can gleam in silvery blossoming harmony.

THOMAS MANN (1875–1955), "DR FAUSTUS"

The clarinet was invented in the first few years of the 18th century by the renowned woodwind maker Johann Christoph Denner (1655–1707), or his son Jakob (1681–1785) of Nuremberg. It was the first reed-blown instrument to have a cylindrical rather than a conical bore. Denner's main achievement was in his practical use of the way that the scale of fundamentals could be made to sound a twelfth higher if a vent hole were pierced at the upper end of a cylinder. This hole was covered by what is now known as the speaker key.

Made of boxwood, the first clarinets were pitched in C and had six finger-holes and two keys. A third key was soon added to extend the range down a semitone and, more importantly, to make possible the playing of the "missing" *b'* at the break – even today,

amateur clarinettists still find this note difficult to produce. The body was divided into three sections, a feature that allowed the use of interchangeable joints of varying length to facilitate playing in different keys.

The first clarinets were played with a reed about 15mm/⅝in wide, tied to the mouthpiece with twine – the barrel of the modern instrument

ABOVE: The first mention of the clarinet was in an advertisement by the Amsterdam publishers Roger & Le Cene in 1706.

did not appear until the 1760s. At first it was common practice to play with the reed uppermost against the top lip. The modern style of placing it on the lower lip was adopted by the Paris Conservatoire in 1831, but did not become universal for many years.

Around 1750, when the fourth (A flat and E flat) and fifth (F sharp and C sharp) keys were added and the foot joint expanded into a bell, the clarinet became more accepted into the orchestra, having previously been used chiefly as a solo instrument, but it did not become firmly established until the mid 19th century. For a time it looked

as if it might replace the oboe and, although the latter has retained its position in the symphony orchestra, the clarinet has succeeded in ousting it from military bands.

In 1790 a sixth key, invented by Jean Lefèvre, was added to give an additional C sharp and G sharp, and the pear-shaped barrel disappeared. In spite of these improvements the instrument was still beset with problems of fingering and intonation, and for these reasons clarinets were built at different pitches. Although the "type" instrument was in C, there was also a B flat clarinet for playing in flat keys and A, B and D models that could be used for sharp keys.

Modern clarinet

In 1809 Iwan Müller (1786–1854), one of the finest clarinettists of his day, brought out the prototype of his 13-keyed model pitched in B flat, which was to become the standard instrument for the next hundred years.

ABOVE: A 19th-century two-keyed clarinet.

Key features

TYPE: single-reed woodwind

PITCH: B flat or E flat

NOTABLE PLAYERS OF THE CLARINET: Anton and Johann Stadler, Heinrick Baermann, Benny Goodman, Frederick Thurston, Gervase de Peyer, Woody Herman, Jack Brymer, Alan Hacker.

In 1817 its development was refined when Müller, who was the first to use pads over the countersunk tone-holes, invented the metal ligature. His tutor was published in 1826, and dedicated to George IV. As an instrumentalist Müller performed all over Europe, his style being described as brilliant and expressive.

The final major modification of the clarinet occurred between 1839 and 1843 when the clarinettist Hyacinthe

Clarinet music

One of the first composers to write for the clarinet was Jean-Philippe Rameau (1683–1764), who scored for it in *Zoroastre* (1749). Its inclusion in the Mannheim orchestra established it as an orchestral instrument, and as such it was used by Mozart, who also wrote three important works for the clarinettist Anton Stadler: the *Kegelstaff Trio* (K498), the Clarinet Quintet (K581) and the Clarinet Concerto (K622). With the improvements to the clarinet that were made in the early 19th century, composers such as Carl Maria von Weber (1786–1826) and Louis Spohr (1784–1851) began to write solos for it. One of the great works of the 20th century that features the clarinet is George Gershwin's (1898–1937) famous symphonic jazz poem, *Rhapsody in Blue*. This original work was written in 1923 in the unbelievably short space of ten days.

ABOVE: *A monk playing an 18th-century two-keyed clarinet.*

Eleonore Klosé collaborated with the maker Louis-August Buffet to simplify the fingering system, using the ring-keys Boehm had developed for his flutes.

Chalumeau

The clarinet was a modification of the chalumeau, a small woodwind instrument with seven holes. Chalumeaux were difficult to play and

LEFT: *The bass clarinet has a compass from D to f". To accommodate its length and make it easier to play, it has a curved bell and has its reed mounted on a curved crook.*

were never popular. Not only was it difficult to obtain the correct embouchure (lip technique), but they were restricted to a range of just over an octave. The sound of the chalumeau was also not to the liking of all, the Hamburg musician Johann Mattheson (1681–1764) describing the instrument's tone as a "dreadful evening symphony". The lower register of the clarinet is known as the chalumeau register.

Bass clarinet

The first bass clarinet was made in 1772 when Giles Lot of Paris produced one with a range of three and a half octaves. In 1793 Carl August Grenser of Dresden presented his *Klarinettenbass*, an instrument built in the form of a bassoon with nine keys. Various other attempts followed, but were all made redundant by Adolphe Sax's bass clarinet of 1838, which resembled a saxophone, with both bell and mouthpiece bent back. Although it has not always been part of the standard woodwind section, many works call for it, including Wagner's *Ring* and Franck's Symphony in D minor.

ABOVE: *Hand positions on the bass clarinet.*

Saxophone

The saxophone is the embodied spirit of beer.

ARNOLD BENNETT (1867–1931)

The saxophone is characterized by a fairly wide body made from a conical tube of thin metal, commonly brass, which is expanded at the open end with a small flare. It has 18–21 tone-holes of graduated size, all of which are controlled by keys. At the mouthpiece end are two speaker keys that enable the instrument to over-blow at the octave. The mouthpiece, which is fitted with a single reed, was originally made of wood, but is now commonly of ebonite or sometimes brass.

The saxophone was patented in 1846 by Adolphe Sax (1814–94). Although Sax's combination of a single bleating reed with a conical body was not entirely new, the saxophone was the first successful instrument of this type. The idea had first been used by William Meikle, a Scotsman who in about 1825 had produced a now virtually forgotten "alto fagotto", a modified small bassoon played with a clarinet mouthpiece.

LEFT: The alto saxophone was invented in 1846 by Adolphe Sax as an attempt to introduce a more powerful group of instruments into military bands to form a link between the clarinets and tenor brasses.

The saxophone family consists of the sopranino in E flat, soprano in B flat, alto in E flat, tenor in B flat, baritone in E flat and bass in B flat. Larger saxophones are made more manageable by introducing a U-bend and tilting the bell slightly forward. From the baritone size downwards, the tubing is doubled by being folded at the upper end.

At the beginning of the 21st century many new models, with only minor differences, are still being brought out yearly. One more radical development was the plastic saxophone, in which all but the keys and mountings are moulded from synthetic materials, but this instrument has not been enthusiastically adopted by players.

Rise in popularity

Since its introduction into French infantry music, the saxophone has steadily gained favour in military bands. Bands such as Jullien's, which introduced the instrument to England in 1850, did much to make the instrument familiar to concert audiences, as did Sousa's band half a century later in America. The saxophone, which became established as a regular member of British military bands in the 1920s, is now also an

ABOVE: One of the most important roles for the saxophone has been in jazz.

Key features

TYPE: single-reed woodwind

PITCH: B flat or E flat

NOTABLE PLAYERS OF THE SAXOPHONE: Sidney Bechet, Marcel Mule, Johnny Hodges, Coleman Hawkins, Lester Young, Charlie Parker, John Coltrane, Stan Getz.

ABOVE: *One of the finest exponents of the alto sax was Charlie Parker (1920–55), whose astounding technique meant that he was idolized by jazz fans everywhere.*

Saxophone music

Georges Bizet's *L'Arlésienne* Suite (1872) includes a famous alto solo, and other composers that have featured the instrument include Ravel (*Bolero*), Prokofiev (*Romeo and Juliet*) and Vaughan Williams (Symphony No. 6). However, Simon Haram, one of the world's foremost saxophone players, is quoted as saying that saxophone players are like jackdaws – they have to steal a lot of stuff.

ABOVE: *The saxophone's popularity has spread all over the world. Here a Tanzanian musician is entertaining his audience.*

established part of the modern symphony orchestra. The alto instrument was the first to be so used, but Richard Strauss's *Symphonia domestica* (1902) called for a saxophone quartet.

Jazz saxophone

Since World War I the saxophone has become extremely popular in music of all kinds, and is now one of the most common wind instruments. Its playing

RIGHT: *The B flat soprano saxophone.*

technique is regarded as fairly simple compared with other reed instruments. Since the 1930s it has played a leading role in jazz bands, and it is in this medium that the instrument's potential has been most thoroughly exploited. Although today's jazz musicians mainly use B flat tenor

and E flat alto saxophones, between the 1930s and '60s, saxophone consorts of the four main types featured strongly in big bands, such as those led by Glenn Miller and Duke Ellington in the United States, Henry Hall in England and Bert Kaempfert and James Last in Germany.

ABOVE: *The most commonly used saxophone is the tenor. This musician is playing for passengers boarding a Mississippi river boat.*

Bassoon

The wedding guest here beat his breast,
For he heard the loud bassoon.

SAMUEL TAYLOR COLERIDGE (1772–1834), "THE ANCIENT MARINER"

Often described as the clown of the orchestra, the bassoon is the bass of the woodwind section. As well as solo work, the bassoon adds colour to the orchestra, as it blends in well with all the other instruments.

In France the word "bassoon" came into use in 1613 to denote the double or bass curtal. Over the next 25 years it was transformed into the separately jointed instrument that is known today as the bassoon. First provided with three swallow-tailed keys – two for the thumbs and one for the little finger – by the mid 17th century the bassoon was being made in four separate sections: the butt, wing, bass and bell. Pitched in C, and made of maple or pearwood, it formed a continuously expanding tube of 2.4m/8ft, which

ABOVE: The bassoon is the bass member of the woodwind section of the orchestra, with the contrabassoon, supported on a spike, playing the lowest notes.

LEFT: The bassoon has a compass of about three and a half octaves. The tube, which is usually made of maple, is doubled.

ABOVE:
Pitched an octave below the bassoon, the contrabassoon has a metal bell as its last section.

was doubled to make it manageable. By 1730 a fourth key had been added, and by 1800 six were common.

During the 19th century many more improvements were made to the bassoon. One of the more notable modifiers of the instrument was Charles-Joseph Sax (1791–1865), who by 1825 had introduced covered tone-holes. Sax continued his work and in 1851, with his son Adolphe, brought out a 23-keyed metal bassoon.

Another important figure in the history of the bassoon is Carl Almenraeder (1786–1843). A performer, teacher, bandmaster and composer, in 1825 he published a treatise in which he described how, by adding certain keys and relocating others, not only could the intonation be improved, but playing in all keys could be facilitated. By 1831 he had founded his own factory in Biebrich, near Wiesbaden, where by increasing the number of keys to 15 he was able to extend the bassoon's compass to nearly four octaves. On Almenraeder's death, his partner Johann Heckel (1812–77) continued to refine the instrument, which by 1843 had 18 keys and a chromatic range of over four octaves. Successive members of the Heckel

Key features

TYPE: double-reed woodwind

PITCH: C

NOTABLE PLAYERS OF THE BASSOON: Paolo Besozzi, Felix Rheiner, Georg Wenzel Ritter, James Mackintosh, Archie Camden, Simon Kovar.

family carried out many reforms to the bassoon, launching a famous model in the 1870s, and it is through their efforts that the instrument reached its present degree of perfection. French and Italian players tend to prefer an alternative French design by Buffet-Crampon, made in rosewood.

Music for the bassoon

An outstanding work in the bassoon's solo repertoire is Mozart's Concerto in B flat (K191) of 1774, and many chamber works for bassoon and strings were written around 1800. Hummel and Weber wrote bassoon concertos; Paganini wrote a Concertino for Bassoon and Horn. The bassoon achieved greater prominence in the 20th century, with solo works such as Elgar's *Romance* (1909) and orchestral

ABOVE: The bassoon player of the orchestra of the Paris opera in 1868.

RIGHT:
To encourage children to take up the bassoon, small faggottini *have been made. This one is seen side by side with a full-size instrument.*

parts like the opening of Stravinsky's *The Rite of Spring* (1913). Shorter compositions for the bassoon in the 20th century have often been given picturesque titles, such as Granville Bantock's *Dance of the Witches*, Gilbert Vinter's *The Playful Pachyderm* and André Bloch's *Dancing Jack*.

Curtal

In the 16th century the need for instruments of a bass register for use with choirs led to the creation of the curtal or dulcian, the immediate predecessor of the modern bassoon. More manageable than the bass shawm because of its doubled tube, the curtal

was named after a short-barrelled cannon of "curtailed" length. By 1600 curtals were being played over much of Europe, from Spain and Italy to Germany and England. Small high-pitched models were particularly popular in Austria and Spain, where they were often played in church ensembles. Court bands also included curtals, and composers such as Giovanni Gabrieli (1555–1612) began writing separate parts for them. Curtals were made in one of two different ways. The more usual method was to bore two channels, connected to each other by a U-bend at the lower ends, into a single block of wood. The other method was to hollow out two sections of wood, then glue them together. In each case, the finished instrument was covered with leather. A slightly flared bell was fitted to the terminal end of the bore, while a short crook with a double reed was attached to the proximal end.

ABOVE: Known since at least 1559, the curtal was less strident in tone than the shawm and as such was often dubbed the dulcian. This replica was made in 1971.

Horn

The horn is perhaps the least efficient instrument of the brass family,
but it produces the most beautiful sound of all.

BARRY TUCKWELL (BORN 1931)

The horn is unique among orchestral instruments, not only in that the keys are operated with the left hand, but because it is also played backwards, with the bell facing towards the rear of the orchestra. It is the most expressive brass instrument in the orchestra, and also the most difficult to play. The normal position for the right hand is with all fingers close together against the far side of the bell and with the thumb close against them. The hand is cupped and can be straightened to sharpen various harmonics, while increased cupping of the hand flattens the harmonics.

ABOVE: Some horns had the tube coiled several times. This 19th-century painting shows two brothers playing horn and drum.

Although still popularly referred to as the French horn, most horns played in orchestras today are in reality the wider bore German horn. Both, however, evolved from the long, coiled *cor de chasse* of the French hunt, and by 1900 had come to resemble the modern instrument closely. F had become the standard pitch and rotary valves were the norm.

Animal horn

The first horns were, as the name implies, made from animal horns. In Africa they were made principally from the horns of antelopes, cattle horns being a poor substitute. One of the oldest types of horn is the Jewish *shofar*, or ram's horn. Made from a ritually killed sheep or goat, the *shofar* is the only musical instrument that has survived into the 20th century in the same form it had in antiquity. The small end of the horn is pierced with a long narrow passage that connects the proximal end with the main cavity of

LEFT: The learner needs a good ear, for the horn has the longest series of harmonics of any brass instrument, the number depending on the skill and lip strength of the player, who must also learn the varying degrees of hand-stopping.

the bore. Two pitches are possible, and are often, but not always, a fifth apart. The *shofar's* use as a martial instrument is documented in the story of the capture of Jericho, when its powerful sound is said to have caused the city walls to fall down. It is still used today in Jewish religious ceremonies such as Rosh Hashanah (the Jewish New Year) and Yom Kippur (the day of atonement).

Hunting horn and post-horn

The horn has been a part of European hunting life since Saxon times. By the 17th century there were two types: in Germany the preference was for a curved shape, while the English hunt

Key features

TYPE: brass aerophone

PITCH: F

NOTABLE PLAYERS OF THE HORN: Denis Brain, Barry Tuckwell.

ABOVE: The shofar *is an early type of horn still used today to mark the Jewish occasions of Rosh Hodesh (the first day of the month) and Rosh Hashanah (the New Year).*

ABOVE: Before valves were introduced, horns were very simple instruments consisting solely of a coiled tube and a large bell into which the hand was inserted.

preferred a straight horn, which could give a more penetrating call. When postal services began to operate in the 15th century, the courier would announce his arrival and impending departure by a distinctive call on a small brass horn.

From crooks to valves

The main problem of the early horns was that, without hand-stopping, they could play only one set of harmonics. One solution, put forward in about 1750 by the Dresden instrument maker Johann Werner, was the slide crook. As each crook was a separate coil of tubing of the correct length for each tonality, by fitting on the appropriate crook the horn could be played in all keys. Useful as this was,

the drawback was that the player had to carry a full set of up to 13 crooks, one for each key, which they had to fit as and when required. Composers allowed for this and, when the music modulated, they gave time for the horn players to change coils before they made their first entry in the new key.

In 1815 the invention of the valve revolutionized the playing of the horn. With the two valves with which the horn was originally fitted, only two extra crooks were now needed. At this time composers wrote for specific orchestras, and it is said that Beethoven wrote the horn solo in the slow movement of his Ninth Symphony for the fourth horn player in the orchestra, as he was the only one playing an instrument with valves.

Double horn

One of the perennial problems for horn players is hitting the wrong note in the high harmonics, where they lie close together. To address this problem in 1898 Fritz Krupse of Erfurt

ABOVE: The double horn enables the player to change the pitch from F to B flat by depressing an extra valve.

RIGHT: An 18th-century German post-horn made in three coils of tubing.

designed a double horn. As its name implies, this is two horns in one, each with its own set of valves but sharing the same mouthpiece and bell. It is pitched in F and B flat, the playing choosing his pitch by depressing an extra valve. The advantage of the double horn was that the twelfth harmonic in F became the ninth in B flat and was, therefore, much safer to play.

Horn music

Mozart wrote four horn concertos, which is all the more remarkable when it is remembered that in his time the horn did not have valves and that pitch depended solely on hand-stopping. Another composer who used the horn to full effect was Richard Strauss. Hindemith and Tippett both wrote sonatas for four horns, and Thea Musgrave wrote a Horn Concerto in 1971. The most ambitious of all works for the post-horn is the popular *Post-horn Galop*, which was composed in 1844 by Koenig, the principal cornettist in the famed Jullien military band.

Trumpet

The quality of tone of the trumpet is noble and brilliant.

HECTOR BERLIOZ (1803–69)

The trumpet has a narrow, mainly cylindrical bore and is lip-vibrated. Forms of the instrument are found all over the world, and with rare exceptions they have traditionally been played by men. They have often been associated with magic and ritual, and with official or military ceremonies.

Egypt and Israel

The ancient Egyptians used metal trumpets 50–60cm/20–24in long and made of silver or bronze; they were sacred and were played only in the worship of Osiris. On their return from exile in Egypt, the Israelites adopted the Egyptian trumpet. It became part of the insignia of the Hebrew priests, who used pairs of silver trumpets to be played in certain rites of the temple.

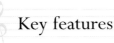

ABOVE: The Greeks compared the sound of the trumpet to that of an elephant, and elephants are still said to "trumpet".

Etruria and Rome

A forerunner of both the trumpet and the alphorn, the Etruscan *lituus* evolved from a curved animal horn attached to a slender wooden cylindrical tube terminating in an upturned bell. The Romans modified the *lituus* by discarding the bulb bell, thus creating a straight wide-bore bronze trumpet about 1.2m/4ft long. This was known as the *tuba*, and was played with a long detachable conical mouthpiece. As well as being used in the civilian arena, this instrument was also played by the cavalry, who used it bent into two folds like a modern bugle, making it easier for a mounted man to play.

Post-classical trumpet

Early post-classical trumpets were made in the same form as the straight Roman instruments with detachable mouthpieces. They were held halfway down with the right hand, while the left hand held the mouthpiece. In the 11th century, the Spanish adopted the straight-tubed Arab *nafir*, which they called the *trompeta morisca*. The crusaders took over the Saracens'

ferocious *cor sarrazinois*, calling it a *buisine*, a term that is an etymological ancestor to *Posaune*, the modern German name for the trombone. The *buisine*, made of brass, copper or silver, terminated in a wide bell.

Medieval Europe

Such was the importance attached to the trumpet in early medieval Europe that the right of owning one was restricted to the aristocracy. Later, because of its noble associations, it became the instrument of the cavalry, a branch of the army that was originally formed from the nobility, where trumpets were used both to sound military signals and to help maintain morale. One such occasion

ABOVE: This 15th-century French miniature depicts the Bible story of the fall of Jericho. The event is signalled by the trumpets of Joshua, which had very long bores.

was the night before the Battle of Agincourt (1415), when the opposing armies were "serenaded by the continuous sound of the trumpets".

Trumpet players were attached to the more important European courts and, as the 14th century progressed, long trumpets appeared with banners displaying the seigneurial arms suspended from the bell to the boss. Such was the prestige of the instrument that, when Charles VI entered Reims in 1380, he was preceded by over 30 trumpeters.

Slide trumpet

It was when trumpets began to be played in ensembles with other instruments that problems of pitch

Trumpet music

Although by the 1560s trumpets were being played between acts in the theatre, they were not formally introduced into the opera band until Monteverdi scored for the instrument in *Orfeo* in 1607. By the mid 17th century they were becoming a regular part of the orchestra, used in works by Pietro Cavalli (1602–76) and Giovanni Legrenzi (1626–90). Purcell's *Dioclesian* (1690) used trumpet fanfares, while Alessandro Scarlatti (1660–1725) frequently included trumpets in his operas. The valved trumpet, developed in the 1820s, was introduced to the orchestra by Gioacchino Rossini (1792–1868), who used it to wonderful effect in *William Tell* in 1829.

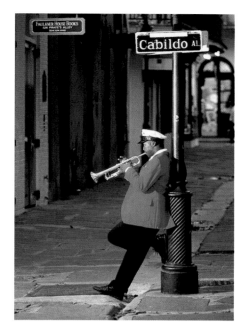

arose. One solution was the slide trumpet, which not only allowed the trumpeter to adjust his pitch easily, but also gave him the first opportunity to play a chromatic scale on an instrument that was otherwise only playable in harmonics. The slide trumpet had an elongated mouthpiece, sometimes over 50cm/20in in length, that was held by the left hand, while the right hand drew the body of the instrument in and out like the slide of a trombone.

A variation on the slide trumpet was designed in the late 18th century by the English trumpeter John Hyde. Hyde's trumpet, in F, had a U-shaped slide that replaced the bend nearest the player and could be pulled out when needed and returned by a spring. Although not fully diatonic, the slide did allow the player to temper the 11th and 13th harmonics that were out of tune with the normal scale.

Keyed trumpet

The various attempts by instrument makers and players to improve the trumpet by altering the pitch with circular tuning bits and crooks only raised the pitch of the whole instrument, which still played only

LEFT: *A trumpeter playing in the streets of New Orleans, Louisiana.*

harmonics. There were several attempts during the 18th and early 19th centuries to create a trumpet that could play a chromatic scale.

One successful innovator was the Viennese instrument maker Joseph Felix Riedel, who made a 15-keyed trumpet to the plans of Anton Weidinger, a trumpeter at the Viennese court. Although the keyed trumpet became popular in Austrian and Italian military bands, it was soon overtaken by the valved trumpet, which began to appear in the 1820s.

Modern trumpet

Although most 19th-century trumpets were in F, military bands preferred E flat trumpets, while in the 1880s trumpets in A, B flat and C started to be produced. During the 19th century various special types of trumpet were made, such as the "Aida" trumpet and the "Bach" trumpet. Today, however, most trumpeters' instrument of choice – whether they are orchestral, jazz or pop musicians – is generally the B flat trumpet, although orchestral musicians occasionally use trumpets pitched in D.

ABOVE: *A Ganter rotary valve B flat trumpet. This rotary valve trumpet has a hand protector on the tubing to protect the surface against wear while it is being held.*

Trombone

The trombones are too sacred for frequent use.

FELIX MENDELSSOHN (1809–47)

The trombone, with its telescopic slide, is the most distinctive member of the orchestral brass section. Invented in the mid 15th century as an answer to the demands of late 14th and early 15th-century composers who were increasingly writing for low pitches, the first trombones were a development of the large S-shaped trumpets that were being built by Flemish makers for the Burgundian court. The instrument's first name was the *trompette-saicqueboute* – the "push-pull trumpet". Different countries abbreviated this descriptive name in various ways: in England it was called the sackbut (first recorded in 1470), in Italy the *trombone* and in Germany the *Posaune*.

These early instruments, which had a softer and mellower timbre than those in use today, were often used –

BELOW, FROM LEFT TO RIGHT: Mutes for brass instruments come in a variety of sizes – trombone mute, French horn mute, trumpet mute, trumpet cup and piccolo trumpet mute.

sometimes coupled with cornetts – as an accompaniment to a single voice, especially in Venetian churches. Indeed, by the early 18th century the trombone was rarely heard outside ecclesiastical establishments. It did not become a conventional part of the orchestra until the late 18th century. The first classical composer to score for the trombone regularly was Beethoven, who used it for the first time in his Fifth Symphony in 1808.

ABOVE: The trombone has seven slide positions; the farther out the slide, the lower the fundamental. The seventh position is like depressing all three trumpet valves.

ABOVE: A trombonist performing in a New Orleans jazz club.

Trombone variations

Although there have been various cosmetic modifications, the principle of the trombone's telescopic slide has remained virtually unchanged. By the 17th century trombones were being made in three sizes: alto in F, tenor in B flat and bass in E flat. During the 17th century various attempts were made to produce ever-larger trombones. One such, built in 1615 by Hans Schreiber, was twice as long as the tenor and consequently pitched an octave lower. Other contemporary contrabass trombones built in Germany include those of Isaac Ehe (1612) and Jan Brueghel (1620).

The double-slide trombone briefly appeared in Nuremberg in the early 17th century and re-emerged in France in the 19th century. Although the basic idea was admirable – to be able to obtain all seven positions with greater ease by diminishing by half the distance between positions – it was found

ABOVE: *The trombone has a distinctive, large bell.*

LEFT: *Most trombonists today prefer B flat and F trombones. By depressing the thumb key, the length of tubing can be altered, minimizing slide action.*

to be impracticable as it proved impossible to make the tube airtight.

The valved trombone was first produced in Vienna in about 1818, and achieved its peak of popularity in the mid 19th century. It was, however, not able to compete with its slide counterpart, and by the end of the 20th century its use was restricted to Latin American, eastern European and Asian bands.

B flat and F trombones

The bass trombone, pitched in G, was so long that the slide had to be operated by a wooden handle.

Although it is still sometimes found in English brass bands, by the 1970s the G trombone had been virtually replaced by the B flat and F trombone, which was introduced as early as 1839 by the Leipzig maker C. F. Sattler. The F trombone consists of a B flat tenor instrument with an F attachment, made of about 1m/3ft of coiled tubing, and brought into play by a rotary valve operated by the player's left thumb.

Modern trombone

Today the trombone is made with one of three bores: France prefers

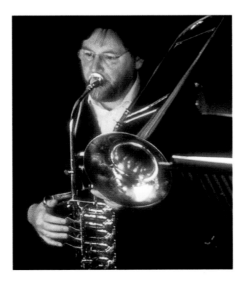

ABOVE: *The valved trombone has never been a widely popular instrument and today it is used more in novelty than serious music.*

a narrow bore, England a medium and the United States and Germany a wide bore. The wider the bore, the warmer and richer the sound. It is only necessary to compare the tone of a pre-World War II narrow bore "peashooter" with that of a modern B flat and F to appreciate the difference.

Key features

TYPE: brass aerophone

PITCH: B flat

NOTABLE PLAYERS OF THE TROMBONE: C. T. Queisser, F. A. Belcke, A. G. Dieppo, Glenn Miller, Tommy Dorsey, Albert Mangelsdorff, Christian Lindberg.

Bent Sørensen

The Danish composer Bent Sørensen (born 1958) wrote a trombone concerto for the Swedish virtuoso Christian Lindberg. The work is described as a *"pianissimo"* rather than a "roaring" concerto and is influenced, as is most of Sørensen's work, by his fascination with birds, bells and jazz. Another solo trombone composition by Sørensen is *The Bells of Vineta*, a piece that imagines the ringing bells of the church, threatened by coastal erosion, sinking into the sea.

Tuba

The tuba is certainly the most intestinal of instruments,
the very lower bowel of music.

PETER DE VRIES (BORN 1910)

The tuba is the bass of the orchestral brass section. English and German orchestras generally use a tuba in F, while those in Italy and the United States prefer the larger CC or BB flat types. In France, the instrument of choice is a very large bore six-valved tenor tuba in C, which was a development of the five-valved tuba used at the Paris Opera House between 1880 and 1892, and which Ravel included in his orchestration of Mussorgsky's *Pictures at an Exhibition* written in 1922.

The orchestral bass tuba was patented by Johann Gottfried Moritz in 1835, and Berlioz enthusiastically asked his publishers to substitute tubas for the ophicleides specified in the score of his *Symphonie fantastique* (1830). In 1832, A. G. Guichard of Paris brought out his newly invented three-valved *ophicleide à pistons* in E flat, and three years later Wilhelm Wieprecht, the bandmaster of the Prussian Dragoon Guards, introduced a five-valved bass tuba in F as a

RIGHT:
The E
flat tuba is
the bass brass
instrument.

replacement for the bass trombone. It was not long before these early tubas had totally replaced the serpent, bass horn and ophicleide. Although today the word "tuba" refers only to the bass instrument, originally the name was applied equally to the whole range. In 1852, for instance, Schubert did not distinguish between the cornet, flugelhorn or tuba. The E flat tuba is still sometimes referred to as a "bombardon".

By the mid 19th century the Bohemian instrument maker Václav

Cerveny had began building tubas with rotary valves, a modification that soon became standard on Austrian and German instruments. In other countries, however, tuba players preferred to retain the piston valve.

Over the years, various large tubas have been produced, including Adolphe Sax's sub-bass in E flat and the sub-contrabass in B flat (1855). Among other giants was Cerveny's *Kaiserbässe*, which was 2.4m/8ft high and had a tube length of almost 13.7m/45ft.

Since World War II tuba players have improved their technique and steadily pushed the range upward. Another important influence is the rise in popularity – especially in the United States – of the brass quintet. Composers who have produced pieces for this ensemble

ABOVE: *Two well-worn rotary valve tubas being played in Ghana.*

Key features

TYPE: brass aerophone

PITCH: F, E flat, B flat or C

NOTABLE PLAYERS OF THE TUBA: William Bell, Howard Johnson, Philip Catelinet, John Fletcher, Roger Bobo.

have treated the tuba as a tenor instrument and many write for it in the same way as for the cello.

The instrument that is known today as the B flat euphonium is really a tenor tuba and until the late 19th century it was uncommon to find anything bigger in orchestras. It was for this instrument that Holst wrote a part in *The Planets* (1916). The first true bass tubas were in F, as used in orchestras, or E flat, as used in brass bands. The BB flat, with its orchestral version in C, is now the normal brass and military band bass and was introduced into the orchestra by Wagner when he scored for a *Kontrabass* tuba in *The Ring* (1876).

Wagner tuba

Invented by Johann Moritz for use in Wagner's *Ring*, Wagner tubas were intended as a bass voice that is a cross between the horns, trumpets, trombones and bass tubas. Built in B flat and E flat with four valves, they were designed to be played by horn players; they have horn mouthpieces and are keyed using the left hand.

Helicon

As the large tubas were rather unwieldy, some builders designed

ABOVE: Two tuba players in a youth band.

them in circular form, resting the bell on the player's left shoulder with the tube passing under the left arm. Such instruments were known as helicons. The disadvantage was that due to the shape, much sound was lost when it was projected to one side. John Philip Sousa (1854–1933) modified the instrument by having the bell project forward over the player's shoulder and, through association, the instrument became widely known as the sousaphone. Today, sousaphones are often made with a fibreglass bell in an attempt to keep the weight down.

ABOVE: An unusual view of the bell of a B flat euphonium.

Tuba music

Since World War II, composers of classical, jazz and avant-garde music have all used the unique character of the tuba, which was given a high profile in popular music with George Kleinsinger and Paul Tripp's *Tubby the Tuba* of 1948. Vaughan Williams's Tuba Concerto was written in 1955. Hindemith, Gordon Jacob, Alex Wilder and Malcolm Arnold have all written solo works, and Walter Hartley and Barney Childs have composed works for tuba ensembles.

ABOVE: The euphonium is a tenor tuba and is mainly found in brass and military bands.

ABOVE: Sousaphones in a Chilean police band, showing the bells facing forwards.

BELOW, FROM LEFT TO RIGHT: These tuba and euphonium mutes are much larger than other brass mutes.

Early Valved Instruments

The two Ajax showing off with a swagger their double thorax amid immense blasts from Sax's horns.

JACQUES OFFENBACH (1819–80), "LA BELLE HÉLÈNE"

The invention of the valve at the beginning of the 19th century transformed the design of brass instruments. Instead of using a set of crooks to change the key of a horn, the player could produce a full range of tones by operating a system of valves to change the length of the tubing in the instrument.

Cornet

After the horn, one of the earliest valved instruments was the cornet. In the 1820s when Jean Hilaire Asté (known as Halary) applied first two, then three valves to the little *cornet de post* – a post-horn with tuning slides and crooks in straight rather than circular form – the instrument became known as the *cornet à pistons*. In England the first manufacturers of the new instrument were Pace and Köhler of London, who called their creation the cornopeon (the "horn of

triumphant songs"). By the mid 19th century, however, the usual generic term for the instrument had become "cornet". Although at first a wide variety of crooks was available, ranging from B flat down to F, by about 1850 B flat was becoming the norm.

The cornet differs from the trumpet in that it has a conical rather than a cylindrical bore. The other essential difference is in the mouthpiece: the cornet's is much deeper, which makes

LEFT: The cornet is the "violin" of the brass band, and a virtuoso player can truly make the instrument sing.

the instrument more flexible and less tiring to play for long periods.

Saxhorn

In 1842 the Belgian instrument maker Adolphe Sax (1814–94) moved to Paris where, under the patronage of Berlioz, he set up a brass and woodwind workshop. In the early 1840s, Sax produced a family of five conical-bore brass instruments, subsequently extended to ten. Although the principle behind the saxhorn was not entirely new, the proportions

Cornet key features

TYPE: brass aerophone

PITCH: B flat or E flat

NOTABLE PLAYERS OF THE CORNET: George Macfarlane, Hermann Koenig, Jules Levy, Howard Reynolds.

ABOVE: Cornets can be made in silver instead of brass, such as this B flat cornet.

Eric Ball

Most of the music written for the saxhorn has been for brass bands. One of the most prolific composers for the medium was Eric Ball (1903–89), whose output included many arrangements and transcriptions as well as original compositions such as *Resurgam* (1950), a wonderful tone poem that depicts the events of Good Friday and graphically portrays the Romans knocking the nails into Christ's hands and feet at the Crucifixion.

adapted by Sax made his instruments superior. Built in upright form, they were generally pitched either in E flat or B flat and were fitted with three vertical valves on horizontal tubing. On early saxhorns these were fitted with Wieprecht's *Berliner-pumpen* valves, but later instruments were provided with slender Perinet valves.

Sax's breakthrough with the saxhorn came in 1843. After a public contest

ABOVE: The piston valves of a B flat cornet.

between an authorized military band and a smaller group, led by the inventor, playing Sax's instruments, the latter were officially adopted and Sax secured a virtual monopoly as supplier of instruments to the French army. The fury this engendered among the more established Paris instrument makers led to attacks on his business and lawsuits that resulted in Sax's financial ruin, but not before the name "saxhorn" had passed into common usage.

ABOVE: A rotary-valved flugelhorn player busking on the Paris Métro.

Distin family

The earliest performers on Sax's instruments included the Distin family. Led by John Distin, who had served at Waterloo as a member of the band of the Grenadier Guards and had subsequently been principal trumpet in the private band of King George IV, the band also included John's three surviving sons. In 1846 Distin established a music shop in London and became Sax's British agent. Four years later the Distins began to manufacture their own saxhorn-type instruments, and also started to publish *Distin's Brass Band Journal*.

Saxhorns became especially popular in British brass bands. The first group to be completely equipped with them was the Mossley Temperance band,

ABOVE: The Distin family playing the set of six coiled circular horns that Sax built for them in 1845. Sax later redesigned his horns with the bell pointing upwards.

which achieved success in the Belle Vue Contest of 1853. The tenor saxhorn in E flat, these days known simply as the tenor horn, is still used in brass and military bands.

Over-the-shoulder horn

Introduced by Alan Dodworth, over-the-shoulder horns were especially popular during the 1850s and '60s in the United States. The advantage of this type of instrument was that the sound of the larger instruments went to the rear of the band rather than up into the air. During static performances some bands had the over-the-shoulder horn players facing backwards, so that the sound was projected in the same direction as all the other instruments.

RIGHT: Over-the-shoulder horns were popular in the mid 19th century with American bands. Today they are found only in living-history bands.

Alphorn

He that blows best, bears away the horn.

PROVERB

The alphorn, as its name implies, is an instrument found in mountainous districts, not only in the Swiss Alps, but also in the Carpathian Mountains of Poland and Romania, as well as in Lithuania and Scandinavia. The instrument is distantly related to the Etruscan *lituus*, whose name survived into the mid 19th century in the Swiss canton of Unterwalden, where the horns were called *liti*.

Construction

No matter where it is found, the alphorn is almost invariably made of wood. It has a conical bore, and the oldest form is the straight expanding tube with a slight flare at the end, while alphorns constructed

ABOVE: *Brightly painted bells of a collection of Swiss alphorns.*

ABOVE: *A 1661 engraving of an alphorn.*

in more recent years usually have an upturned bell.

Although ash, lime and hazel have been used in the manufacture of alphorns, the wood of choice was usually a young fir growing out of a mountainside and curving upwards from its roots, thereby giving a natural upturned bell. After seasoning, the long poles were longitudinally halved using an axe or saw, then hollowed out and glued back together. In Switzerland the method of making the alphorn changed in the 19th century, when the bore was formed from a single log by burning out the centre. The bell was made separately and added to the end. By about 1850 the total length of the alphorn had become standardized at about 3m/10ft, but modern Swiss instruments range from 1.5m/5ft to 4m/13ft in length and are made in two detachable sections.

Switzerland

Originally a herdsman's instrument, the Swiss alphorn can be traced back to the 14th century, when it had an average length of about 1.5m/5ft. Because of its superior carrying power, it was used as a signalling instrument to warn villagers of danger, and, in later years, to summon them to church. It is this use of the alphorn that was quoted by Beethoven at the end of his *Pastoral Symphony* in 1808. In 1826 an innovation occurred when Ferdinand Huber of Switzerland had three alphorns made of different sizes and tuned to different keys, for use in two and three-part ensemble performances.

In modern Switzerland the alphorn is now principally used to entertain tourists, if possible siting it where it will set up an echo on the opposite side of a valley. It is also used to call

cattle down from the mountains, and a traditional melody played for this purpose is known as a *ranz des vaches* (which means something like a procession of cattle). Different tunes of this type exist in each district, of which the Gruyère version is one of the most famous. The tunes are characterized by short motifs frequently repeated, giving them a mesmerizing effect. They now have words and are sung in the manner of folk songs, but the intervals used indicate that they were originally composed for the alphorn, which can play only harmonics.

Northern Europe

In Lithuania, alphorns were used both for signalling and in folk music, and were played in processions and at weddings. In the western Carpathians they are played only by women and children, and among the Mari people of the Urals 1.5m/5ft wooden alphorns are especially made for the spring festival. The Polish version of the alphorn is the *trombita*; made of pine, it can be up to 4m/13ft long. A feature of the instrument is that, while the bells of most alphorns rest on the ground, the bell-end of the *trombita* is supported on a post.

In Moldova and Romania the alphorn is called the *bucium*, of which there are five kinds that vary in length from 1.5m/5ft to 3m/10ft. They are either straight or curved and are bound with bark, roots or gut. Although they are usually made of wood, in the north of Romania the *bucium* is often made from metal, sometimes with the tubing coiled back on itself.

ABOVE: *What more epitomizes Switzerland than an alphorn player in his local costume, the sound resonating across the valleys?*

Pipes

Into the street the Piper stept, Smiling first a little smile,
As if he knew what magic slept, In his quiet pipe the while.

ROBERT BROWNING (1812–89), "THE PIED PIPER OF HAMELIN"

Simple blown instruments, consisting of cylindrical or conical tubes without mechanism, have evolved in many cultures and are widely played as folk instruments.

Aulos

The best-known double pipe is the aulos, an ancient Greek reed instrument that dates from at least 2800 BC. Each pipe consisted of a slender cylindrical tube made out of cane, wood or ivory, about 50cm/20in long, with from three to six tone-holes. Two pipes were played as a pair, the musician holding one in each hand.

At the proximal end of the pipe was a bulb of wood or ivory that served as the staple for the reed. As the whole reed was taken into the mouth, it is unclear from illustrations whether auloi were single or double-reed

ABOVE: A variation on the aulos was when one pipe terminated in a bell. The aulos was mentioned by Homer as an instrument of the countryside.

instruments, all the original reeds having long since disintegrated. In order to support the lips and cheeks, male players – who apparently blew harder than their female colleagues – wore a *phorbeia*, or leather mouth-band tied around their heads.

The aulos was played on many different occasions. It was part of the orgiastic cult of Dionysus, and was used to accompany choirs and at marriages and funerals, at which it was played in processions. It was also played in celebration of famous people or victorious athletes, as well as in musical contests between performers, such as those held at the Pythian games at Delphi.

LEFT: A pupil learning to play the aulos. This early 5th-century BC vase painting depicts an aulos in which the left pipe is longer than the right.

Pan-pipes

The pan-pipes consist of a set of vertical tubes of different resonating lengths joined side by side. The tubes are stopped at the lower end while the player blows across the upper ends. They are made from various materials and are found all over the world. In most societies the pan-pipes have always had a lowly status, and are often portrayed as a characteristic instrument of herdsmen.

Classical Greek pan-pipes, known as a *syrinx*, consisted of a set of tubes all of the same length; each tube was

Aulos music

Auletes competed at the Pythian games by composing and playing the Pythian *nomos*, a solo performance that was descriptive of Apollo's legendary victory over the Python of Delphi. The music was presented in five sections, which had to illustrate the different stages of the battle.

The winner in 586 BC was Sacadas, who created "sounds like those of the trumpet and gnashing like that of the serpent as it grinds its teeth after being pierced by arrows".

blocked with wax to the depth necessary to give the required notes. By the Hellenistic period, however, especially in Etruria and Rome, the tubes were graded in length. The pipes were usually stuck together with wax and the assembly was reinforced by a cloth binding or a wooden frame.

ABOVE: An area where the pan-pipes are still found is South America, where they are an integral part of Bolivian and Peruvian folk music. Some of these pipes are very large.

Occasionally pan-pipes were made from a solid block of wood, ivory or other material into which the holes

were bored. The pipes were held in both hands and moved from side to side as the player blew across the top.

Bladder pipe

Known from the 9th century, the bladder pipe was played by blowing through a short blowpipe into an animal bladder in which a reed was enclosed. This bladder served, like the bag of the bagpipes, as a wind reservoir. Out of the bladder came the chanter, with a varying number of finger-holes. Although the bladder pipe became virtually obsolete during the Renaissance, a descendant of the instrument survives in Poland, where it is still played in rural districts.

ABOVE: This representation of a bladder pipe is from Agricola's Musica Instrumentalis Deudsch *of 1529.*

Picco pipe

One of the more unusual musicians who toured Europe in the 1850s was Picco, a blind Sardinian minstrel who played a three-holed pipe only 8.5cm/3½in long, which he called his "pastoral tibia". Picco, who evoked "strains that would charm Apollo", played not only simple folk tunes but also variations on the *Carnival of Venice*, and was said to manage a range of three octaves. His popularity led to the commercial production of "Picco" pipes. Another person who played a small pipe in the mid 19th century was the Hungarian Kransky Baschik. Even smaller than Picco's pipe, Baschik's instrument could be played in octaves and thirds.

RIGHT: According to the legend surrounding the pan-pipes, one day the god Pan was pursuing the nymph Syrinx who fled to the river and, in an attempt to escape from her pursuer, transformed herself into a reed. Unable to distinguish her from the other reeds, Pan cut several at random and formed them into what are now known as pan-pipes.

Cornett

The sound of the cornett is like a ray of sunshine piercing the shadows.

MARIN MERSENNE (1588–1648)

Spelt with a double "t" to differentiate it from the 19th-century valved instrument, the cornett's origin can be traced back to at least the 9th century, when holes were pierced in cow and goat horns so that tunes could be played on them. The instrument was certainly known in 14th-century France, for romances of the period mention the *cor à doigts*. It was a wooden lip-vibrated wind instrument with finger-holes and a cup-shaped mouthpiece that was customarily played at the side of the

LEFT: A late 16th-century six-holed, curved cornett.

mouth. The soft tone of the instrument made it – along with trombones – an ideal accompaniment for voices in churches, but it was also used to accompany dancing, both indoors and outdoors.

Construction

By the 13th century the cornett had five finger-holes and a bell made of animal horn. A later version had six finger-holes on the upper side and a thumb-hole on the underside. It was fitted with a separate mouthpiece, commonly made of ivory, bone or horn.

By the 16th century slender curved cornetts, which got their name from the Italian word for "little horn", were being carved from roughly shaped

blocks of hard, close-grained wood. The blocks were halved lengthways and channels gouged into each half to make a cylindrical bore when they were glued back together. Finally, black leather was glued over the wood to seal any possible leaks.

Use of the cornett

Classified as valveless trumpets, medieval cornetts were made both straight and curved. The Germans preferred the former, while most of the rest of Europe settled for the latter. There were three main sizes of cornett: the small treble (cornettino),

ABOVE: A 17th-century illustration of a cornett player by Wiegel.

ABOVE: This 19th-century painting by John Spencer shows an angel playing a cornett.

the treble and the tenor. In its heyday – between 1550 and 1650 – the treble cornett was used more than any other wind instrument for virtuoso-playing.

Cornetts were used with trombones and organs to accompany choral music, especially in Venice where, in 1600, they formed the nucleus of the band led by the composer and organist Giovanni Gabrieli (c.1553–1612). Some Italian curved cornetts were very ornate, with the bell end carved in the shape of a beast's head. In England, cornetts were used to support the treble voices of the choir of the Chapel Royal, while in France cornetts and trombones were the usual instrumentation for ceremonial music up to about 1650.

RIGHT: A mid 16th-century German engraving of a woman holding a cornett.

Decline

The cornett was tiring to play and presented problems in getting a good embouchure; in spite of Mersenne's remarks, it was often not played well. The higher register was similar to that of a trumpet and the lower like a trombone, while the indistinct wailing sound of the middle register was very unattractive when played in isolation. When used with other instruments the cornett could achieve special effects, however it began to fall out of use from about 1650. It was inevitable that the finest players of the instrument would start to turn their attention to the developing oboe.

By the end of the 18th century the cornett was no more than a rare curiosity. One of the last pieces written especially for the instrument was Matthew Locke's *Music for his Majesty's Sagbutts and Cornetts* (1661), while the last composer actually to score for the cornett was Christoph Willibald Gluck (1714–87), who used it in his *Orpheus*, composed in 1762. The last bastion of the cornett was in German *Turmmusik*, in which it lasted well into the 19th century. It was revived in the 20th century by early music specialists.

ABOVE: This 15th-century painting shows three English musicians on a balcony (top right) playing cornetts to accompany a dance.

ABOVE: Replica cornetts are made for living-history groups by Otto Steinkopf of Berlin (straight cornetts) and Christopher Monk of Surrey, England (curved cornetts).

Bugle

The diabolical clamour produced by the call to arms sounded by the bugles and drums.

ALEXIS DE TOCQUEVILLE (1905–59)

The word bugle is derived from the Latin *buculus*, meaning "bullock", a reference to the fact that the first bugles were made out of short cattle horns. Originally the bugle was a hunter's instrument, but by the 15th century town watchmen and soldiers had begun to use it. Made of brass, copper or silver, the bugle retained its horn shape into the 18th century, when it began to be made with an upward-pointing bell.

In the 18th century the shape evolved into a large semicircle, which was held to the body by a leather harness. This form, called in German *Halbmond*, was introduced during the Seven Years War (1756–63) as a distinguishing instrument for the Prussian *Jäger* battalions. In the early 19th century the tubing began to be arranged in an elliptical coil, and in 1814 it was adopted as the badge of the British Light Infantry. The regular infantry B flat bugle, with twice-wound tubing and a small bell,

ABOVE: *A silver-plated bugle. As a protection against loss, the mouthpiece is attached to the instrument by a chain.*

was first authorized in 1858. In the United States this type is known as a cavalry bugle.

Keyed bugle

In the early 19th century Joseph Haliday (1772–1857), the bandmaster of the Irish Cavan Militia, transformed the bugle into a keyed instrument. Haliday subsequently sold the patent to the Dublin instrument maker Matthew Pace, who made the first keyed bugle as a compliment to the Duke of Kent, the then Commander in Chief of the British army. Henceforth the instrument became colloquially known as the Royal Kent Bugle. The earliest instruments had five keys, but a sixth was soon added and later examples had up to 12 keys.

When the keyed bugle was played by the band of the Grenadier Guards at a military review held in Paris after the battle of Waterloo in 1815, the Russian Grand Duke Konstantin was so impressed with the instrument that he

ABOVE: *A bugle major of the Royal Sappers in 1823.*

ABOVE: *A 19th-century brass bugle.*

ABOVE: *The flugelhorn is a cross between the cornet and bugle. It is mainly seen in brass bands and some jazz combinations.*

commanded John Distin, the band's chief musician, to have one of the new instruments made for him. Distin, who was later to manufacture instruments himself in London, approached the Paris instrument maker Jean Hilaire Asté (Halary). In 1821 he took out patents to cover three forms of keyed bugle: the clavi-tube, quinti-tube and ophicleide. In its various forms, the keyed bugle was the first fully melodic treble brass instrument and immediately became popular for solo work, until superseded in the middle of the century by the flugelhorn and the cornet.

Ophicleide

A much more efficient bass instrument than the serpent or bass horn, Asté's ophicleide of 1821 – named from the Greek for "keyed serpent" – was made of metal, the long tubing bending back on itself, with nine keys covering the large tone-holes. It was often unkindly called the "chromatic bullock". The first composer to score for the ophicleide was Gaspare Spontini (1774–1851), the *Generalmusikdirektor* to the king of Prussia, who used the instrument in his opera *Olimpie* in 1819. It soon entered many orchestras and bands, including the one led by the famous French bandleader Louis Jullien, who used it to augment the trombones.

With the invention of valves the construction of brass instruments was revolutionized, and in 1832 the Parisian brass instrument maker A. Guichard brought out his three-valved ophicleide, which had tuning slides for C and B flat. Although the ophicleide was eventually replaced by the tuba in the middle of the 19th century, it survived, especially in Italy, into the early 20th century.

ABOVE: A mounted bugler blowing a large-bell instrument.

ABOVE: This 19th-century French comical caricature shows a young boy learning to play the ophicleide, the largest wind instrument of the time.

Serpent

What the devil is that?

GEORGE FRIDERIC HANDEL (1685–1759), ON FIRST HEARING A SERPENT

The serpent, so named from its winding S-shape, is believed to have been invented by Canon Edmé Guillaume of Auxerre in about 1590, as an improvement on the bass cornett, to accompany plainchant in churches. Used to double men's voices, it blended perfectly, adding depth and fullness to the sound. Like the cornett, it was made of wood, with a cup-shaped ivory or horn mouthpiece mounted on a metal crook. It had a conical bore with six finger-holes but no thumb-hole.

Manufacture

There were two main methods of constructing a serpent. One was to hollow out two complete halves from

ABOVE: A serpent player from Bonanni's Gabinetto Armonico of 1723.

ABOVE: This 13-key serpent was made in London, c.1850.

solid blocks of wood, usually maple, and then glue them together to make a tube before covering the whole with leather. The alternative – the method preferred in England – was to build up the instrument from fairly short overlapping half-sections of wood, which were then glued together and covered with leather.

Although serpents were usually made of wood there are rare instances of metal instruments being made, such as

those built in about 1800 by Carl August Grenser of Dresden. Sadly, no metal serpent is known to have survived.

One of the largest serpents was that built by the Wood Brothers in about 1840. Used in York Minster, it was twice the size of conventional instruments, containing nearly 4.8m/16ft of tubing.

Upright serpent

The main problem with the serpent, which was over 2m/6ft long, was getting the finger-holes within reach of the player's hands. This was the reason for the serpentine contours of the instrument, but an alternative solution was that provided in 1788 by J. J. Régibo, a musician of the church of St Peter in Lille, who built an upright serpent with straight double tubes. Régibo's instrument, which was capable of being dismantled into three sections, also had the advantage that it was

Key features

TYPE: woodwind aerophone

PITCH: E, D or C

NOTABLE PLAYERS OF THE SERPENT: Abbé Aubert, Abbé Lunel, Louis Alexandre Frichot, André, Jepp.

louder and easier to play than conventional models. It opened the way for a number of bassoon-shaped serpents, including the later English models that are recognizable by their short overlapping sections, giving U-bends rather than the older S-curves.

The serpent in the orchestra

By the mid 17th century the serpent had left the confines of the church and was being used in secular instrumental ensembles. By 1756 it was employed in the orchestra of the Comédie Italienne and was spreading to Germany, the Low Countries and England. By the 19th century the serpent had become firmly established in orchestras, with both Mendelssohn and Wagner scoring for it. In French orchestras the serpent was often substituted for the contrabassoon. It was at about this time that the serpent was first made with keys; at first it had only three or four, but by the end of the instrument's existence 14 had become the norm.

Great skill and musicianship were required to play the serpent, since every note depended on the player's embouchure. Various fingering charts were published during the 18th and 19th centuries, all of which differed widely.

ABOVE: A Royal Marine Band of 1826. The seated musician is playing the serpent.

Military bands

In the 18th century the serpent gained a foothold in English and German military bands, where it became known as the *serpent militaire* as opposed to the ecclesiastical *serpent d'église*. The military version generally had a metal mouthpiece. One notable version of the military band serpent was the ophibaryton, which had a straight bell in the form of a painted dragon's head. Although some bands in Spain were still using the instrument as late as 1884, the serpent fell into disuse with the invention of the valved tuba in the 1830s.

RIGHT: Early serpents such as this one had finger-holes instead of keys.

ABOVE: This 17th-century drawing by Bracelli shows a sackbut on the left and a serpent on the right.

Bagpipes

Twelve Highlanders and a bagpipe make a rebellion.

PROVERB

Nobody is ambiguous about bagpipes – they either love them or hate them. They probably originated in Sumeria and perhaps independently in Greece. They were known by the Romans, and Arab references to the instrument date back to the 11th century. Their main characteristic is the continuous sound that is achieved using the air reserved in the bag, so that the player can breathe while playing. To articulate the melody, and ensure that each note is not tied to the next, the piper interpolates a grace note before each note of the melody. Most bagpipes have a limited range, with a compass of about nine tones.

The bag is inflated by air from the mouth or a set of bellows operated by the player's arm. The blowpipe, reeded chanter and drones, which are usually tuned in octaves and fifths, are inserted through the sides of the bag. Early bags were made from either the whole skin of a small animal, or the stomach or bladder of a larger one. Whole skin bags usually have the chanter inserted into the natural neck and the drones and blowpipe into the forelegs. Modern bags are usually made of tanned sheepskin cut to shape.

Scottish Highland pipes
The distinctive feature of the Highland bagpipes, with their loud and

BELOW: Believed to have been introduced to Scotland by the Romans, the Highland pipes have been used as a martial instrument from at least the 15th century.

penetrating tone, is the long blowpipe that allows the player to stand erect rather than leaning forwards. There are three single-reed drones, two tenor and one bass, and a double-reed chanter. Scotland is the most active of pipe-playing countries, and Scottish pipes have been exported to France and India.

Northumbrian pipes
Although bagpipes were once common in England as well as Scotland, today they are found only in Northumberland, where the bellows-operated small-pipes, intended for indoor use, are played seated with the drones lying across the knees. A feature of these pipes is that the chanter has a closed end, enabling the piper to play staccato and repeat a note without interpolating grace notes.

Kathryn Tickell (born 1967) is recognized as one of the leading Northumbrian pipers of the present generation, and has been appointed the official piper to the Lord Mayor of Newcastle upon Tyne.

Irish pipes
The mouth-blown Irish war-pipe fell into disuse in the 18th century when it began to be replaced by the Scottish Highland pipe, although a new version was made during the 20th century. The bellows-blown union pipes, which are played seated, were probably introduced in the early 18th century. The modern pipe, which has a double-bore chanter with two reeds, has become so complex that it is often referred to as the "Irish organ".

Musette
Originally a pastoral instrument, the French bellows-blown musette

LEFT: A 14th-century English bagpipe with a single drone and chanter. This instrument pre-dates the Northumbrian pipes – it is not bellows-operated. Instead, the player inflates the bag by means of a blowpipe.

ABOVE: *The Irish union bagpipes were introduced in the 18th century and, unlike the Scottish variety, they are played in a sitting position.*

was popular in the 17th century at court, where it was used to accompany dancing. By the 18th century, with its ivory pipes inserted into a bag of matching silk and velvet, the musette had become a fashionable and delicate "toy" of the nobility and as such disappeared in the wake of the French Revolution.

Zampogna

Native to southern Italy and Sicily, the *zampogna* has two drones and two chanters arranged for playing harmony. At Christmas in the streets of Naples, two-man teams called *zampognari* serenade images of the infant Christ set up at the roadside.

Eastern European pipes

Today there are two main types of pipes in Poland: the bellows-operated *dudy*, whose drone pipe folds back on itself and terminates in a curved bell, and the *dudy zywieckie*, which is mouth-blown and played solo or with a violin.

In some parts of Latvia and Estonia bags were often made of sealskin or a seal's stomach, which were unaffected by dryness or damp. In the 18th century the playing of such instruments was discouraged, as it was thought that they led to disorder and crime. They did, however, survive into the 1940s and have since been revived by several folklore groups.

In south-eastern Europe the end of the chanter was sometimes carved into the shape of an animal's head. The Czech *kozial*, commonly called "wedding pipes", can be traced back to the 14th century, while the Bosnian and Croatian *diple* is played outdoors on festive occasions. The bellows-blown Hungarian *duda*, which terminates in a cow's horn, has a small finger-hole opposite the thumb-hole, which raises any note by a semitone, thereby allowing modulations.

Indian bagpipes

The traditional Hindustani *masak* is the simplest bagpipe of all. It consists of a single-reed cane pipe and a blowpipe tied into a whole goatskin. Another

ABOVE: *The Italian single-drone bagpipe, the* zampogna, *is native to southern Italy and Sicily. Both Handel and Bach alluded to the instrument.*

ABOVE, CLOCKWISE FROM TOP LEFT: *Four different types of bagpipes — Irish Uilleann pipe, French cornemuse, Italian calabrian and French musette.*

Indian bagpipe, the southern Indian *bajana scuti*, was used mainly to accompany devotional music until replaced in the mid 19th century by the harmonium.

Bagpipes music

Until the 19th century there was no written music for the Highland bagpipes, as it was mainly transmitted by aural tradition. Although written music is now used, the many types of grace notes that feature in bagpipes music mean that the notation only approximates to what is to be played. Apart from traditional folk tunes, some pipe majors write special tunes in celebration of important events.

Mouth Organ

A cherub in a box.

ANONYMOUS

The concept behind the modern, horizontally held mouth organ came from Christian Friedrich Buschmann (1805–64) of Berlin, who realized in 1821 that melodies could be played on a set of pitch-pipes that he had made for use when tuning an organ. Various other people experimented with the idea, and the first instrument that looked like the modern harmonica was produced by Christian Messner, a young German clockmaker who began to construct similar instruments to Buschmann's, which he sold at country fairs and inns. At about the same time the first commercially produced mouth organs appeared in Vienna, one of which was Ernst Schmidt's apollolyra, with its 44 reeds controlled by keys.

Harmonica

In Tossingen, Christian Weiss and Matthias Höhner (1833–1902) started manufacturing harmonicas in the mid 1850s. Although their early models were all handmade, Höhner soon adapted the new methods and techniques of mass production and it was not long before his business had grown beyond all expectations. By 1879 he had made over 700,000 harmonicas – of which over 60 per cent had been exported to the United States.

Although harmonicas are made in various sizes and compasses, all consist of a set of free reeds mounted in a grooved metal box, which is moved from side to side in front of the player's mouth. Sounds are produced by both blowing and sucking and, if the instrument is diatonic, only one key can be played on any one model. The chromatic harmonica, which is used as a performing instrument, was first produced in the early 1920s.

Although virtuosi such as Larry Adler (born 1914) have given the harmonica a wider appeal, the instrument has always been considered as more of a toy than a serious instrument. Since World War II, however, several symphonic composers have scored for it. In the 1960s the mouth organ became popular with folk singers such as Bob Dylan and Donovan. To keep their hands free to play the guitar, they held the mouth organ in a frame worn around the neck.

LEFT: A modern harmonica made by Höhner. The sound is produced by both blowing and sucking air through the rows of reeds inside the instrument.

Melodica

Another type of mouth organ is the melodica, an innovative vertical form of the instrument produced from 1959. The two main types are the piano melodica, which has a miniature keyboard played with one hand, and the soprano melodica, which is operated by a series of push keys, one hand playing the diatonic and the other the chromatic tones.

ABOVE: The harmonica has always been very popular among young people. This photograph shows a class of girls being taught to play the famous Höhner harmonica.

ABOVE: The piano melodica has a miniature piano-like keyboard, which is played with one hand while blowing into the mouthpiece.

BELOW: The modern chromatic Chinese sheng *has 17 pipes and is played polyphonically in triads. It is now a regular feature of the Chinese orchestra.*

Sheng

The modern mouth organ has evolved from the classical Chinese *sheng* that dates back to the Chou dynasty (1122–221 BC), and consists of a gourd into which are inserted a short blowpipe and up to 36 bamboo pipes of varying length, each with a finger-hole and a free reed cut from a length of bamboo that vibrates when the finger-hole is closed. The pipes are arranged in an incomplete circle representing, according to popular legend, the folded wings of the mythical phoenix.

A new type of mouth organ, the *paisheng*, appeared in China in the 1960s. It is the size of a small piano, complete with keyboard, and has a range of four octaves. Used in the concert hall, the player sits in front of the instrument at the keyboard and fills the wind-chamber by blowing through a long blowpipe.

ABOVE: Bob Dylan was one of the youth idols of the 1960s. He usually wore his mouth organ in a frame around the neck so that he could play the guitar at the same time.

Didgeridoo

The spectrum of sound which can be produced by the didgeridoo evokes association with sounds perceived in the womb.

DR WOLFGANG STROBEL

The didgeridoo is an end-blown straight natural trumpet used by the indigenous peoples of Australia. Depending on the region, didgeridoos are made of various types of eucalyptus wood, such as yellow box gum tree, bloodwood, Red River gum, stringy bark or woollybutt. To be suitable for making a didgeridoo, the trunk or branch must have the right diameter (7.5–15cm/3–6in), length (1.2–2m/4–6ft) and, of course, have been hollowed out by termites. As the didgeridoo builder cannot see that the trees are hollow from the outside, he peels off a piece of bark and taps the tree with his knuckles. Once a tree is selected, it is chopped down and the bark is peeled off.

The next stage involves using long chisels to scrape out any layers of wood that have not been devoured by the termites. The builder then thins the end of the interior walls to a depth of 30–40cm/12–16in to make a funnel shape. Although the didgeridoo is played without a separate mouthpiece, a rim of beeswax or eucalyptus gum is sometimes fitted to the mouth end.

LEFT: A didgeridoo is made from a scraped-out tree trunk or branch. By means of circular breathing, a player can produce a continuous sound.

Decoration

Didgeridoos are decorated only for special occasions; generally they are plain. When they are decorated, the motifs are subject to religious taboo and are seen only by the initiated. The decoration is removed immediately after the ceremony and in some cases the didgeridoo is destroyed. On the other hand, some musicians decorate their instruments with totemic decoration, in which case the motif is down to the artist's imagination and has no religious significance.

Method of play

Didgeridoos are played by men and boys, often together with clapping sticks, to accompany singing and dancing as well as for funeral ceremonies. Although it is known for players to perform standing and sometimes moving around with the dancers and singers, the best position for playing the didgeridoo is seated with one leg bent to the side and the other stretched forward, with the foot helping to support the instrument. Sometimes, for added effect, the end is inserted into a tin-can resonator. Other performers prefer to support it off the ground between their feet. It is a very difficult instrument to play, and virtuoso players are recognized and highly valued members of society.

The pitch of the didgeridoo varies according to the length of the tube. To

ABOVE: Didgeridoos are now being mass-produced for tourists in workshops like this one.

ABOVE: *A native Australian playing a didgeridoo in Sydney, Australia.*

Gondwanaland, formed in 1978, features an electronically amplified didgeridoo whose unique rhythmical sound forms a bridge across thousands of years of musical history. The band uses no less than ten different didgeridoos played by Charlie McMahon, each of which is tuned to a different key.

McMahon has also played the didgeridoo with the London Philharmonic Orchestra, and invented an instrument that he calls the "didgeribone". As its name suggests, it is a cross between a didgeridoo and a trombone, and consists of two wooden tubes placed one inside the other. The inner tube slides in and out to create different tones, as with a trombone.

produce the characteristic continuous drone, frequent breaths are snatched though the nose while the air, which is stored in the cheeks, is continuously expelled down the tube. Although generally only one tone is available, a good player can produce another tone a fourth higher. Changes in the shape of the mouth can be made to change the timbre, and the tongue is used to give vibrato effects and achieve rhythmic patterns. Voiced sounds, which may imitate bird and animal noises, are superimposed on the fundamental drone.

Popular music

The didgeridoo is also used in pop music. The Australian band

ABOVE: *A selection of painted didgeridoos.*

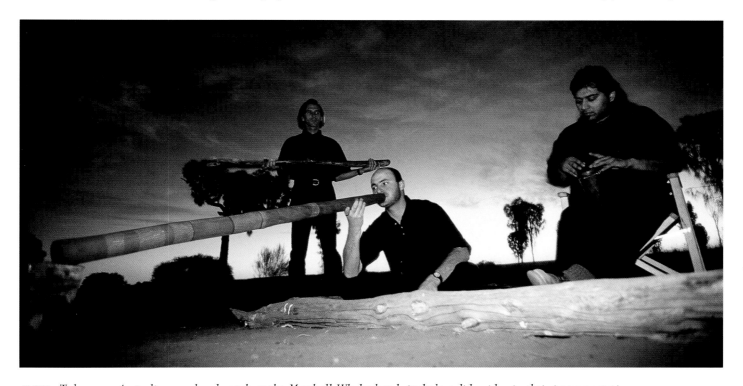

ABOVE: *Today some Australian pop bands, such as the Marshall Whyler band, include a didgeridoo in their instrumentation.*

✤ Percussion ✤

Rhythm and Drama

The percussion acts as a central heating system.

IGOR STRAVINSKY (1882–1971)

Percussion in music is universal. There is not a country in the world that does not make percussion instruments of some kind to provide a rhythmic backbone for its music. Drums are probably the world's oldest musical instruments, but percussion is used for many effects that are not simply rhythmic: many instruments, such as cymbals, shakers and jingles, make more continuous, but exciting, noises, while a single stroke on a gong may create a dramatic climax to a musical work.

There are two main types of percussion instruments: those that are tuned to a definite pitch, such as timpani, xylophone or tubular bells, and those whose pitch is indefinite, such as the triangle, bass drum or tambourine. Orchestral percussionists play an ever-increasing number of instruments as composers search for original musical effects, and each player may need to play ten or more instruments in a single work. To manage a large percussion section, professional players have to master a range of techniques, as well as making purely practical arrangements to enable them both to reach the instruments and read the music on the concert platform without tripping over each other. The most specialized percussionist in the orchestra is the timpanist.

Magic and myth

Long before the drum became a musical instrument, its noise-making qualities were no doubt credited with the powers of making thunder and chasing away devils, not to mention frightening the enemy. In ancient Greece soldiers beat on shields made of tightly stretched ox-hide – a custom perpetuated by Zulu warriors well into the 19th century.

Like so many other musical instruments, the earliest use of the bell was in magic and ritual. Its power to ward off evil is illustrated in the *Book*

BELOW, FROM LEFT TO RIGHT: A ridged guiro, wooden beater and wood block. The guiro can be struck or scraped and the wood block is struck to produce a short, untuned note.

of *Exodus*, written between the 9th and 5th centuries BC, when Aaron is instructed to wear bells of gold when he goes into the "holy place". Among the Bobati people of Zaire, bells were rung as a guard against evil influences entering the chief's body whenever he drank or smoked. In East Africa the Teso people wear bells around their ankles to appease the spirit of the storm, while the Bakrewi attach bells to the entrances of their houses to ward off evil.

Religious significance

Rattles often have a magical and religious significance, and a rattle or shaker is one of the accoutrements of

ABOVE: Russia is a country of large bells; these two men are erecting three bells.

BELOW, FROM LEFT TO RIGHT: The jingle stick and tambourine are two forms of the same instrument. They can be struck to produce a percussive sound, or shaken to prolong the ringing.

ABOVE, FROM LEFT TO RIGHT: An orchestral percussion section showing timpani, congas, bass drum, gong, cymbals, claves, glockenspiel and tambourine.

ABOVE: The cog ratchet rattle has been used for many years and for many reasons — from scaring birds off the fields to supporting a favourite football team.

the shaman. In China the thunder god Zin Shin was surrounded by a revolving wheel to which alternate barrel drums and kettledrums were fixed, the god striking them with a drumstick held in one hand. Ancient Japanese belief connected the playing of percussion with the invention of music, the myth being that the gods beat the measure upon "the mother of all the castanets".

Ever since their invention, drums have been used in rituals. Some were classed as sacred objects, while others were status symbols and emblems of royalty. In ancient Mesopotamia the hide of a sacred bull was used as the drum head, while a seal of the third millennium BC shows the goddess Ishtar standing before an altar that

looks like an upturned hourglass drum. The practice of using the drum as an altar has been carried into modern times, with soldiers in the field using an upturned drum as the focus of acts of worship.

Ancient scrapers were made from animal bones or ridged gourds, and have survived into modern times in folk instruments such as the guiro of Venezuela, a hollow gourd with a serrated surface. Related to the scraper is the cog rattle or ratchet, which was used in medieval religious ceremonies during Holy Week. Ratchet rattles are still used in some German festivals, particularly in the South. The cog rattle's tribal attributes re-emerged in the mid 20th century when it was taken up by football supporters.

ABOVE: Maracas are hollow gourds filled with seeds. They are used in Latin American dance music, shaken to provide the rhythms.

ABOVE: A rainstick is a wooden or plastic tube containing pellets that make the sound of rain when the tube is turned over.

ABOVE: A selection of hand shakers. At the top are a ganza and a multi-guiro, and at the bottom is a torpedo. They can be struck with beaters as well as being shaken.

ABOVE: A native American shaman beating an octagonal buffalo-hide frame drum in the fields of Washington State.

Timpani

When drums speak out, laws hold their tongues.

THOMAS FULLER (1608–61)

The timpani are the most important members of the Western orchestral percussion section. They can uniquely be tuned to a definite pitch and are used both as rhythmic and as melodic instruments.

Early kettledrums

Large kettledrums were developed during the 14th and 15th centuries in Germany. They were played as a pair, slung on either side of a horse. Such was the prestige of owning kettledrums in Germany and Sweden that they became the preserve of the aristocracy; no one under the rank of baron was permitted to own them. Kettledrums entered certain cavalry regiments that were owned

LEFT: Pedal-operated timpani are a main feature of the symphony orchestra. Pedals can change the tuning much faster than the old system of hand-tuning screws or taps.

At this time the instruments were tensioned using square-topped screws turned with a loose key. The first advance was to replace the screws with taps. They were quicker and quieter to operate, but the timpanist still had to stop playing to re-tune, and the composer had to allow for this each time his score called for a key change.

There were various other attempts to make the life of the timpanist easier. These ranged from Gerhard Cramer's central screw (1812), which operated all the other tuning screws simultaneously to a method of rotating the barrel of

ABOVE: This 17th-century engraving by Weigel shows a pair of early kettledrums from Germany being played with two wooden sticks in an outdoor setting.

and to a large extent manned by the nobility. By the early 1600s they had followed the trumpet into church music and shortly thereafter into the orchestra.

Tuning

Before the military kettledrum was able to play a full part in the modern orchestra, it had to undergo various radical changes. Early kettledrums were expected only to contribute the tonic and the dominant of a tonality, which rarely changed. However, from the late 18th century composers such as Beethoven wrote music that expected the drummer to modulate right in the middle of a piece of music, a process that even for the most experienced players took one or two minutes.

ABOVE: A 19th-century kettledrummer of the French Lancers. Carried on either side of the horse, the drums are dressed with banners bearing the regimental crest.

the drum itself, devised in 1821 by J. Stumpff of Amsterdam.

Adolphe Sax endeavoured to build a kettledrum with holes of different sizes in the shell. These were covered by keys that could be opened to produce different pitches. Sax also tried doing away with the shell altogether. Although this was intended to reduce the weight of the drums, the resulting framework was so heavy that the instruments weighed more than ordinary ones!

Pedal system

Modern orchestral timpani are tuned by a pedal that acts on a central screw, allowing the drummer to change tonality while continuing to play with both hands. This method was developed in the early 1880s by Carl Pittrich, a player in the Dresden Orchestra. Although Pittrich was not the first to produce pedal timpani, his were the first successful models. The Americans William Ludwig and Robert C. Danly brought out their balanced-action mechanism, with the pedal held by a spring, in 1925. Pedal timpani are known as "machine drums", and they have allowed composers like Bartók to include *glissandos* in their timpani parts.

Even with machine drums, a separate drum is needed for each different note when they follow each other in quick succession. The modern orchestral set consists of at least five pedal timpani in graduated sizes, giving a range of about two octaves. The large bowl-shaped resonating chambers are made from copper. Fibreglass is a much lighter, cheaper alternative, but gives an inferior tone. Plastic heads have now replaced calfskin.

India

Kettledrums in India are chiefly used in the *nahabat*, the noisy band that plays at state ceremonies and in processions. These bands often include a pair of silver kettledrums over 150cm/5ft in diameter and weighing about 205kg/450lb, which are mounted on an elephant. Each drum has its own player, who strikes the drum head with a silver stick. The small pairs of hand drums called *tabla* and *bayan* are miniature versions of the kettledrums.

Nakers

An early form of kettledrum is the nakers, a pair of small drums up to 25cm/10in in diameter, one pitched higher than the other. They were adapted from the Arab *naqqara* during the crusades of the 13th century. In Europe, these portable drums were used both for military music and in consort with trumpets and pipes.

ABOVE: *Drums are known in every part of the world. In India there are many types of folk drum, including the small kettledrum that is played strung around the neck.*

ABOVE: *The 15th-century Italian musician on the left is playing the nakers — small drums with barrel-shaped wooden, metal or clay bodies covered with animal skins.*

ABOVE: *A set of modern pedal-operated orchestral timpani with plastic heads.*

Side Drum

There is no instrument the sound of which proclaims
such vast internal satisfaction as the drums.

GEORGE MEREDITH (1828–1909)

The side drum gets its name from its playing position in military bands, where it is slung from the shoulder and worn on an angle at the player's side. It consists of a cylindrical shell of wood or metal covered at each end with a head of calfskin or plastic. Although the depth of the shell varies according to the purpose of the instrument, modern marching-band side drums usually have a depth of about 30cm/12in.

The orchestral side drum or snare drum is 10–30cm/4–12in deep with a diameter of 35–40cm/14–16in. In the 19th century, however, it was much deeper, at about 50cm/20in. It is played with wooden sticks, usually of hickory or ebony, with slim, rounded heads known as "acorns".

RIGHT:
Although
the side drum is generally
played with wooden sticks,
for special, softer effects
orchestral and jazz drummers
sometimes use wire brushes
instead. Evocative names
for particular rhythmic
ornamentations include
"paradiddle",
"flamadiddle" and
"ratamacue".

picks up sympathetic vibrations from other instruments, which can cause the snares to buzz very audibly. To resolve this, a quick-release lever allows the drummer to release the snares almost instantaneously when the drum is not being played. Playing the side drum with the snares released gives a tom-tom effect.

Tabor

An early version of the side drum was the 12th-century French tabor. This was a small and light cylinder drum, which was buckled on to the chest or left arm. The outside of the upper membrane was fitted with a snare, and it was this that was hit rather than – as is customary now – the membrane itself. Tabors,

ABOVE: *This 15th-century Italian paining shows an angel playing the side drum by hitting the snare head.*

Snares

Giving the drum its characteristic timbre, the snares consist of eight or more strings of gut or thin wire coiled on a silk core, stretched across the lower head. Today an open coil of wire is often used, particularly by jazz players, which instead of producing a sharp rhythm adds a buzz to the sound. The snares must be at the right tension to produce the best sound and are tightened by screw devices.

One problem with snares in the orchestra is that the side drum easily

RIGHT:
The tabor
was played
to accompany
dancing, and
would have been
accompanied
by bagpipes.

ABOVE: *A regimental side drummer of the Fifteenth Kings Regiment of Light Dragoons ("The Hussars") in 1768.*

which were used to keep time for dancing, were beaten by musicians who usually simultaneously played a three-holed pipe.

The name "tabor" is also given to a long, narrow drum, with or without snares, which is sometimes used in orchestral music and is otherwise known as a tambourin.

Military side drum

The side drum came into fashion in the late 18th century when Janissary bands, which imitated the Turkish music played by the Ottoman sultan's bodyguard, became popular in Europe. A feature of these bands, which says more about the moral values of the day than about musical taste, was that side drums were usually played by young black men, who dressed in the most

exotic manner and performed incredible acrobatic feats with their drumsticks as they played.

Playing technique

The main difficulty of playing the side drum is that the initial sound is of short duration. A longer sound is obtained by the roll, which is a rapid reiteration of strokes. This is a very skilled act and it requires a great deal of practice to produce an even roll with two strokes from each hand. It is much easier to play a roll on a drum with modern snares, as the traditional type make a snap rather than the contemporary buzz.

ABOVE: *This side drum has been turned upside down to show its wire snare.*

ABOVE: *A member of a Chinese girls' band playing a shallow side drum in Beijing.*

Bass Drum

A drum is a woman.

LEFT: *A rod-tensioned orchestral bass drum. The instrument is struck with a felt-covered beater and damped with the other hand.*

The bass drum, the largest orchestral drum of indefinite pitch, remained a rarity in Europe until the 18th century, when it became well known through the Turkish Janissary bands that were fashionable at the time. The orchestral bass drum is played from a standing position, supported on a stand or a swivel frame which can be adjusted to suit the percussionist. It is struck with a large felt-headed stick, and the usual technique is to strike the drum with a glancing blow midway between the centre and the rim. Sometimes a double-headed beater is used, played with a rapid oscillatory movement of the wrist. This technique is called for in Dukas's *L'Apprenti sorcier* (1897) and Stravinsky's *The Firebird* (1910) to produce a bass drum roll.

Davul

The bass drum played in the modern orchestra is a descendant of the 14th-century Turkish davul. Introduced into Europe in the 18th century with other Janissary instruments, the davul was played with two different beaters: a heavy, spoon-shaped club and a light stick. The davul is still played, accompanied by a shawm, by buskers in modern Istanbul. In Europe it was first played in military bands, and was beaten on one head with a solid club and on the other with a switch of birch twigs in imitation of the Turkish style. It was introduced into the orchestra by Michael Haydn (1737–1806) in his *Turkish Suite* (1777) and was also used in Mozart's *Die Entführung aus dem Serail* (1782) and in Joseph Haydn's *Military Symphony* (Symphony No. 100) of 1794. In the scores for these works, the use of the two different beaters was distinguished by the direction of the stems of the notes. Today, this distinction is lost if felt-headed or lambswool beaters are used for both heads.

Military bass drum

The military bass drum, which consists of a cylindrical shell of wood or, more commonly today, metal or laminated wood, has a diameter at least twice as great as its depth. The average parade bass drum has a depth of about

ABOVE: *The orchestral bass drum is often supported on a tilted stand facing the performer.*

ABOVE: An orchestral bass drum, seen from the player's perspective.

ABOVE: Rock and pop groups, such as this 1950s band, often include a drum kit with a bass drum that is struck with a foot pedal.

Giant bass drum

The British firm of Distin & Son built a giant bass drum with a diameter of 240cm/8ft for the 1857 Crystal Palace Handel Festival. It was broken up in the late 1950s. One of the largest bass drums in existence today is in Disneyland in California. Built in 1961 by the Remo Company, it has a diameter of 320cm/10½ft, but it is never played.

30cm/12in and a diameter of about 70cm/28in. It is carried with the shell resting against the player's chest and the two heads facing sideways, and is played with hard felt beaters. The heads, which were originally of calfskin, are now more commonly made of plastic, which avoids the problems formerly experienced by drummers when marching in wet weather. The heads are lapped on to hoops placed over the open ends of the shell and secured by counter hoops. The tension of the heads is adjusted by thumbscrews, rods or rope.

The military bass drum player sets and maintains the marching tempo, as well as signalling to the rest of the band to stop playing using two fast successive beats called a "double tap".

Gong drum

Orchestras used to have their own kind of bass drum known as the gong drum. The advantage of this over the double-headed bass drum was that as it had a single head, so it was easier to stop vibrations and thus play short notes. On the other hand, as single-headed drums have a definite pitch, it had to have a very large head. Today the gong drum has largely been abandoned in favour of a double-headed drum with a diameter of about 150cm/5ft and a depth of about 50cm/20in.

ABOVE: A band bass drum with a royal crest painted on the shell.

Other Drums

*You're not supposed to rape the drums,
you make love to them.*

BILLY HIGGINS (BORN 1936)

A drum can be any hollow body over which a membrane, or head, is stretched. When the head is hit, the ensuing vibrations are amplified by the body. Thousands of different drums – both pitched and unpitched – have evolved all over the world, to provide a rhythmic foundation for music and dance, to send signals, work magic or stir up emotions in battle.

Tambourine

This ancient instrument, which has remained virtually unchanged since Roman times, consists of a shallow hoop, usually covered with a

ABOVE: The tambourine is an instrument of the dance and has been so since at least the 17th century when it was played by the singer and dancer Barbara Campanine.

ABOVE: A trio of Cuban conga players.

parchment head. Circular metal jingles set into the hoop sound continuously when shaken or briefly when the head is struck or rubbed with the thumb.

Tom-toms

Unsnared small drums with wooden shells and double heads, tom-toms are usually double-tensioned. The smaller ones are clamped together in pairs, and the drums are supported on legs or attached to the bass drum of a drum kit. Although tom-toms are usually of indefinite pitch, they can be tuned roughly within the range of E to B flat. Sets of chromatic tom-toms are now made.

ABOVE: Congas are made in a wide variety of sizes; this one is a medium conga.

RIGHT: Although bongos are authentically played with the fingers or hands, wooden sticks can be used for a louder sound.

Bongos

Usually played in pairs, bongos are found in most Latin American countries. In Cuba they are made from short sections of hollow tree trunks with drum skins nailed over the larger ends, then held near a source of heat so that they become taut. Factory-manufactured bongos are made in pairs and are held between the knees. There is usually an interval of about a fourth between the two small drums. Bongos are the highest-pitched hand drums of Latin America, and are widely used in popular music.

Congas

Conga drums or "tumbas" are the lowest-pitched Latin American drums. They are single-headed drums with a long tapering wooden shell. Like the bongo, the conga has a depressed rim that leaves the head free for finger-style playing.

Timbales

Built with shallow shells made of brass or copper, single-headed timbales are supported on an adjustable stand and are played in pairs with thin wooden sticks. They are of Latin American origin. Although each one of a pair is of the same depth, they each have a different diameter that can range from 23cm/9in to 36cm/14in. Timbales give a bright, penetrating sound that is metallic with a pronounced ring.

ABOVE: *The timbale drum is predominantly used in Latin American dance music.*

Tabla

The Indian tabla is an instrument consisting of two small, single-headed hand drums, the *tabla* and the *bayan*.

ABOVE: *The Indian tabla player uses every joint and knuckle of his fingers and thumbs to produce a wide variety of sounds on the two drums (*tabla *and* bayan*).*

They produce a mellow, round sound of well-defined pitch. The *tabla* is the higher-pitched of the two, with a wooden shell and a diameter of about 15cm/6in. The head is made of three layers of skin, with a central black patch of a paste of flour and iron filings made according to an ancient recipe. The *bayan*, the bass drum, has a metal shell and a diameter of about 23cm/9in. It also has a black patch on the head.

There is also an Arabic drum called a tabla, which has an egg-cup shape and is made variously out of wood, earthenware or metal. It is either laid horizontally across the left knee or held under the left arm, and is beaten with the hands.

RIGHT:
Steel drum pans can be played on the march, hung around the neck, or, as in this case, resting on a stand.

Steel drums

Originating in Trinidad in the 1930s and '40s, steel drums were first developed as instruments for use in processional and carnival bands, and were originally made by cutting down

RIGHT, CLOCKWISE FROM TOP LEFT: *The drum kit consists of a ride cymbal, floor tom, two toms, snare drum, crash cymbal, hi-hat cymbal and bass drum.*

ABOVE: *Steel drum bands take part in many festivals. Here a band in the Virgin Islands is seen playing at an Easter sunrise service.*

oil drums. A steel drum usually has a range of two octaves, and there are five steps in tuning it. First the head is pounded into a concave shape, after which the units are marked out by grooving with a steel punch. It is then tempered by burning, and the barrel is cut to the required length. Finally, the drum is tuned using a small hammer. Struck with a rubber-headed panstick, the tenor, or "ping-pong", plays the tune while the rhythm, guitar and bass pans provide the rhythm.

Drum kit

Dance, pop and jazz-band drummers generally sit at a drum kit that includes a variety of percussion instruments, including a bass drum of about 60cm/24in diameter that is played with a foot pedal. Other parts of the drum kit, such as the snare drum, cymbals and blocks, are played with sticks or brushes.

Cymbals and Gongs

*One single cymbal clash by Bruckner is worth all
the four symphonies of Brahms with the serenades thrown in.*

HUGO WOLF (1860–1903)

The cymbals are possibly the most spectacular percussion instruments of the orchestra. Generally made from copper or brass concave plates, the dramatic activities of the extrovert cymbalist never fail to attract the audience's attention.

Ancient cymbals

Cymbals were known in ancient Israel, where they were played during the dedication of the Ark. In Egypt small cymbals, only about 15cm/6in in diameter, were used from about the 8th century BC. From there the cymbals travelled to Greece, where they were originally used as a ritual instrument associated with the cult of the goddess Kybele. They passed into

ABOVE: *This 15th-century painting shows a player holding a pair of cymbals vertically by their handles, the prevailing mode of playing in the West.*

ABOVE: *Orchestral cymbals are held in the centre by leather hand-grips that pass through holes in the circular plates.*

martial use and subsequently into the Greek theatre. The Greek *kymbala*, from which the modern name is derived, spread to Etruria, and so on to Rome and its empire.

Orchestral cymbals

The cymbals were almost forgotten in the West until the introduction of "Turkish" music in the second half of the 18th century. So unusual were cymbals at this time that when the French composer André Grétry (1741–1813) scored for them in his *L'Amitié à l'épreuve* (1770), it had to be explained to the performers how they were to be played. Nine years later Christoph Willibald Gluck used cymbals in *Iphigénie en Tauride* while, in the last quarter of the 18th century, the "clashpans" found their way into European military bands.

Cymbals began to be used regularly in orchestras in the early 19th century. Some composers used them simply as noisemakers, but others realized their full potential. One such composer was Berlioz, whose *Grande Messe des Morts* (1837) required ten cymbals, while his symphony *Roméo et Juliette* (1839) called for two "antique cymbals" tuned a fifth apart. Made of thick bronze and copied initially from those discovered in the ruins of Pompeii, antique cymbals or *crotales* are capable of being tuned to a definite pitch. They are sometimes arranged in a chromatic series and played with sticks. Other composers who have used the antique cymbals include Claude Debussy in *Prélude à l'après-midi d'un faune* (1892) and Igor Stravinsky in *The Rite of Spring* (1913).

Special effects

Cymbals are not just clashed together, but are capable of achieving many

ABOVE: *As well as being crashed together loudly, cymbals can be slid lightly across each other to produce a soft note, or struck with a drum stick.*

ABOVE: *Orchestral cymbals are heavy, and care is needed when preparing for an entrance.*

in pairs to the thumb and forefinger or middle finger of each hand, are played in many countries, especially Egypt. Finger cymbals of a different type, like thimbles, are worn by Chinese dancers on the thumb and middle finger of each hand. Both kinds are also widely used in Western orchestral music.

ABOVE: *Finger cymbals are attached in pairs to the thumb and forefinger or middle finger of each hand. These are still played in many countries, including Egypt and Greece, where the dancers prefer the two to be about a semitone apart.*

effects. In the "slide", the edge of one cymbal is slid across the other, giving a quiet, sustained effect. The faces of the two cymbals can also be scraped together in a "roll *a due*". In his Five Orchestral Pieces (1909) Schoenberg asks that a cello bow be drawn over the edge of the cymbal, while Bartók's Sonata for Two Pianos and Percussion (1937) calls on the percussionist to stroke the edge of the cymbal with the blade of a penknife. In Debussy's *La Mer* (1905), a coin is scraped across the surface of the cymbal.

Modern cymbals

Since World War II, orchestras have come to prefer thinner cymbals with a lighter sound than the 19th-century instruments. Modern cymbals, made of an alloy of copper and tin, are usually considerably larger than earlier ones, and range between 30cm/12in and 65cm/26in in diameter, the most common being about 40cm/16in.

Finger cymbals

Usually made of brass or silver, finger cymbals originated in Asia as dancers' accoutrements, and they are still used this way. Miniature cymbals, attached

ABOVE: *Bangladeshi dancers performing a traditional Manipur dance using small cymbals.*

Hi-hats

Sometimes the cymbals are operated by a foot pedal. Originally, pedal cymbals were merely a pair of matched plates attached to wooden jaws held open with a spring, the player clashing the two together with the foot. Today, however, pedal cymbals – which are known as hi-hats (in dance bands) or choke cymbals (in orchestras) – are mounted on top of a stand so that they can be either played with the foot or clashed with a stick. They are occasionally found in the orchestra, but are a more common feature of small bands.

Jazz and pop bands

Since the 1920s, jazz bands have preferred Chinese-made cymbals because they make a louder clash with a shorter period of resonance. They have an upturned rim and a squared-off central section. Pop bands use various types of cymbals, such as the snap cymbal (which produces a quick splash of sound), the sizzle cymbal (which produces a sizzling sound due to the loose rivets inserted into the rim) and the ride cymbal (in which a constant reiteration of strokes does not build up into an echoing roar).

Indian cymbals

Various types of cymbals are used in India. The *cakva* of Maharashtra are about 9cm/3½in in diameter. Held by

ABOVE: Hi-hat cymbals are played mounted on a column and either struck with a stick or clashed together by a foot pedal.

ABOVE: Cymbals are an important part of the modern drum kit.

ABOVE: In the 18th and early 19th centuries regimental bands often gave the cymbals to black musicians in the belief that they added "colour" to the band.

cloth handles, they are used in dancing and folk-singing. The *bartal*, on the other hand, is a large and heavy metal cymbal native to Assam. When clashed, the deep resonant tone of the *bartal* can be heard for over 15 seconds.

Another type of Indian cymbal is the *ilatalam*, which is mainly used in temple music, dance dramas and shadow-puppet plays. Found in the Kerala region, these flat instruments, made of brass and 12–15cm/5–6in in diameter, are played in two distinct ways. One method is to clash a pair horizontally together and then slip the edge of one against the rim of the other to obtain a prolonged ringing sound. The other method is to hold them vertically in the hollow of one hand and clash them by contracting the fingers towards the palm.

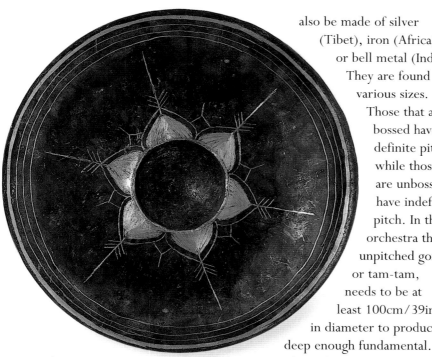

ABOVE: *The tam-tam is a shallow suspended bronze gong with a long and colourful reverberation. Those with a shallow rim are from China, while those with a deeper rim come from Burma.*

also be made of silver (Tibet), iron (Africa) or bell metal (India). They are found in various sizes. Those that are bossed have a definite pitch, while those that are unbossed have indefinite pitch. In the orchestra the unpitched gong, or tam-tam, needs to be at least 100cm/39in in diameter to produce a deep enough fundamental.

Apart from the *chempung* of Sumatra, which is played resting on a bed of banana leaves, gongs are generally freely suspended and are struck in the centre with either a beater or the fist.

ABOVE: *Detail of a traditional Chinese gong, showing the mallet striking the centre of the instrument.*

Gong

For those of a certain age the gong will forever be associated with the opening credits of Rank films, in which a gigantic gong is struck by a muscular man. The player on the soundtrack of this famous sequence was the eminent percussionist James Blades.

Gongs are usually made of thin bronze with a turned edge, but may

Gong chimes

The Chinese *yun lo* is a set of small bronze gongs suspended vertically in an upright frame in three rows of three, with a single one at the top. Although they are all of the same diameter, they vary considerably in thickness. Originally they were Confucian and Buddhist cult instruments. Today, however, their

use is restricted to funeral processions. Sets of tuned gongs are also made in the West for orchestral use, with a range of up to four and a half octaves.

ABOVE: *The gong plays an important role in many religions. Here a monk is about to strike a gong suspended in a Chinese temple.*

ABOVE: *A tam-tam mallet.*

RIGHT: *The gong is an Asian instrument with its origin in 6th-century China, where it was used to ward off evil spirits. Until the beginning of the 20th century Chinese servants preceded their masters and mistresses beating a single gong, the rank of the personage being indicated by the number of strokes.*

Castanets

*My feet were alright
but I could not manage the castanets.*

MIKHAIL GLINKA (1804–57)

Castanets are percussion instruments of indefinite pitch that are either clicked rhythmically or sounded in a sustained roll. The name of the instrument comes from the Latin *castanea*, meaning chestnut, the wood out of which they were traditionally made. Today, however, other hardwoods, such as boxwood or walnut, are preferred. Each castanet is made from a single piece of wood, cut in half and hollowed out in the centre to form a hemispheric cavity. The two halves are united by a cord that is looped over the thumb for playing.

LEFT: *Castanets have been used to accompany dancing from the earliest times. They came to Spain with the Arabs, but did not spread to the rest of Europe until the 16th century.*

Ancient castanets

Clappers have been known for over 5000 years; in their most primitive form they were simply two sticks beaten together. Examples have been found made of wood, ivory or metal, and clappers originated both as a substitute for hand-clapping to accompany dance and as a noise to dispel devils. Hinged clappers, operated by one hand, have been traced back to the early third millennium when they were used by dancing girls in Sumer.

Vessel clappers, made from materials such as hippopotamus teeth, began to appear in Egypt from about 2000 BC. In some of these instruments the natural hollow inherent in the material formed the vessel, but in others the cavity was enlarged to increase the volume of sound. A hole was pierced in each shank to tie a pair together. Such instruments were always played by women to accompany dancing. These clappers evolved into prototype castanets, which made their first appearance – even though they were much longer than today's – in popular music-making in Greece and Egypt in about 500 BC. In a modified form they are still used by Copts in religious services. Castanets are also known to have been used in ancient Rome.

Spain

In Europe the castanets are primarily a dance instrument associated with flamenco in Spain, where they are believed to have been introduced while it was a Phoenician colony. Certainly a popular folk instrument, the castanets have

RIGHT: *What would a Spanish dance be without the rhythmic sound of the dancers' castanets?*

virtually become Spain's national instrument. Although they are traditionally made of wood, it is recorded that during the Roman occupation the dancers of Cadiz played castanets made from metal.

Often used with a guitar to accompany dances – especially the

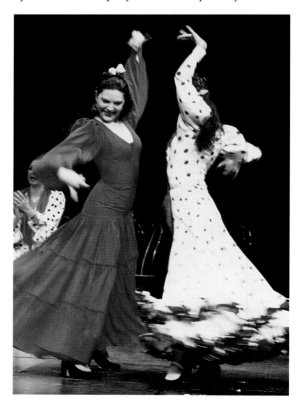

saraband — Spanish castanets consist of two almost circular discs, hollowed in the centre of the striking side and connected by an ornamental cord. The two castanets of a pair are of different pitches. The lower-pitched one (the *macho*, or "male") is held in the left hand, while the higher-pitched one (the *hembra*, or "female") is held in the right hand. The cups are held downwards and are manipulated by the fingers, using the middle two fingers of the left hand and all four fingers of the right hand. By 1588 both the dance

LEFT: Of all national dances, the Spanish flamenco must rank as the most difficult to perform; the dancer not only has to concentrate on his or her steps, but also has to keep time with the castanets.

RIGHT: Orchestral castanets are attached to a handle. The player shakes the handle, striking the shells on the free hand.

and the instrument had spread northwards into France, for in that year it is reported that the Duc de Richelieu, with castanets on his fingers and bells on his shoes, danced the saraband at a court ballet.

Orchestral castanets

True castanets are difficult to master and most modern orchestras use pairs, sometimes made of Bakelite, attached to long handles for ease in clicking. Many composers have scored for castanets in their Hispanic works, such as Georges Bizet's ever-popular opera *Carmen* (1873), Emmanuel Chabrier's *España* (1883) and Jules Massenet's *Le Cid* (1885).

Other composers have used the castanets to create special effects. Richard Wagner used them to create a great emotional impact in the lead-in to the "Venusberg" music in *Tannhäuser* (1845). Richard Strauss scored for them in the "Dance of the Seven Veils" from *Salome* (1905), and Benjamin Britten used them to imitate the sound of a night bird in *Let's Make an Opera!* (1949). The *castagnettes de fer*, for which Darius Milhaud scored in *Les Choëphores* in 1915, sounded like small cymbals or clappers.

LEFT: Castanets are not the sole preserve of Spanish folk music. As this lithograph of 1840 shows, they are also found in Italy.

Triangle

Triangles and similar non-musical instruments
are forbidden to cornettists, be they master or apprentice.

STUTTGART REGULATION OF 1721

The triangle was originally used as a folk instrument, and its value as an orchestral instrument was first realized in 1710 when it was employed by the Hamburg Opera. Seven years later it had entered the Dresden Opera. In both cases it was probably used to accompany folk-dancing.

Ancient triangle
The triangle is a descendant of the Egyptian *sistrum*, which was used in the worship of Hathor and Isis, and to ward off evil spirits. There were two main forms of the *sistrum*: the metal arched version and the faience "shrine" *sistrum*, which had as a central feature a head of the goddess Hathor. The metal version was shaped like an inverted U and was often made of silver with

ABOVE: This 18th-century English scene shows a small boy playing the triangle, accompanied by a tambourine and flute.

ABOVE: The method of playing a triangle was described by Jacques Cellier: the triangle hung from the left thumb and was struck by a steel stick held in the right hand.

a straight wooden handle protruding from the bottom. Loose-fitting metal rods or wires jingled when shaken, and small loose metal discs were hung on the rods to create additional sounds.

European folk triangle
In medieval Europe triangles were used for religious purposes and dance music. In northern Europe these early instruments, larger than they are today, were of trapezoid form and usually had a series of loose rings, or jingles, threaded on to the lower bar. Before 1660 three rings were standard, whereas after this date as many as five appeared. By the 19th century the rings had disappeared completely. Italy and Bohemia favoured a stirrup shape devoid of rings.

For many years the "lowly" triangle was frowned upon and considered a

beggar's instrument, chiefly in use among vagrants and gypsies. Such was the musical snobbery of the early 18th century that cornett players in Stuttgart were actually forbidden to play the "paltry instrument".

The triangle in the orchestra
As an orchestral instrument the triangle was first scored for in about 1750 in an overture by Johann Friedrich Fasch (1688–1758). When the fashion for Janissary music arose in the mid 18th century, the triangle was substituted in the orchestra for the Turkish crescent, or bell tree (otherwise known as a "jingling Johnny"), which was used by military bands to create exotic effects with the cymbals and bass drum. Mozart scored for it in *Die Entführung aus dem Serail* (1782), Haydn

ABOVE: So that it is always in reach, the orchestral triangle is usually suspended over one of the side drums.

in his *Military Symphony* (1794), and Beethoven in his Ninth Symphony (1823). Originally used only to provide rhythm, in the mid 19th century the triangle claimed its place as an indispensable member of the orchestra when Liszt raised it to the rank of a solo instrument in his Piano Concerto in E flat of 1853.

Many composers have since used the triangle to great effect, but none more picturesquely than Edward Elgar. In the eleventh of his *Enigma Variations* (1899) it is used to depict the tinkle of the medal on the collar of the bulldog Dan as he shakes himself after a plunge into the River Wye.

Construction

The modern triangle is a steel rod bent in the shape of an equilateral triangle, left open where the ends meet so as to allow the whole length to vibrate. It is usually suspended by a thin thread or wrist strap, so as not to interfere with the vibrations. The triangle is beaten with a rod of the same material. Although the sound it makes is not loud, because of its enharmonic overtones its indefinite pitch can be heard above the full orchestra. Were the gap closed to make a complete triangle, it would have a definite pitch. Orchestral percussionists generally use a range of triangles in different sizes.

ABOVE: *The blurred beater in this picture indicates that this orchestral performer is playing a rapid trill on the triangle.*

ABOVE: *Although the triangle is traditionally struck on the bottom bar, for special effects it can be struck almost anywhere.*

ABOVE: *This late 15th-century painting shows angels playing open tambourine and triangle.*

Xylophone

I must own that the skill of Michael Guzikow [Polish xylophonist] beats everything that I would have imagined, for with his wooden sticks resting on straw he produces all that is possible with the most perfect instrument.

FELIX MENDELSSOHN (1809–47)

The xylophone was introduced into the orchestra in 1874 when the French composer Camille Saint-Saëns scored for it in *Danse Macabre*, intending it to represent the rattling bones of the dead. Although little original orchestral music has been written for the xylophone, it has a small but useful solo repertoire.

The xylophone is a set of tuned wooden percussion blocks, which are laid in a row parallel to one another and are played by being hit with sticks or knobbed beaters. Tuning is achieved by reducing the length of the block to raise the pitch, or filing the underside at the centre of the block to lower it. As no vibrations occur at the ends of the blocks, they are either placed on straw ropes or pierced and fixed to a frame, without impairment of tone. Up to the 1920s xylophones in Germany were built using the former method, a feature that caused them to be called *Strohfiedel* ("straw fiddles").

The modern xylophone owes much to the work of Hermann Winterhof who, in 1927, invented the "arcuate notch". This is an arc cut on the underside of each key, both to improve the quality of tone and to give greater definition of pitch. Modern instruments are built in various sizes capable of playing up to four octaves, with rosewood keys arranged in two

ABOVE: The xylophone has tuned wooden bars with tubular resonators suspended underneath, and is played with wooden, rubber or plastic beaters.

rows like those on a piano keyboard. Suspended under each key is a tubular metal resonator that gives the instrument its characteristic sound.

Europe
The xylophone has been known since at least the early 16th century, when Hans Holbein painted his *Dance of Death* showing Death carrying a xylophone suspended horizontally, like a tray, from a cord around his neck. However, the instrument did not become popular until the 1830s, when the Polish xylophonist Michael Joseph Gusikow brought it to the attention of the public with his concerts. Gusikow gave the instrument an enduring popularity in folk music.

Asia
The xylophone is believed to have originated in South-east Asia. One Asian version is the *mokkin* of Japan,

ABOVE: The marimba was developed in the United States around 1910. It is similar to the xylophone but is pitched an octave deeper, giving it a characteristic mellow sound.

ABOVE: *The marimba can be played with four beaters instead of two. Playing in this way produces soft, deep chords.*

ABOVE: *The* rang nat *is a type of metallic xylophone — known as a "metallophone" in Java and Bali — used in Javanese Gamelan bands. Also seen in this photograph are some gong chimes, or* khong vong yai.

which, although it has between 13 and 16 keys, is used as a rhythm rather than a melody instrument, chiefly in *kabuki* music. In Burma the *pattala* has up to 23 keys, which are finely tuned by fixing wax pellets to the undersides. The xylophones and metallophones of Indonesian percussion orchestras are many and varied, ranging from single-octave models to large multi-octave instruments that are played using two beaters. As early as the 7th century, Balinese *gambang* players were using four beaters, two in each hand, held to form a V.

Xylophone music

Works composed especially for the xylophone include *Fantasy on Japanese Wood Prints* (1965) by Alan Hovhaness (born 1911), Sonata for Xylophone (1967) by Thomas Pitfield (born 1903) and various works by the astronomer Patrick Moore (born 1923), who is also an accomplished xylophonist. Other works that include prominent xylophone parts include Igor Stravinsky's *The Firebird* (1910) and the monumental *Gothic Symphony* (1931) by Havergal Brian (1876–1972).

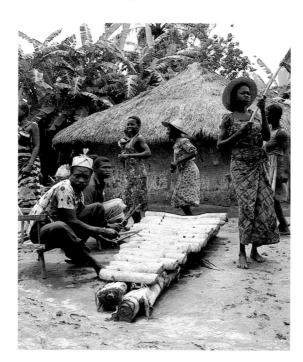

ABOVE: *In Zaire and other central African countries, xylophones are made by placing logs sliced into increasing sizes over a base of two long logs.*

Africa

From Asia the xylophone migrated to Africa. Here the simplest form is the pit or ground xylophone which, as the name implies, is a pit in the ground over which the ends of wooden bars are placed on bundles of grass. This primitive instrument is still played in parts of the continent, an example being the eight-keyed *ndara* of Uganda. The log xylophone, found in East and West Africa, as well as in Indonesia and Papua New Guinea, is composed of a few keys placed across the outstretched legs of the player. In a more developed form, gourds are suspended from the keys to augment the sound. In Nigeria a small portable version has ox-horn resonators.

Bells

Gay bells or sad, they bring you memories
of half forgotten innocent old places.

W. B. Yeats (1865–1939)

In one form or another, bells are known all over the world. Ancient Egyptian priests wore small closed silver bells as protective amulets when they were in the temple, a practice continued in the Christian church: as late as the 11th century, Archbishop Lanfranc of Canterbury wore a cope edged with 51 bells.

The practice of fitting animals with bells to ward off evil dates back to at least 520 BC, when they are mentioned in the *Book of Zachariah*. In Siberia small bells are still fitted on to the yokes of horse-drawn vehicles to scare off wolves and devils.

Ancient Greek soldiers attached bronze bells to their shields in an effort to terrify the enemy. It must have been an awesome sound for, owing to the density of bronze, their bells would have clanged rather than emitting the clear ringing tone that is expected today. The Greeks also issued bells to watchmen and sentinels for use in alerting the population in times of danger.

The custom of ringing a "passing bell", with the object of keeping evil spirits away from the dead, dates back to at least the 8th century. The Bayeux Tapestry, made in the late 11th century, clearly shows two boys, each carrying a pair of hand bells, accompanying the coffin of Edward the Confessor for exactly this reason.

Casting

Early bells were cast using the *cire perdue* or "lost wax" method. A clay or brick model of the inside surface of the

ABOVE: A late 7th-century BC bronze bell found in Bologna, Italy.

bell was made. Over this, a layer of wax was built up to the shape and thickness of the finished bell. Once the wax had set, it was covered by another layer of clay and the entire mould was thoroughly baked. As the clay hardened the wax melted and drained away, leaving a vacant space into which the bell metal was poured to form the actual bell. The Whitechapel Bell Foundry in London, which still casts church bells and a five-octave range of hand bells, was founded in 1420.

Some early bells were not cast but made from thin iron plates hammered into circular or rectangular sheets and riveted together before being dipped into molten copper to seal the joints.

ABOVE: The bells of the Church of San Francisco in Córdoba, Spain. Bells are traditionally hung high in church towers so that they can be heard over great distances.

Church bells

Early church bells were of a long, thin beehive shape. During the 12th and 13th centuries, however, the form of the bell evolved into a slightly conical sugar-loaf shape, which by the beginning of the 14th century had reached the fatter, wider appearance that is familiar today.

One of the earliest references to ringing church bells in England is found in Rutland. Here, in the church of St Andrew in Stoke Dry on the early 12th-century south pillar of the Romanesque chancel arch, is depicted a man pulling on a bell rope. Although it was not until the 16th century that bells regularly began to carry inscriptions, at Littleborough, Nottinghamshire there is a bell made in about 1170 that bears the inscription "Santa Maria".

The mechanics of the church bell are relatively simple. The crown of each bell is fixed to a headstick of metal, which is in turn attached to a large wheel. The rim of the wheel is grooved to hold the bell rope which, when pulled, raises the bell, causing it to swing until its mouth is high enough for the clapper to strike it.

Change-ringing

Britain differs from the rest of Europe in that church bells are rung in changes. A change is the ringing of a set of bells in all possible combinations. Thus a set of three bells contains six changes (123, 231, 213, 321, 312 and 132). Each set of changes constitutes a peal. A peal of three bells consists of six changes, while a peal of four bells contains 24, one of eight bells contains 40,320 and so on.

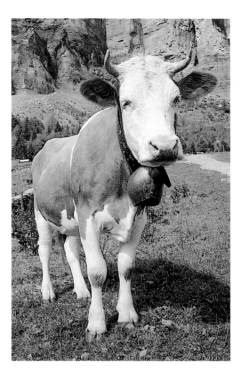

ABOVE: The custom of fitting animals, such as horses and cows, with bells was originally to ward off evil, although on a more practical level it is also useful for the farmer to be able to hear them moving around.

ABOVE: The earliest known carving (12th-century) of church bell ringers.

ABOVE: An engraving of an 18th-century French bell foundry showing a bell being hoisted from its casting mould.

Hand bells

Hand bells, as the name implies, are relatively small bells fitted with a handle that enables them to be held in the hand for ringing. The oldest known hand bells come from China and date from about 1600 BC. Chinese hand bells were, however, in existence before this, for there are earlier written references to their use in religious music. In 9th-century Japan small hand bells struck with hammers were used to accompany the singing of *goeka*, a kind of Buddhist plainsong. This tradition lives on, and at the beginning of the 21st century there are many enthusiasts who form several thousand *goeka* societies in Japan, and hold regular conventions.

Modern Western hand bells are normally made in sets numbering between six and 60, covering a range of up to five octaves, and are usually rung by groups of between four and 15 ringers. Generally each player holds one or two bells in each hand. Sometimes, however, the bells are laid on a table and are lifted and rung as they are required.

By the mid 19th century almost every village in England had its own hand-bell team that played at local fairs, entertainments and during the Christmas season. In the 20th century, hand-bell ringing again became popular, this time in the United States. In 1954 the American Guild of English

ABOVE: A modern handmade set of bell chimes.

Hand-bell Ringers was founded and today there are more than a thousand teams representing over 10,000 ringers.

Bell wheel

One of the earliest ecclesiastical uses of small bells is the bell wheel, or *Zimbelstern*, examples of which are recorded from the 10th century. Mainly found in France, Germany and Spain, and to a lesser extent in Britain, this contraption consisted of a number of small silver bells attached to a large wheel. The wheel was originally revolved by means of either a rope or a hand-crank, but by the 13th century clockwork was also used, and some were attached to the church organ and operated by a stop.

One of the finest bell wheels was the "Star" of Fulda Cathedral in Germany. This wonderful creation, which was suspended from the nave ceiling, was 7.3m/24ft in diameter and had no less than 350 bells attached to its 14 rays. In 1781 tragedy struck when its rope broke, causing it to crash down upon the assembled congregation. Since its restoration, it still has 150 of its bells and is operated by a treadmill.

Bell chimes

Although tuned sets of bell chimes have been in existence for at least 3000 years, it was not until the 11th century that they reached Europe. The first depiction of the instrument, in an illustrated Bible of about 1070, shows a musician hammering a seven-bell chime with one hand while tapping a frame drum with the other hand. During the 13th century some chimes, which were connected to town clocks, were mechanized, the time being sounded by bells that were struck by hammers operated by a cogwheel.

LEFT: Hand-bell groups were very popular in the 19th century. One such band that toured extensively was the "Swedish Bell Ringers".

Carillon

The art of making bell chimes was perfected in the Low Countries and northern France, where the bells were suspended from a framework inside a tower. Hammers were automatically released by iron pegs set into a large wooden barrel (later a metal cylinder) that was turned by weights and pulleys. As the barrel revolved, the pegs tripped levers that were in turn connected to the hammers by wires.

ABOVE: The carillon at the church of Corneille sur Risle, France.

ABOVE: A 13th-century illumination depicting a man playing a bell chime with crudely made hammers. By his side is another musician playing a viol in the style of the period.

Two of the earliest town clocks fitted with bells were that in Mons (1328) and the astronomical clock in Strasbourg Cathedral (1354). The latter's pegs were fitted in such a way that the bells could play several tunes.

From about 1500 a keyboard was added to the Antwerp carillon, making it possible to play the bells manually. During the 16th century the compass of the carillons extended downwards, involving larger, heavier bells. As these were impossible to play by hand, a pedal board was added. The number of bells continued to increase and, by 1612, St Paul's church in Liège boasted a carillon of 24 bells.

As the popularity of the carillon grew, so did the demand for longer and more varied tunes. Once the cylinder had made a single complete revolution all its music had been played, so to accommodate longer tunes larger cylinders were made, some reaching over 2m/6ft in diameter.

The most famous carillon builders of the 17th century were the Van der Gheyn family and the Hemony brothers, Pierre and François, who came from Lorraine but worked in Amsterdam. In 1655 Pierre Hemony built the largest carillon yet, a machine containing 52 bells. He was such a perfectionist that he required his bells to contain the overtones of three octaves, two fifths, a major third and a minor third.

Today the world's foremost builder of carillons is the British bell foundry Taylor & Co., in Loughborough. Their creations have been installed in bell towers all over the world, including their home town, where a 47-bell carillon was built in 1923 as a memorial to those men of the town who died in World War I.

ABOVE: These traditional Swiss cow bells are accompanying a procession of alpine singers.

Bells in the orchestra

Bells have been used in orchestras since the 18th century. One outstanding use of bells took place in 1882 at the first performance of Tchaikovsky's *1812 Overture*. Although the ambitious Tchaikovsky had wanted to have all the church bells of Moscow peal out in the grand finale, the city fathers deemed the idea impractical so the composer had to be content with the bells of Uspensky Cathedral, in which the concert took place.

Many 19th-century composers, however, preferred to use other instruments to imitate the sound of the bell. Rimsky-Korsakov, for instance, used a combination of triangle, cymbal and gong combined with pizzicato and sustained chords from the strings and wind in his *Russian Easter Festival*

LEFT: Orchestral sleigh bells recreate the sound of the bells placed around the necks of sleigh-pulling Russian horses.

overture in 1888. Generally, however, modern orchestras use tubular bells, but since the 1970s synthesizers and other electronic instruments have been increasingly used to imitate bells.

Tubular bells

Tubular bells originated in South-east Asia. When they became known in Europe the chimes were at first made of bell metal, but this proved expensive. In 1886, after various experiments, a British instrument maker, John Hampton of Coventry, produced tubular bells made of bronze. Today chimes are usually made of brass. Ordered in graduated lengths to give a range of up to two octaves, they all have the same diameter and are suspended from a frame.

ABOVE: Modern orchestral tubular bells.

ABOVE: Tubular bells mallets.

Glockenspiel

The European concept of the glockenspiel originated in the Netherlands, where it was introduced from Indonesia in the second half of the 17th century. The European instrument was originally a miniature carillon, and its earliest known use was in 1739 when Handel used one in a production of *Saul*. Today it is more commonly made of a series of graduated steel bars, arranged in two rows like the black and white keys of a piano, and played with moderately hard beaters.

ABOVE: By the 16th century some bell chimes were connected to a keyboard, thereby making it possible to play the bells manually.

ABOVE: Tubular bells are sounded by being hit at the top with hard mallets. A foot pedal operates a felted damper to stop the sound when required.

ABOVE: The modern glockenspiel has steel bars covering two and a half octaves.

The keyed glockenspiel, in which small metal hammers strike the bars from below, arrived in the orchestra before what is now the standard instrument took its place in the mid 19th century, and Mozart, Tchaikovsky, Saint-Saëns and many other composers included it in their scores. Nearly all these parts are now played on the conventional glockenspiel, which has a superior tone and dynamic range.

Bell-lyra

The portable glockenspiel was designed in the 19th century specifically for German marching bands. Originally a single row of metal cups, it is now made with a series of metal bars arranged like a piano keyboard that are hung in a lyre-shaped frame set on a wooden handle. Tapped with a metal beater, it is carried in front of the player, level with the head.

Celesta

Similar to the keyed glockenspiel, the celesta resembles an upright piano. The metal bars are struck by felt-covered hammers activated by a simple piano mechanism, and there is a sustaining pedal. It was invented by Auguste

Mustel of Paris in 1886 as an improvement on the "dulcitone", an instrument consisting of a series of tuning forks operated by a keyboard, which he had constructed some 20 years earlier.

According to legend, Tchaikovsky was walking down a street in Paris when he heard a celesta being played. He was so enchanted by the sound that he used it to represent the Sugar-plum Fairy in *The Nutcracker* (1892). Béla Bartók scored for the celesta in his *Music for Strings, Percussion and Celesta*, which was published in 1936.

ABOVE: The celesta is played like a piano but has a bell-like sound. Although mainly used in classical orchestras, it is also occasionally used in popular music.

Vibraphone

The vibraphone is a cross between the glockenspiel and the xylophone, and was invented in the United States in 1921. Beneath the alloy bars are tubular resonators fitted with resonating lids that are made to vibrate by means of an electric motor. The vibraphone produces a bell-like sound and has been scored for by composers such as Benjamin Britten and Luigi Dallapiccola (1904–75). It quickly became popular as a jazz instrument, first played by its leading exponent Lionel Hampton (born 1909).

ABOVE: The vibraphone has a foot pedal that opens and closes the resonating tubes.

Bells music

Among the earliest composers to score for bells were Nicholas Dalayrac (1753–1809) in his opera *Camille* (1791), and Luigi Cherubini (1760–1842) in *Elisa* (1794). Rossini called for a bell in the second act of *William Tell* (1829), and Giacomo Meyerbeer (1791–1864) demanded a specially made large bell for *Les Huguenots* (1836).

Keyboards

Striking Chords

The most difficult things written by one perfectly versed in the difficulties of the keyboard are far easier to play than the easiest things conceived by an amateur.

ROBERT SCHUMANN (1810–56)

Early keyboards had only natural notes (the "white" notes) identified by the first seven letters of the alphabet (A–G), which were often marked on the appropriate keys to allow the player to differentiate between otherwise identical keys. In time a B flat was inserted between the A and B keys, which were cut away for the purpose. In Germany the B flat is still referred to as B, while the B is known as H. By the 15th century the keyboard had become fully chromatic, with the five raised sharp and flat notes forming an upper row as they do today. The oldest surviving chromatic keyboard dates from 1361 and is found on the organ of Halberstadt Cathedral in Germany.

With the introduction of sharps and flats to the keyboard, the old modal system – which had been built around the different notes of the diatonic

ABOVE: The keys of the harpsichord differ from those of other keyboards in that the "naturals" are black and the "accidentals" are white.

ABOVE: This painting is from the cover of a virginal. It shows a band of musicians in the midst of the autumnal wine-making festivities. Built by Paul Wissmayr for Lucas Behaim in 1619, Behaim himself is seen playing the bass viol.

"natural" scales – slowly died out and its place was taken by the familiar major and minor scales that were better suited to harmony. In the Middle Ages there had been six modes, but now there were just two, each available in 12 keys.

Although Pythagoras's natural intervals had been adequate for the simple melodies and harmonies of the modal system, based on a handful of common chords, they caused problems when the chromatic keyboard was introduced. The reasons for this are found in mathematics. On a seven-octave keyboard there are 12 fifths. Pythagoras showed that the frequency ratio of an octave to its fundamental was 2:1 and that of a fifth was 3:2.

To cover the seven octaves, $(2:1)^7$ could be expected to equal $(3:2)^{12}$. However, $(2:1)^7$ produces 128 and $(3:2)^{12}$ gives 129.75.

Mean-tone temperament

A partial solution was adopted in the 16th century when mean-tone temperament was developed by Francisco Salinas (1513–90), a music theorist at the University of Salamanca, to "temper" or adjust the intervals of fixed-pitch instruments to fit them for practical performance. The system was founded on the accuracy of the major third. Taking C' as the fundamental, the fourth fifth reaches e. However, this e did not make an exact major third with the c immediately below it.

Mean-tone temperament flattened the *e* so that an exact major third was formed, and in so doing the four fifths that had been passed through were also slightly flattened. This method of tuning was fine for the major scales of A, G, D, C, F and B flat, and the relative minors of the last three, but not for other scales, because it made the distance between the semitones unequal, so that a passage played in one key sounded discordant when played in another. Keyboard composers before the 18th century therefore wrote in comparatively few keys and used very little modulation.

Equal temperament

The problem was solved by dividing the octave into 12 equal semitones, creating equal temperament. In so doing, each semitone was slightly adjusted from its natural position. By this means, for example, D sharp and E flat became identical, although

ABOVE: A 1920s rosewood baby grand piano with ivory keys, made by Steinway.

according to "natural" tuning they differ slightly. When fixed-pitch instruments were tuned in this way, they could be played in any key, and modulation into any other key was possible.

This system had originally been suggested as early as the 16th century, but was not adopted until the 18th, when it was still opposed as an impure compromise. Bach's 48 Preludes and Fugues, published in two books in 1722 and 1744 as *The Well-tempered Clavier*, were written in all the major and minor keys as an endorsement of the system of equal temperament.

ABOVE: The organ at the Royal Festival Hall in London was built with meticulous workmanship by Harrison & Harrison and was inaugurated in 1954.

ABOVE: The grand piano is an important orchestral and solo instrument.

Clavichord

*Who dislikes noise, raging and fuming, whose heart bursts in sweet feelings,
neglects both the harpsichord and the piano and chooses the clavichord.*

CHRISTIAN SCHUBART (1739–91)

LEFT: *This clavichord was built
by Georg Schmahl of Ulm in
1807. Although not as
ornate as some of this
maker's earlier creations,
the natural keys are
covered in plumwood.*

The clavichord is of deceptively simple construction, consisting of a small shallow box without stand or legs. Behind the keyboard, the strings are attached to hitch-pins at the left of the box, then pass across the back halves of the keys and over the bridge to the tuning pins on the right. When a key is depressed the tangent (a small upright brass blade set directly in the key) gently touches the corresponding string, making a vibration node at the point of contact; to the right of this strike point the string crosses the bridge that transmits the vibrations to the soundboard. The superfluous section of the string to the left is deadened by a strip of felt that is woven between the strings.

The loudness of the tone depends directly on the force used by the player on the key, and the tangent remains in contact with the string while it is sounding. The loudest possible sound is produced by depressing a key quickly, but at its loudest the clavichord is too quiet to be anything other than a solo instrument. Its soft, ethereal tone is, however, ideal for domestic use in small rooms.

Fretted clavichord
Until the early 18th century all clavichords were "fretted": each string was struck by the tangents of several keys. An individual string for each note was unnecessary, as notes as close as a tone or a semitone apart were rarely played together in the predominantly melodic music of the time. In the bass octave each of the notes usually had its own string; two or three keys shared a string in the middle register, while the treble strings were shared by two, three or four keys.

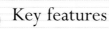

Key features

TYPE: keyboard

PITCH: concert

RANGE: *E' to e"*

ABOVE: *This finely detailed painting, executed by the Dutch master Jan Muyckens in 1648,
shows a gentleman seated at a clavichord. The instrument is resting on a table and the lid
has been raised to show the action.*

The first clavichords had a compass of two and a half octaves, but by the 17th century this had risen to four, with a short octave in the bass in which no keys were provided for unnecessary chromatic notes as a device to save space. Essentially domestic instruments, clavichords were also used by organists when practising.

Unfretted clavichord

In the early 18th century German clavichords began to appear unfretted, that is with a separate string for each note. Larger clavichords with a five or six-octave compass were built, and superb examples of decorated casework were made. Although this would appear to have been an improvement, it did not prove popular, for more strings meant a larger, heavier and therefore more expensive instrument.

Germany

Although the clavichord gave way to virginals and spinets throughout much of Europe in the 16th and 17th centuries, it remained popular in Germany, Scandinavia and Spain. By 1650 northern Germany was the centre of clavichord-making and manufacturers were building clavichords that cost about one-quarter

ABOVE: A 17th-century Dutch painting by Gerrit Dou of a woman at the clavichord.

of the price of a harpsichord. By the mid 1700s the German clavichord had become a symbol of the *Empfindsame Zeitalter*, standing for noble simplicity as a bastion against the encroaching ostentation of the piano.

Germany also developed its own style of playing. As the tangent remains in contact with the string, a slight variation of finger pressure on the key

RIGHT: An unfretted clavichord made by the Bavarian instrument maker Christian Gottlob Hubert in the late 18th century.

ABOVE: This simple line drawing is said to date from about 1440 and shows a musician playing the clavichord at a table.

can alter the tension of the string. By caressing the key a *bebung* effect was produced that gave warmth and feeling to the note in much the same way as the violinist uses vibrato.

Even in Germany, however, the clavichord finally had to give way to the piano, and by 1820 it was virtually extinct, until it was recreated in the 20th century for the playing of early music.

Clavichord music

Sixteenth-century music composed for the clavichord usually consisted of dances such as Hugh Aston's *Hornepype*, the *Quatorze gaillards* published by Pierre Attaingnant in 1531, and the *Intavolatura nova di varie sorte de balli* issued in Venice by Gardane in 1551. Music was still being composed for the clavichord in the 18th century by composers such as C. P. E. Bach (1714–88), Christian Neefe (1748–98) and Friedrich Rust (1739–96), who wrote pieces that included special effects for the instrument such as strumming and drumming on the strings.

Harpsichord

*One should have an easy manner at the harpsichord and
avoid either staring fixedly at any object, or looking too vague.*

FRANÇOIS COUPERIN (1668–1733), "L'ART DE TOUCHER LE CLAVECIN"

The harpsichord can be dated back to at least 1397, when there is a record in Padua of the invention of an instrument called a *clavicymbalum*, a name that was translated as "virginal" in England. It did not become known as the harpsichord, from the Italian *arpicordo*, until 1607. The new instrument was the first to use a mechanical plucking action to activate the strings; this system was also used in the virginal and the spinet.

Mechanism

The harpsichord is a mechanized version of the psaltery. Each key operates a wooden rod, or "jack", on which is mounted a quill plectrum. As the key is depressed, the jack rises and the plectrum plucks the string. The jack is

Key features

TYPE: keyboard

PITCH: concert

RANGE: *c'* to *c''''*

**NOTABLE PLAYERS OF THE
HARPSICHORD:** Wanda
Landowska, Arnold
Dolmetsch, Thurston Dart,
Christopher Hogwood.

so constructed that on its way down, when the key is released, the plectrum is pivoted back and avoids the string. As the jack descends a felt damper quietens the string.

Because the strings run at right angles to the keyboard, it is possible to mount more than one jack on each key, and more than one string to each note, each with its own jack. Each set of strings is called a "choir". By moving the jacks to one side, using a stop, one or more choirs can be left unplucked, so that the volume of sound produced is reduced. Apart from this facility, the player has no control over the level of sound, as the string is always plucked in the same way. However, additional

*LEFT: A harpsichord made in 1756 by Jacob
Kirckman of London. The interior surfaces
are decorated with holly and walnut
marquetry, while the case is veneered
with burr walnut.*

stops modify the sounds in other ways, such as the "harp" stop that mutes some strings to give a pizzicato effect, or the "lute" stop that operates extra jacks nearer the ends of the strings to give a nasal sound.

Two-manual harpsichord

From the 1670s, the development of double manuals allowed performers to change from louder to softer passages without interrupting their playing. The lower manual worked two choirs, while the upper manual worked a single choir for quiet passages. In French harpsichords, the two mechanisms could be coupled to operate all three choirs together for maximum volume.

ABOVE: A beautifully decorated harpsichord.

Styles

The earliest surviving instruments are Italian, including one dated 1515. They have single manuals and separate outer cases, and may have had only a single set of strings.

Flemish harpsichords, principally made by the Ruckers family of Antwerp from the mid 16th to late 17th centuries, were played all over Europe. They were beautifully decorated with printed papers, and in some instruments the paintings inside the lid were by Rubens. Many Ruckers harpsichords were later rebuilt for the French market by Pascal Taskin, who inherited the French firm of Blanchet, the royal harpsichord makers.

The major English makers of the 18th century were Burkat Shudi (1702–73), who was joined in 1761 by John Broadwood (1732–1812) and Jacob Kirckman (1710–92). While French instruments were elaborately painted and gilded, English harpsichord cases were relatively austere, but were finely veneered in walnut and sycamore or, later, in satinwood and mahogany.

Innovations

During the 18th century there were many attempts to modify and improve the harpsichord. Jean Marius's *clavecin brisé*, or folding harpsichord of 1700, was made in three hinged sections. The century also saw ever-larger harpsichords with three and even four

ABOVE: Harpsichords are often beautifully decorated, with gold panelling and painted scenes.

registers, together with a complex system of stops to provide different tone-colours. In 1769 Shudi patented the "Venetian swell", a device that opened and shut like a Venetian blind over the strings and soundboard, to produce *crescendos* and *diminuendos*. The quill plectrum was replaced by one made of hard leather.

Decline

In 1768 Johann Christian Bach's London recital made the piano instantly fashionable and ended the supremacy of the harpsichord. Although the harpsichord was still being built in Dublin as late as 1824, it was soon overtaken by the new, more expressive instrument. By 1837 it was almost extinct, for when in that year the pianist Ignaz Moscheles gave a "historical" recital in London, he had difficulty in finding a harpsichord on which to perform.

The modern revival began in the 1880s, when the French piano makers Erard and Pleyel built copies of 18th-century harpsichords, and in London Arnold Dolmetsch began to present recitals of Renaissance and Baroque music on antique instruments.

ABOVE: Detail of a modern harpsichord keyboard built by Colin Booth in 1993.

Virginal

*To teach men's daughters on the virginal is
as harmless a calling as any man can follow.*

SOLOMON ECCLES (1618–83)

Although virginals were the most popular keyboard instruments in Elizabethan households, the name is not, as many believe, a compliment to the "Virgin Queen". Descended from the psaltery, the instrument has been known since at least 1460, 50 years before Elizabeth's birth. The etymology of the word "virginals" (like "scissors", it is often used in the plural) is uncertain. It may be from the Latin *virga*, meaning "rod" or

ABOVE: A 1976 replica of a 1623 Ruckers virginal from Antwerp. Apart from their musical quality, instruments from Antwerp are notable for the elaborate decoration of their interiors with printed paper and painting.

"jack", or may even be a reference to the young ladies who most commonly played the instrument.

By 1500 virginals were being played throughout Europe. They are mentioned in a proverb that was inscribed on the walls of Manor House, Leckingfield, Yorkshire, in about 1500, while on the other side of Europe the court organist at Buda played the virginal to entertain the prince at mealtimes in 1501. Henry VIII is known to have purchased five virginals in 1530, while in 1549 the Innsbruck court bought an instrument made by an organ builder from Königsberg. Virginals were extremely popular as domestic instruments in the

Low Countries, England, Austria and Germany. In England they eventually gave way to the spinet and in Germany to the clavichord.

Shape

Strung with 32 metal strings lying parallel with the keyboard, the virginal had the form of a clavichord coupled with the sound of a harpsichord, since the strings were plucked. Each string was longer than that of its neighbour, forming a triangle inside the case, with the long bass strings at the front. In Flemish virginals the keyboard was placed either to the right or left of the centre of the long side, a feature that determined the timbre of the instrument. When it was placed to the right, the strings were plucked nearer their centre, and this produced a nasal tone that was described as "grunting

ABOVE: Detail of the inside of a virginal with delicately painted flowers and embellishments. The highest standards of craftsmanship went into the lavish decoration of the domestic instruments.

ABOVE: A 16th-century engraving showing a woman playing a virginal.

Key features

TYPE: keyboard

PITCH: concert

RANGE: *c'* to *c''''*

LEFT: A Young Lady seated at a Virginal, *painted in about 1670 by Jan Vermeer. Many Dutch masters painted scenes like this, indicating the importance of chamber music in domestic life.*

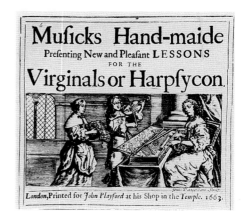

ABOVE: A handbill of 1663 advertising lessons for people wishing to learn the virginal or harpsichord.

ABOVE: The keyboard of a virginal is similar to that of a piano. This instrument typically has an intricately decorated panel above the keys.

without a lid. Flemish virginals, which were chiefly made in Antwerp, had recessed keyboards made of thicker softwood and were furnished with a lid. English virginals, all surviving examples of which were made between 1640 and 1680, combined features of both the Italian and Flemish styles. They were exceptionally deep and featured a vaulted lid.

Double virginal

An extremely popular form was the double virginal, invented in Antwerp. Nicknamed the "mother and child", it combined a large keyboard cheek by jowl with a smaller one half the size. The smaller one

was set in a recess between the soundboard and the bottom of the case, usually to the left of the larger keyboard. Although it could also be played on its own, during performance the "child" could be withdrawn and placed on top of the "mother" so that the latter's keyboard played both instruments, the "child" sounding an octave above the "mother". These were built in the late 16th century, and in 1584 a Leipzig musical instrument dealer named Krause had in his stock *"1 neu Instrument mit 2 Clavieren"* ("one new instrument with two keyboards").

BELOW: This virginal is beautifully decorated with glass.

like pigs". This form was called a *muselar*. With the keyboard to the left, in the form called a *spinett*, the sound was brighter.

There were three main centres of virginal-making: Italy, Belgium and England. Italian-made virginals, which were characterized by a projecting keyboard like the contemporary Italian spinet, were made of cypress wood

Spinet

Called upon one Haward, that makes virginalls, and did there like of a little espinette, and will have him finish it for me: for I had a mind to a small harpsichon, but this takes up less room.

SAMUEL PEPYS (1633–1703)

The spinet, a small version of the harpsichord, is believed to have got its name from either the Italian word *spina* or the French *épinette* ("thorn"), both references to the plectra with which the instrument's strings are plucked. Another theory is that it is named after one of the early builders of the instrument, the Venetian Giovanni Spinetti, one of whose surviving instruments is dated 1503.

The spinet has the same action as the harpsichord, but is built on a smaller, domestic scale. It was popular in France from the late 15th century. As well as being mentioned in an Avignon contract of 1503, the instrument is also included in the household accounts of the Countess of Angoulême in the mid 1490s. Although early instruments were built of thin cypress wood, without a lid, by the 18th century the cases were being made of thicker wood, such as Brazil or pine, and were complete with lids. Smaller spinets, termed "spinettinos", were also made.

The spinet was not introduced into England until Charles II's return from France at the Restoration in 1660. It soon proved very popular, and by the

LEFT: A typical early English example of a bentside spinet built in London in about 1770. This compact harpsichord, whose keyboard occupies much of the case, is made of walnut, with Italian-style interior trim in cypress.

end of the century an English school of spinet-building had developed, and the instrument was beginning to replace the virginal. Most English spinets had a compass starting with G, whereas continental spinets tended to begin on F.

For those who could not afford a harpsichord or did not have room for one, the spinet was the next best thing. It flourished longer in England than anywhere else, only disappearing when it was replaced by the square piano in the early 19th century.

Shape

The spinet's single set of strings is arranged across the instrument (in

Key features

TYPE: keyboard

PITCH: concert

RANGE: *c'* to *c''''*

ABOVE: This finely decorated 16th-century polygonal spinet was built by the Italian maker Annibale dei Rossi. He and his son Ferrante were recorded in 1595 as improvers and modernizers of clavichords.

contrast to the harpsichord where the strings are set at right angles to the keyboard). The oblique stringing of the early models produced a trapezoid shape, while the characteristic Italian spinet of the 16th and 17th centuries was five or six-sided, with a keyboard projecting from the long side.

Small spinets of the Italian pattern were most popular in France in the 16th and 17th centuries. These were usually about 80cm/32in (tuned to an octave above concert pitch) or 102cm/40in long (tuned to a fourth above concert pitch).

In Germany there were rare cases of wing-shaped spinets being made with two manuals for use by organists and teachers.

In 1631 Girolamo Zenti invented the bentside or "leg of mutton" spinet, a development that achieved great popularity in England. So named because of its wing shape, it was made in the shape of a triangle with unequal sides, with the keyboard set into one of the shorter sides. It was a conveniently compact shape, being both shorter and narrower than a harpsichord of equal range.

ABOVE: An engraving entitled Dame am Spinett *by Johann Sartorius.*

Double-strung spinet

As a rule the spinet was not capable of changes of tone-colour or volume. An attempt to rectify this was the double-strung spinet. Examples of this rare type are the two-manual octave spinet built by Israel Gellinger, and Cristofori's *"cembelo traverso"*. Variations were obtained in these instruments by moving the keyboard in or out, so that both or only one set of jacks would be lifted when the keys were depressed.

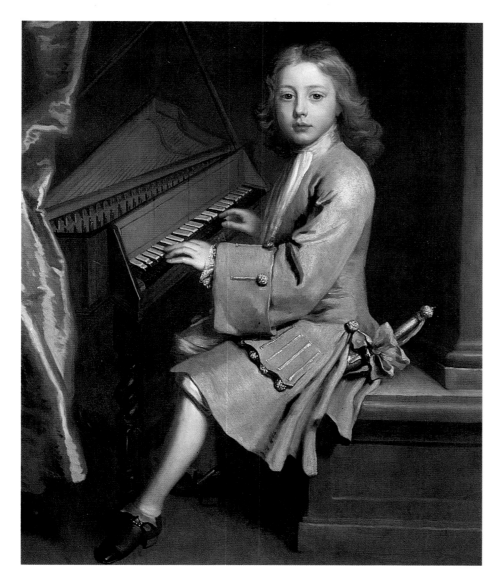

ABOVE: An 18th-century painting of a young man playing the spinet by Jonathan Richardson (1665–1745). Like the harpsichord, the "natural" keys of the spinet are black and the "accidentals" are white.

ABOVE: This spinet was made by one of the main English keyboard makers of the 18th century, Thomas Hitchcock of London.

Piano

The pianoforte is the most perfect of all musical instruments: its invention
was to music what the invention of printing was to poetry.

GEORGE BERNARD SHAW (1856–1950)

The months of May and June 1768 saw the turning point in the history of the piano. On May 19, Henry Walsh gave the world's first public performace for solo piano in Dublin; two weeks later, on June 2, at the Thatched House, St James's Square, London, Johann Christian Bach (1735–82) – J. S. Bach's youngest son – performed on a square piano. These were not the first occasions that the instrument had been heard in public, for a year earlier Charles Dibdin had used a piano to accompany a song sung during the interval of a production of *The Beggar's Opera* at Covent Garden. However, the kudos given to the piano by Bach's recital made the instrument fashionable overnight.

Bartolomeo Cristofori

The pianoforte was invented around 1709 by Bartolomeo Cristofori (1655–1731), a harpsichord builder and keeper of the royal musical instruments in Florence. The early Cristofori pianos, which looked and sounded like contemporary harpsichords, had a range of four octaves, half that of a modern grand. Indeed the very name, *gravicembalo col piano e forte*, implied that it was considered merely as another type of harpsichord, there being no real desire at the time to create an entirely new instrument. Surviving Cristofori pianos, with their thin strings and

LEFT: An ornate 19th-century grand piano built by Joseph Schneider.

hard hammers, do in fact sound very like harpsichords.

The main difference between the piano and the harpsichord was that the strings of the former were struck

ABOVE: This sturdy grand piano was presented to Ludwig van Beethoven by the London firm of John Broadwood & Sons in 1817.

by hammers rather than being plucked by quills, as in the harpsichord. When the piano key was pressed, the hammer struck the string and immediately came away, allowing the string to vibrate and sound until the key was released, activating a damper to silence it. The earliest music published specifically for the piano was a sonata composed by Lodovico Giustini in 1732, the year after Cristofori's death.

Square piano

Actually an oblong shape similar to the clavichord, the square piano was first made in 1742 by Johann Sacher, a Bavarian instrument maker. Although these instruments took up less space and were cheaper to produce than grand pianos, the main problem was that the bass strings had to be short and were therefore weak in tone as well as volume.

In Britain, square pianos were made by Johannes Zumpe from 1760, and it was one of his instruments on which J. C. Bach gave his London recital. An early French builder of square pianos was Sébastien Erard (1752–1831) who introduced various improvements to the Zumpe design including the *agraffe* in 1808, a device that improved the tension of the strings, and, in 1821, the double escapement action that

ABOVE: *Franz Liszt playing a piano built by Ludwig Bösendorfer.*

ABOVE: *This 1726 Cristofori piano represents the climax of the Italian's work. It is double-strung and has a four-octave compass as well as a synchronized damper.*

ABOVE: *This square piano built by Adam Beyer of London in 1777 is decorated with two sorts of mahogany.*

increased the speed at which notes could be repeated.

Although upright pianos gradually became more popular in European homes during the 19th century, square pianos survived for many years, particularly in the United States, where they grew large and elaborate.

The piano in the home

By the end of the 18th century the piano had become more than just a fashionable toy, and was a living force

Frédéric Chopin

Without doubt one of the greatest composers for the piano who ever lived was Frédéric Chopin (1810–49), the son of a French father and a Polish mother, who moved to Paris in 1831. His music was a kaleidoscope of three distinct traditions: German classicism, Italian *bel canto* and Polish folk music, and he composed almost exclusively for the piano. No other composer has enjoyed such lasting and continuous popularity with so many people, and his music is still found on almost every piano in the world. Chopin can truly be said to have dipped his pen in moonbeams and flooded the world with melodies.

in culture and entertainment in the homes of the wealthy. As a sign of the piano's increased popularity as a domestic instrument, in 1797 James Harrison launched his *Piano-Forte Magazine*. Each issue included a note, signed by Harrison, promising a new piano to any reader who purchased the entire 250 numbers and could produce the signed certificates that were included in each issue.

ABOVE: *The First Piano Lesson by Jules Alexis Meunier (1863–1942) depicts an early 19th-century young lady receiving piano tuition from her teacher.*

Upright piano

Larger than harpsichords, early horizontally strung pianos took up a lot of floor space, and to address this problem Domenico del Mela of Gagliano built the first vertical piano in 1739. The piano was simply turned upright on a stand, with the strings and soundboard towering above the keyboard. About 1800 it was realized that the soundboard could be dropped towards the floor, placing most of the string length behind the keyboard in front of the player's knees, thereby decreasing the overall height of the instrument. The strings were tuned at the top and the hammers arranged to strike from the front. In 1811 the "cottage" piano appeared in London. It was just over 1m/3ft tall, with diagonally arranged strings.

In the 1830s the problem of the short bass strings was solved with the invention of the overstrung piano, in which the shorter strings ran vertically and the bass strings crossed obliquely over them allowing for greater length. This method of stringing soon became the norm for all pianos and is the method still used today.

ABOVE: Der Appollosaal, Berlin, is one of the centres in the reinstated German capital where piano recitals are given on a fairly regular basis.

Sound

As the 19th century dawned, there were two distinct piano sounds. There was the light action and sensuous tone of German and Austrian instruments, on which musicians such as Mozart had performed, and there was the firmer action and stronger tone of English instruments, particularly those made by John Broadwood. It was one of the latter that Beethoven used, for as his deafness increased he could no longer hear what he was playing on a Viennese instrument.

Pedals

In 1759 Weltmann in France had invented a piano-harpsichord combination with knee levers that were used to effect registration, but pedals were introduced by John

ABOVE: Upright pianos have two pedals. The left one is the "soft" pedal and the right the "sustaining" pedal.

Broadwood, the pre-eminent British maker, in 1783. There were usually two pedals to operate two stops, *forte* and *una corda*, but many experiments were made with other devices to modify the tone. Some pianos had as many as four extra pedals. The *forte* or sustaining pedal lifted the dampers so that the sound was sustained after the key had fallen back, while the *una corda* or "soft" pedal shifted the action sideways so that the hammers struck only one string for each note. One special stop created a bassoon effect

LEFT: This small upright piano was built by the renowned firm of Clementi of London in 1825. The instrument is veneered in rosewood with pleated silk panels in the front.

with a strip of parchment passed through the strings, and in deference to the craze for "Turkish music" some pianos were built with small drums, bells, cymbals and triangles inside the case, all controlled by pedals.

Strings

The instrument on which J. C. Bach had played in 1768 sounded very different from a modern piano. Beethoven and Mozart would not recognize their music now, as the "modern" piano sound did not begin to appear until about 1850. The strings of early 19th-century pianos were still quite light and thin and at much lower tension than today's models, in which the strings are so rigid and tense that they behave more like bars. This thinness gave the instruments more harmonic overtones than a modern piano, a characteristic that gives early pianos an "out-of-tune" tone quality, reminiscent of ragtime pianos of the 1920s. To increase the volume of sound, makers increased the thickness of the strings. This meant that the tension also had to be increased to maintain them at the same pitch.

ABOVE: *An inside view of a modern Steinway grand piano.*

ABOVE: *Instruments by Erard, one of the great makers of pianos (and harps) were used by players from Beethoven to Ravel. Built in 1866, this is an early example, veneered in costly Amboyna wood.*

ABOVE: *Piano fingering is very important, both to reach the notes and to interpret the music. There are nearly one hundred keys but only ten fingers to play them with.*

Frame

Added tension in the strings meant that the frame had to be reinforced. Although the first iron frame appeared as early as 1800, it was not until 1828 that Adolphus Babcock of Boston produced the first square piano with a full iron frame, cast in a single piece. The first iron frame for a grand piano was made in Boston in 1843 by Jonas Chickering. In the 1860s Steinway's cast iron frames were first seen in Europe, and almost all makers followed suit.

Unusual sounds

During the 20th century many new sounds and colours were brought out of the piano. Erik Satie (1866–1925) put sheets of paper between the strings for a performance of *La Piège de Meduse* in 1914. John Cage altered the tone of the piano by attaching objects such as paper, nails and milk bottles to the strings. One composer, David Bedford (born 1937), asked a performer to scream inside the piano to make the strings vibrate, while La Monte Young (born 1935), for reasons best known to himself, asked the pianist to bring a bale of hay and a bucket of water on to the stage for the piano to eat and drink.

ABOVE: *By the end of the 19th century there was a piano in almost every middle-class home. Singing around the piano was an enjoyable family activity.*

Organ

When the full Organ joins the tuneful Quire
Th' Immortal Pow'rs incline their Ear.

ALEXANDER POPE (1688–1744)

The organ is without doubt capable of producing the greatest effects, and is truly worthy of Mozart's praise as the king of instruments. Devised in Alexandria in the 3rd century BC, by the 2nd century AD the organ had become one of the main instruments of Rome and was heard in almost all aspects of Roman entertainment, including the theatre, games, gladiatorial contests, circus and banquets. Even Nero is believed to have played the organ.

Water organ

The direct ancestor of the modern pipe organ is the hydraulis, or water organ, believed to have been invented by Ctesibius, an Alexandrian engineer who is also credited with the invention of the water-pump, water-clock and water-powered artificial singing birds.

Although water was not the motive force in the hydraulis, it acted to maintain an even pressure of air, which was supplied by a hand-pump. The sound was produced through a set of bronze pipes, graded in length like the contemporary pan-pipes; indeed, the hydraulis was sometimes described as a *syrinx* played with the hands. Originally there was only one row of pipes, but by the 3rd century AD the instrument was being built with four, six or even eight ranks of pipes. It was said to be so loud that hydraulis players had to plug their ears. Ctesibius can truly be called the "Father of the Organ", for his basic conception of the provision

of a continuous wind supply to an array of tuned pipes controlled from a keyboard remains unchanged to this day.

The main drawback of the water organ was that it required precision engineering and needed constant

LEFT: This beautifully painted positive organ was built in about 1600.

maintenance, as it was prone to corrosion. By AD 200 the water tank had been eliminated in favour of a windbag inflated by bellows and compressed air.

Church organ

The European "organ revival" of the 10th century came about because the instrument was reintroduced from Byzantium. Between the 10th and 13th centuries the organ became almost exclusively a church instrument in western Europe. Organs were erected in places such as Cologne Cathedral (AD 950), where one was used "for purposes of teaching the

LEFT: A 4th-century illustration of a water organ, or hydraulis. The player stood at the keyboard while his assistant operated the long lever that worked the pump. Under the pipes was a keyboard that operated perforated sliders. When a key was pressed, a slider was pushed into position to release pressurized air from the wind canal and thereby sound the note. When the key was released, a spring pulled the slider back, shutting off the air supply and stopping the note.

science of music", and the Benedictine Abbey in Bagas, Spain (AD 972), where the instrument was placed near the entrance. At the consecration of the Bagas organ special mention was made of the fact that it could be "heard from afar", which has led to the theory that it was used for summoning the congregation, much like modern church bells. In England, an organ was built at Winchester in about AD 990.

By the 10th century, foot-operated bellows began to appear and the sliders, which all looked the same and therefore had the name of each note written on them, terminated in handles. For several centuries these relatively small organs constituted the typical church organ. By the 13th century all instruments other than organs were excluded from various churches in Spain, Italy and France. In the 15th century many new churches were built, most with an organ as part of the regular furniture.

ABOVE: *The beautiful and ornate organ in Roskilde cathedral, Denmark, was built in 1554. This is an organ of the type known as "swallow nests", because they were suspended against a church wall.*

ABOVE: *Grinling Gibbons decorated the interior of the church of St James, Piccadilly, in London in the 1680s. One example of his craftsmanship is the gilded organ case that is surmounted by musical angels.*

During the 13th century the sliders began to be replaced by keys. The early keyboards had wide keys that decreased in width from the wide bass keys to the narrower treble keys.

During the 14th century, with full chromaticism and larger compass, the keyboard began to take on its modern appearance, with the accidentals (the "black" notes) in an upper row.

In the 14th century the organ compass, which hitherto had not exceeded two octaves, increased until a chromatic compass of three octaves was achieved. By now, organs were becoming common and were no longer restricted to the major churches. By the end of the century some of the larger and more important churches, such as Meaux, Leyden and Westminster, had two organs: a great organ in the west end and a smaller positive organ in the choir.

Classical organ

Two manuals began to appear in the 14th century, enabling the same organist to control both the main organ and the small positive organ. This led to the rapid development of the organ and its performing potential, which ensured its pre-eminence in Europe until the mid 18th century.

A large organ may have thousands of pipes, divided into groups, or stops, each of which is brought into play by pulling out a knob on the console. Each pipe produces a characteristic sound, depending on its shape, whether it is made of wood, tin or an alloy, and whether it is a flue or reed-pipe. In early organs all the pipes were open flues but during the 16th century reed pipes, with resonators of brass or wood, came into use. Various types of reed are used to create distinctive sounds, some imitating orchestral instruments or the human voice.

ABOVE: Detail of the pipes of the English house organ pictured above right.

RIGHT: Built by John Byfield of London in 1766, this is an outstanding example of an almost unaltered English house organ, with original glass doors and superb limewood carvings. The case is solid mahogany.

A series of up to five five-octave manuals and a 32-note pedalboard control valves that release air from the wind-chest into the various sets of pipes. The sets and their relative manuals are usually known as the Choir, Great, Swell, Solo and Echo.

Noted organ builders

During the late Renaissance, organ-building reached new heights of refinement. Organs were sumptuously decorated with inlaid wood, ivory and gold. The organ in the palace of Frederiksborg in Denmark, built in 1612 by Esaias Compenius, has solid silver stops shaped like human faces.

In Britain the period of the Commonwealth (1642–60) saw the Puritans execute the "speedy demolition of all organs". At the Restoration an influx of Dutch and émigré English builders arrived. The most noteworthy was Father Bernard Schmidt (died 1708) who introduced the "echo" organ in 1684. It was Schmidt who built London's Temple Church organ (1682–84), an instrument that was regarded as "a luxury unique in England", as well as organs for Westminster Abbey and St Paul's Cathedral. John Snetzler arrived in Britain from Switzerland around 1740. His work includes the organ used in Dublin for the first performance of Handel's *Messiah* in 1742, and that for the Lutheran Savoy Chapel in London.

Gottfried Silbermann (1683–1753) was a friend of J. S. Bach. He was

influenced by Casparini, who had built organs in northern Italy, especially Venice, and he also trained in Paris. He built a total of 45 organs in Saxony, all carefully sited for the best acoustical effect, and they remain unsurpassed. Silbermann's organs have a distinctive silvery sound, praised by Mozart as "magnificent beyond measure".

Portative organ

Emerging in the 13th century, the small portative organ was used mainly for secular purposes but also found its way into religious processions, in which it was carried suspended from a strap around the neck. It was positioned at right angles to the body for playing, allowing the player to operate the bellows with the left hand and the keys with the right. Like many "folk" instruments of its time the portative organ was fitted with drones – two tall pipes (bourdons) at the treble end.

ABOVE: This marble relief depicts, among others, a putto playing a portative organ; the right hand plays the keys and the left hand operates the bellows.

Positive organ

By 1425 the positive organ was being used in churches that either could not afford a large fixed organ or needed an additional chamber-size organ for occasional use such as for a service in a side chapel. It was distinct from the portative organ in that it was "moveable" rather than portable. It usually had two rows of flue pipes, a single manual and no pedalboard. An assistant was needed to operate the bellows while it was played.

Fairground organ

Gavioli of Paris started building fairground organs around 1870 to imitate a military band. One of the largest ever built had 104 keys, with large figures on each end of the front operating a bass drum and a side drum. Made by Charles Marenghi of Paris, this monstrous construction was said to reproduce the sounds of over 1200 instruments and was illuminated by hundreds of varicoloured electric lamps.

Cinema organ

Organs built by the American Wurlitzer Company in the early 20th century were designed to replace a small orchestra and to provide the perfect accompaniment to silent films. Every possible percussion instrument was imitated, including drums, telephone bells, surf, horses' hooves and even police sirens. In the United States the cinema organ died out with the advent of sound films, but in Britain it was retained and used to give short recitals before the films began.

BELOW: An elaborate Dutch fairground organ, still a feature of many carnivals.

French organ

In the 19th century many old organs were enlarged and improved. In France, Aristide Cavaillé-Coll, who pioneered electrically powered pneumatic tracker action, created flexible and expressive organs that inspired French composers to write a flood of large-scale secular works for solo organ. The organ symphony originated with Charles Widor (1844–1937), professor of organ at the Paris Conservatoire and organist at Ste Sulpice (1869–1933). César Franck (1822–90) was another leading figure in the French organ world and Widor's predecessor at the Conservatoire. He was organist at Ste Clotilde (1859–90) and wrote several pieces for the instrument, including *Six Pièces* (1862), *Trois Pièces* (1878) and *Trois Chorales* (1896). Franck's style is easily recognizable through its harmonic idiom and method of construction.

ABOVE: A three-manual Wurlitzer cinema organ, looking like the deck of a jet aeroplane. The hands are kept busy with the stops and the feet have to master all the pedals.

Accordion

The accordion is an instrument with the sentiments of an assassin.

AMBROSE BIERCE (1842–1914)

The accordion is a hand-held free-reed aerophone, in which the sound is produced by tempered steel reeds that vibrate when air is forced through them by a set of bellows. On one side of the bellows there are rows of buttons or a keyboard on which the melody is played, while on the other side there are buttons for the bass notes and chords.

LEFT: The long rows of buttons for the right hand of the accordion produce the melody, and the buttons for the left hand play the bass notes and chords.

Early accordions

In 1821, Christian Buschmann (1805–64) of Berlin patented his *Handäoline*, an instrument that was worked by lever-like keys. Seven years later, Cyrillus Demian (1772–1847), a Viennese musician, brought out his *Akkordion* (German for "harmony"), which, although similar in principle to Buschmann's instrument, had accompanying chords. Made in rosewood with inlays of ivory and mother-of-pearl, the instrument was copied by various other musicians, who, not being able to use the copyrighted name, referred to their versions by the generic term *Handharmonikas*. One of the most important advances in the history of the accordion occurred in 1852 when Monsieur Busson of Paris introduced piano-type keys to the instrument.

Piano accordion

Although by the beginning of the 20th century the bass keyboard had been sufficiently developed to provide accompaniments in all keys, the piano accordion was still an instrument of the people, its use being restricted to popular and rural entertainment in cafés, dance halls and music halls. By 1931, however, the accordion was beginning to be taken seriously, for in that year a music school for accordionists was established in the German town of Trossingen, a location chosen for its vicinity to the famous Höhner accordion factory. The British College of Accordionists was founded in 1936.

ABOVE: The piano accordion has become a folk instrument in most of Europe. Sweden is no exception.

ABOVE: In 1852 Monsieur Busson of Paris introduced piano-type keys to the accordion. The advantage of the new instrument was that it could be played informally by ambulant performers. This diminutive instrument is one of Busson's first and does not have the chord and bass keys of the more developed types.

ABOVE: *A busker playing a piano accordion in Prague's Golden Lane.*

Modern accordion

Today's instruments have up to 140 basses actuated by seven rows of buttons and a keyboard compass ranging from two to four octaves. The usual 120-button Stradella fixed-bass keyboard, first developed by the Italian Mariano Dallape in 1876, consists of two rows of bass notes and four rows of chord buttons. Some models have a converter switch that enables chords to be played in any inversion. In Italy, a small variant of the accordion, the *organetto*, has almost replaced the *zampogna*, a type of bagpipe whose repertoire it shares.

Bandoneon

In Argentina, Uruguay and Brazil, South American tango bands often feature the bandoneon, a double-action square-shaped type of accordion. Invented in the 19th century by

ABOVE: *The double-action bandoneon is used in the tango bands of Latin America. This example was made by Wilhelm König in 1914.*

Accordion music

In 1948, when the Trossingen school became an official state academy, the first principal was Hugo Herrmann who, in 1927, had written *Sieben Neue Spielmusiker*, the first original composition for the solo accordion. Although the accordion is mainly played as a solo instrument or as part of the instrumental line-up in folk bands, many major composers have scored for it. These include Sergei Prokofiev (1891–1953) in *Cantata for the 20th Anniversary of the October Revolution* and Paul Dessau (1894–1979) in *Die Verurteilung des Lukullus*. Roberto Gerhard (1896–1970) also used the accordion in various works such as his Nonet and Concerto for Eight.

Heinrich Band of Krefeld, Germany, the early models had more than 88 notes. Today's instruments, however, are usually restricted to 71.

Concertina

Based on much the same principle as the accordion, the concertina, invented by Charles Whetstone (1802–72) in 1829, consists of two hexagonal casings, each containing a small button keyboard. The casings are connected by bellows that, when extended or contracted, cause a flow of air to activate the free reeds of the instrument when one of the keys is pressed.

There are two main types of concertina: the English, in which there

ABOVE: *The concertina is unusual in that it has 14 keys to the octave and is tuned to mean rather than equal temperament.*

is a uniform tone – the same note being sounded on both extension and contraction of the bellows – and the German, which sounds different notes on extension and compression.

Although it was played by people such as Giulio Regondi (1822–72), a guitarist and player of the *mélophone*, and Richard Blagrave (1826–95) whose playing was once described as a "first-rate workman on a miserable tool", the concertina was never a popular instrument and its use today is almost solely restricted to folk music, although composers such as Charles Ives (1874–1954) and Percy Grainger (1882–1961) did occasionally score for the instrument.

ABOVE: *South America has many accordion aficionados. This young man is playing at the Vallanato Festival in Colombia.*

Harmonium

It is astonishing what an effect the sound of some simple air played on an harmonium on a Sunday evening has on the loiterers in the streets.

MUSICAL OPINION, JUNE 1905

LEFT: Built by the leading firm of Alexandre of Paris in 1859, this harmonium was widely used both in homes and churches.

The harmonium, which resembles a small organ, was often used as a substitute for its big brother in small churches and chapels, as well as being popular as a household instrument. A distant relation of the mouth organ, it consists of a series of free reeds operated by a keyboard and activated by a wind supply from foot-operated compression bellows.

Early French harmonium

The harmonium evolved from Gabriel Grenié's *orgue expressif*, a free-reed keyboard instrument of about 1810. The register of Grenié's instrument was supplied by bellows worked by two pedals. The "expression" was a stop that enabled direct contact between the bellows and the wind-reservoir by means of the pedals, thereby permitting dynamic gradations for the first time in the history of the organ.

In 1834 an improved version by the eminent French organ builder Aristide Cavaillé-Coll was exhibited at the Paris exposition. Built in the form of a small, square piano, Cavaillé-Coll's instrument, which was called the *poïkilorgue*, had a range of one and a half octaves. In 1843 Grenié's pupil Théodore-Achille Muller patented a portable model that could be folded up into a rectangular box.

Although the French were the leaders in making and perfecting the harmonium, experiments were also being carried out in Bavaria. Here, in 1815, Bernhard Eschenbach devised a free-reed keyboard instrument that was capable of "expression", which he called an *Aoline*.

Improvements

The harmonium achieved its ultimate popularity in the form patented by the Parisian Alexandre-François Debain (1809–77) in 1842. Debain's harmonium incorporated a three-octave keyboard with sets of reeds of different thicknesses and widths. One of the new features was that each key controlled a valve that regulated the amount of wind produced by the compression bellows. This made possible, for the first time, the production of different tones. Further improvements, added by Debain in 1848, included the shifting keyboard, a device that permitted transposition by any interval, while playing the music as noted. In 1854 Victor Mustel added a divided expression stop worked by knee-levers.

Experimental harmoniums

Because of its ability to sustain a constant tone, the harmonium was well suited for acoustical experiments

ABOVE: The popularity of the harmonium in the 19th century was mainly due to its price. This New Cottage Harmonium cost seven guineas, a fraction of that of a piano.

and demonstrations of different tuning systems. The best known of these experimental harmoniums was that designed by Shohé Tanka and built by Johann Kewitsch of Berlin in 1889. Such was the accuracy of Tanka's instrument that it was tuned to pure intervals, with no less than 20 keys to the octave. This, however, was child's play compared with Banquet's experimental harmonium, which was constructed to produce 53 microtones to the octave.

India

The harmonium was introduced into India by missionaries around the mid 19th century to accompany hymn-singing. Since the 1920s small portable harmoniums have been made in India and Pakistan; Palitana in Gujarat is the centre of manufacture of the reeds. Harmoniums are very popular, and many homes have one. They are widely used to accompany devotional music, to the dismay of aficionados of traditional Indian music, as their

fixed pitch is at odds with the flexible intonation of Indian vocal and instrumental music They have also led to the demise of indigenous instruments such as the *bajona sruti*, or Indian bagpipe.

As is common with Indian musicians, the harmonium player sits on the floor, playing the keyboard with one hand and operating the bellows with the other. Harmoniums are, however, now giving way in their turn to the ubiquitous electronic keyboard.

Indian harmoniums

LEFT, BELOW AND RIGHT: Small portable harmoniums have been very popular in India, with many homes owning one. The musician usually sits on the floor, playing the keyboard with one hand and operating the bellows with the other.

Mechanical Instruments

*A good melody is such a one as would grind
about the streets upon the organ.*

THOMAS ARNE (1710–78)

In the years before recording and broadcasting, instruments that played pre-set tunes became popular. When no musician was available, turning a handle could provide music, whether at home, for street entertainment, dancing, or for church services.

Barrel organ

The barrel organ made its appearance in Italy in the early 1700s. One of the first makers of the instrument was Giovanni Barbieri of Modena; his name was perpetuated by the French, who called the Italian's invention *orgue de Barbarie*. However, by 1774 many had obviously forgotten the Italian's pioneer work, for in that year an advertisement appeared offering for sale *"Un veritable orgue de barbarie fait par les sauvages."*

These early constructions were small enough to rest on the player's left hip

LEFT: This 19th-century English barrel organ has three barrels. Two play dance music and popular songs, while the third provides hymn tunes.

while the right hand turned the handle. The barrel organ's mechanism consisted of two or more ranks of organ pipes placed above a set of bellows in an enclosed cabinet, while the music was supplied by a pinned cylinder or barrel that was mounted on a metal spindle. Each pin raised a trigger-shaped key that opened a pallet, allowing wind to enter the required pipe. Each tune required one complete rotation of the barrel.

In the 19th century, with the demand for longer and more complicated music, barrel organs became larger and larger. In 1887 Michael Welte patented an instrument in which the barrels were pegged spirally and rotated 12 times during one piece of music, making it possible for quite long compositions to be played.

Street organ

In the early 19th century an Italian named Gavioli, who was established in Paris, started making portable organs in which the barrel was replaced by perforated cardboard strips, concertina-folded and based on the

THE STREET ORGAN.

LEFT: The organ grinder was once a familiar sight in the streets of most European towns, surrounded by children. The music made a welcome break in an otherwise monotonous day.

card patterns used by jacquard weavers. Gavioli's organs were often mounted on handcarts and wheeled about by "organ grinders", who were invariably accompanied by little monkeys. These organs were very successful and were seen on the streets of most European cities until well into the 20th century.

Church barrel organ

Until the introduction of the harmonium, many small churches and chapels used a "barrel and finger organ" as a substitute for a conventional organ. These were so-called because they had a conventional keyboard at the front and a barrel movement at the back. The barrels were pegged with hymns, chants, psalms and even voluntaries so that if no organist was available for a service, music could still be produced by turning the handle.

ABOVE: Early barrel pianos, operated by turning a handle, were quite small domestic instruments.

ABOVE: An orchestrion or "orchestral organ", showing the internal mechanisms, including the pipes and barrel.

Orchestrion

The main drawback of the barrel organ was its monotonous sound, and in an attempt to rectify this the orchestrion was invented. Intended for indoor use in wealthy households, the orchestrion was composed of ranks of organ pipes of differing timbres that were constructed to imitate the sounds of orchestral instruments. It was an elaborate assembly with refined cabinet work and had as many as eight ranks of pipes with a chromatic compass of over five octaves, plus percussion instruments such as cymbals, drums and triangles.

One of the first successful orchestrions was built in Holland in 1789. Said to be capable of imitating a whole orchestra, it was encased in a 3m/10ft cube and was complete with four manuals and a pedalboard for obtaining *crescendos* and *diminuendos*. The componium, a Dutch invention of 1821, could compose variations on a theme, using two movable barrels.

Apollonicon

In 1817, Flight & Robson of London exhibited their massive apollonicon, which had been constructed the previous year. No less than 7.2m/24ft in height and 6m/20ft wide and deep, it had nearly 2000 pipes, disposed in 46 registers. It had five manuals that could be played either mechanically or, when detached from the main body, manually by five performers, all facing the public. It was displayed and operated in the window of the company's London showroom for some years, but was not a financial success and was dismantled in 1840.

Music box

Small musical movements were first made in the late 18th century for snuff boxes. By the 1830s the music box was established in its standard form, with tuning combs that had as many as 250 teeth covering a range of about six octaves. Many of these boxes were finely decorated and embellished with marquetry and mother-of-pearl. The early combs were fitted to cylinders, but by the 1890s disc-operated boxes were appearing, with discs up to 85cm/34in in diameter. They were eclipsed by the arrival of the gramophone.

ABOVE: This internal view of a music box built in the last year of the 19th century in Sainte-Croix, Switzerland, shows the steel comb whose tuned tongues are plucked by pins on the clockwork-driven cylinder, as well as the bells and drum.

Electronic Keyboards and Computers

The synthesizer is no more inhuman than the piano.

MILTON BABBITT (BORN 1916)

LEFT: The electronic keyboard has become one of the most important instruments in many small bands. The sound of almost every instrument of the orchestra — and other sounds — can be achieved.

One of the first electronic instruments was Thaddeus Cahill's keyboard-operated "dynamophone" or "telharmonium", the first full-size version of which was completed in 1906. It supplied current to telephone receivers fitted with cardboard horns, and was used for daily concerts. Although the aim of the instrument was "to generate music electrically with tones of good quality", Cahill's pioneer work was too far ahead of its time and his invention was eventually sold for scrap, but his ideas were the basis of later developments during the 1920s and '30s.

Theremin

The Russian scientist Lev Theremin invented the theremin in 1924. Its signals were produced by oscillators, and were modified by the position of the player's hands. Volume was controlled by the proximity of one hand to a metal loop, and pitch by moving the other hand towards or away from an antenna protruding vertically out of the instrument. Although some musicians were able to demonstrate its vocal qualities, it was very difficult to play and as such did not become widely used. The radical composer Edgar Varèse (1885–1965) used two theremins in *Ecuatorial* (1934) but later replaced them with the more reliable *ondes Martenot*.

Ondes Martenot

The *ondes Martenot*, invented by the French musician and engineer Maurice Martenot (1896–1980), was produced in 1928. Although its oscillating valves are similar to those of the theremin, it is very much easier to control the pitch produced, as the player is guided by a five-octave keyboard. A substantial number of works have been written for it, and it produces haunting sounds.

Hammond organ

The American Laurens Hammond invented the Hammond organ in 1935, with the intention of replacing the pipe organ for both church and domestic use. Like the conventional organ, it has two small manuals and a pedalboard, but produces sounds electronically. This versatile organ became very popular in the 1960s,

RIGHT: The eponymous Hammond organ, with its ability to produce (albeit limited) special effects, was a forerunner of the modern electronic keyboard.

especially with rock musicians. Special stops and tabs control the manuals and produce effects such as "wah-wahs", *glissandos* and arpeggios.

Synthesizer

The first synthesizer of major importance was the RCA Mark II, which was acquired in 1959 by the Columbia-Princeton Electronic Music Center in New York. It had been developed at the Sarnoff Research Center, New Jersey, from the Mark I of 1955 by Harry Olsen and Herbert

ABOVE: Composing music has come a long way from the quill pen of Purcell to the MIDI keyboard and computer of the modern composer.

ABOVE: A mixing desk is standard equipment in the modern recording studio.

Belar. Using transistors instead of valves, it was much smaller than the Mark I, a colossal machine that almost filled a room with controls for the multitude of oscillators, mixers, filters and amplifier.

Since 1966 much smaller synthesizers have been made available commercially, including the Moog Sonic Six and the Buchla. Originally developed for producing tapes for recordings, by the mid 1960s synthesizers had reached the concert platform as chordal instruments for live performances, and were especially popular with rock bands.

Although the synthesizer keyboard looks like that of a piano, it behaves in a different way: it controls not only the pitch of a note (which may not be the same as that on a piano), but also its length. Some keyboards are touch-sensitive so that, depending on the way the keys are depressed or released, different functions may be performed.

Some modern synthesizers, such as the Kawai CP150, have dummy keyboards to give the performer the feeling of playing a "real" piano. The

Kawai CP150 has a unique weighted action with wooden keys that simulate a hammer action by using a dummy hammer within the mechanism. The effect is so natural that in time the action beds down and settles in, just like a real piano keyboard.

Digital revolution

Today almost every recording studio has an abundance of computer-related equipment. The music is digitally saved on to a hard disk and then edited on a mixing desk using sophisticated

ABOVE: This mixing desk, a Virtua Digital Console, has eliminated the need for long rows of buttons and dials.

software before the final version is mastered on to digital audio tape. This Musical Instrument Digital Interface (MIDI) deals with all aspects of the performance, including pitch, velocity and duration. As well as the MIDI keyboard, there are conventional MIDI instruments that connect electronically with the mixing desk. Even acoustic instruments can have tiny microphones attached to convert analogue pitch into digital information. Such is modern technology that it is almost possible to play a flute concerto on a kazoo.

ABOVE: The computer combines all the functions of a mixing desk and multi-track tape machine to create a "virtual studio".

The Voice

The Human Instrument

Song is man's sweetest joy.

ARISTOTLE (384–322 BC)

The fundamental musical instrument is the human voice. Singing is the most natural and spontaneous mode of musical expression, and since it is almost always linked to a text it can unambiguously express thought as well as emotion. As the singer is his or her own instrument, the voice is never altogether distanced from the personality. However, a good voice does not make a singer unless it is combined with accurate rhythm, good sense of pitch and enunciation. As in other instruments, the sound of the voice is the result of amplified vibrations. The vibrations of the

ABOVE: Boys' choirs have been a feature of Christian ritual for a thousand years. As women were banned from taking part in the service, when polytonal music developed it was the youthful soprano voices that sang the top line of the music, while men sang the alto and baritone lines.

vocal cords resonate in the cavities of both the chest (in the lower register) and the head (in the upper register). The singer automatically adjusts the shapes and sizes of these cavities to produce the required notes.

Vocal ranges

When men and women sing together, men usually sing an octave lower: the normal range of women's voices is in the treble clef, and the men's is in the bass clef. Each voice has its own natural range of pitch. The highest woman's voice is the soprano, and the lowest the contralto, or alto, with the mezzo-soprano lying between the two extremes. These pitches are also within the range of boys' voices (known as trebles).

The lowest male voice is the bass and the highest is usually the tenor, with the baritone between them. Some male singers have a natural extension at the top of their range which allows them to sing in the alto, or countertenor, range.

Madrigals

The early church forbade women to participate in services, so treble parts were sung by boys and countertenors.

ABOVE: Diana Ross was a founder member of the Supremes, one of the singing groups that emerged from Detroit in the 1960s.

Until the 15th century most music was written for high voices, but with the expansion of polyphony, songs began to feature two parts below the tenor and the qualities of the bass voice became better appreciated.

By the 16th century all secular music used vocal ranges that were comfortable for male voices, with countertenor parts never going above *d"*. When women joined singing groups, madrigals with parts as high as *g"* appeared. Madrigal singers and composers became increasingly interested in secular music and the ornamentation – forbidden in church music – that could be added to it.

Opera

The birth of opera between 1575 and 1625 resulted in an entirely new kind of singer. The madrigal singer had a relatively limited range, rarely exceeding an octave and a half. Opera singers began to extend their range, both up and down, to accommodate the composers who were experimenting in new forms of vocal music, just as instrument makers were experimenting in the construction of musical instruments.

Voice production

Singing styles and techniques before the advent of sound recordings are even harder to study than instrumental playing styles, as once the singer has died their voice is forever lost. There is no surviving instrument to help with research into the lost sound.

Although styles of singing changed, the Italian method of voice production, known as *bel canto* ("beautiful singing"), remained the same from the time of Monteverdi to that of Rossini. The main characteristic of *bel canto* voice production is the forward-placing of the voice, with a concentration of resonance in the nasal cavities to give a light, florid effect.

ABOVE: The music of a cathedral choir is a joy to hear in a candlelight setting.

ABOVE: The British mezzo-soprano Anne Murray (born 1949) was especially praised for her Covent Garden performance of the title role in Handel's Xerxes *in 1985.*

In the 20th century there were two main developments in singing. One is the *verismo*, or realistic style, as perfected by Enrico Caruso (1872–1921). Operatic composers around 1900 – particularly Italians such as Pietro Mascagni (1863–1945) and Giacomo Puccini (1858–1924) – began to write operas with more contemporary, realistic plots, for which the artifice of the traditional *bel canto* vocal style was unsuitable.

The second development was due to the invention of electronic amplification. Until the 1920s there was little difference between classical and popular singing. However, as popular singers began to use microphones, new singing styles developed. There was now no need to project the voice as before. Because it was easier for sound engineers to amplify a soft voice, early radio performers who sang with light, intimate voices were preferred.

ABOVE: The London Philharmonic Choir in rehearsal.

Choirs

Let the pealing organ blow To the full-voiced quire below
In service high and anthems clear.

JOHN MILTON (1608–74)

Organized choral singing has been known for at least 3000 years, since it is mentioned in Homer's *Iliad*, composed in about 850 BC. The ancient Greek chorus, from which choirs derive, included dancers as well as singers, and participated as a group in religious festivals. Some of these groups were very large, and could comprise up to 600 people. In Greek drama, the chorus provided a moral commentary on the action. Tragedies had a chorus of between 12 and 15 people, while comedies had from 24–50.

Polyphony

Choral music, in the form of plainsong, was an essential component of services in the early church. Early medieval choirs were small: they usually consisted of from four to eight boys and from 10 to 18 men, women being absolutely excluded from church services. One of the largest choirs of the 12th and 13th centuries was that of Notre Dame in Paris, which consisted of almost 30 singers.

As polyphonic composition gradually replaced unharmonized chant, the range of voices widened. The earliest surviving mass, by Guillaume de Machaut (c.1300–77) is written in four parts. Antiphonal music, which was developed at St Mark's in Venice by Andrea and Giovanni Gabrieli, involved a solo voice and a choir, or two or more contrasting choirs, who sang verses and responses from different parts of the church. The increasing richness and complexity

ABOVE: A 14th-century French church choir. These singers are sharing a single manuscript copy of their text and musical line.

Vienna Boys Choir

The Hofmusikkapelle, which evolved into the world-famous Wiener Sängerknaben (the Vienna Boys Choir), was founded in 1498 by the Holy Roman Emperor Maximilian I. Its original purpose was to provide musical training for the choir of the Hofburg in Vienna. Now, however, it is a private boarding school. The 150 boys are divided into four choirs, each of which tours Europe and the United States for three months of the year.

ABOVE: The world-famous Vienna Boys Choir.

ABOVE: To say that the Welsh love singing is like saying that fish like swimming. Almost every village has its own choir, an institution that binds the communities together.

century, choral singing has been an important focal activity of the *eisteddfod* since it was first introduced in 1825. For many years virtually the only songs the singers knew were hymns, but by the second half of the 19th century cantatas, oratorios and works by contemporary Welsh composers such as Joseph Parry (1841–1903) and David Jenkins (1849–1915) were added to the repertoire.

During the 20th century many outstanding choirs were formed, and choral festivals have included Harlech (1867–1934), Cardiff (1892–1910) and the Three Valleys Festival (1930–39). Since 1947 choral singers from all over the world have flocked to Llangollen for the annual International Eisteddfod.

ABOVE: A girls' choir performing at a concert.

of polyphony culminated in works by the Roman school, led by Giovanni Perluigi da Palestrina (1525–94).

Church choir

The sung mass became one of the most important forms of church music. Composers of all periods have written settings of it, and choral singing has a central role in almost every religious service. Renaissance choirs sang in a minimum of four parts, often six, eight or more. The choirs grew larger, and were accompanied by instrumental groups. After the Reformation, Protestant choirs were modelled on the Catholic pattern, and women therefore continued to be excluded, preserving the tradition of using boys' voices. This tradition is only gradually being challenged.

Choral societies

The overwhelming popularity of Handel's oratorios in late 18th-century Britain – especially *The Messiah* (1742) – led to the formation of new choral societies, which did include women, in almost every town. At first only religious music was sung, including, as well as Handel, Haydn's *Creation* (1799) and later Mendelssohn's *Elijah* (1846), but secular music eventually crept in, such as the popular songs of Gilbert and Sullivan's Savoy Operas.

Choral singing reached extraordinarily high standards in Germany, where choral societies grew up in the industrial towns, a movement that was fostered by numerous choral festivals, such as those held at Frankenhausen, Mannheim, Magdeburg and Halle. Excellent folk choirs still flourish today.

Male voice choir

One country synonymous with choral singing is Wales. Growing up with the enormous rise in the urban population in the early 19th

ABOVE: The choir of St John's College Chapel, Cambridge.

Soloists

Let but thy voice engender with the string
And angels will be born, while thou doest sing.

ROBERT HERRICK (1591–1674)

The earliest solo singers were poet-composers who sang their own songs, and few singers were famous as soloists before the mid 16th century. However, they acquired greater importance as secular music became more highly ornamented. At the same time, women began to perform as singers, and a preference for the soprano voice was established. The birth of opera, which drew its earliest performers from the ranks of popular court singers of madrigals, eventually led to the rise of the professional opera star. Although many singers restrict their singing to one medium, such as opera or recital work, some have made a name for themselves in both.

ABOVE: Adelina Patti was famous for her wealth and for never attending rehearsals, but was a great actress.

ABOVE: Jenny Lind, "The Swedish Nightingale", was the pop idol of the mid 19th century. She was in such demand that tickets for her concerts were usually sold out within hours of being put on sale.

Male voices

One of the best examples of operatic singers "going solo" is the outstanding success of Luciano Pavarotti (born 1935), José Carreras (born 1946) and Plácido Domingo (born 1941) – three men whose successes in opera have been equalled if not excelled by their appearance as "The Three Tenors" at concerts held in conjunction with the three football World Cup finals in Italy (1990), the United States (1994) and France (1998).

Without doubt the most popular tenor of his generation, Pavarotti, with his trademark white handkerchief in his left hand, has brought operatic arias to enormous audiences. His recording of *Nessun dorma*, an aria from Puccini's *Turandot* that was used as the theme song of Italia '90, hit the pop charts worldwide. Many people who had hitherto felt alienated from opera realized the beauties of the music they had so long resisted.

Some classically trained male singers have deliberately pursued a solo career rather than performing in opera. These include the Austrian Richard Tauber (1892–1948), the Irish singer Josef Locke (1917–99) and the German Ivan Rebroff, whose fantastic voice ranges from the ultra bass, which must be one of the deepest known, to a high falsetto.

Female voices

One of the most popular singers of the 19th century was Jenny Lind (1820–87), known as the "Swedish Nightingale", whose appearances often caused more excitement than a royal visit. On more than one occasion when Lind was singing in London the House of Commons was unable to continue business as there were not enough MPs present to constitute a quorum – they were all at her concert. Her singing was so pure that her audiences could hardly believe that such powers existed in the human voice. She was married to the conductor Otto Goldschmidt, who often accompanied her on the

piano. Another factor that endeared her to the public was her custom of donating part of her salary to a charitable institution in whichever town she performed.

Another 19th-century diva was the *coloratura* soprano Adelina Patti (1843–1919), who began her career as a child prodigy in the United States. Hearing her voice so affected Rossini that he rewrote the role of Rosina in *The Barber of Seville* for her. He once said to her: "Madam, I have cried twice in my life. Once when I dropped a wing of chicken into Lake Como, and once when for the first time I heard you sing."

Joan Sutherland (born 1926) is arguably the 20th century's finest *coloratura* soprano, and made many of the great roles of Delibes, Massenet, Rossini, Donizetti and Bellini her own. She conquered the world in 1959 with

her performance in Donizetti's *Lucia di Lammermoor*, her rich and agile voice making her one of the most popular singers of the time. She gave her

farewell performance on New Year's Eve 1990, in a guest appearance with the American mezzo-soprano Marilyn Horne and Luciano Pavarotti in the Covent Garden production of Johann Strauss's operetta *Die Fledermaus*.

Kiri Te Kanawa (born 1944) had begun her recording career by the time she was 20. One of the most famous sopranos of modern times, she made her debut as the Countess in *Le nozze di Figaro* at Covent Garden in 1971.

ABOVE: One of the most remarkable "discoveries" of the 1990s was "The Three Tenors". The trio of Plácido Domingo, José Carreras and Luciano Pavarotti brought opera to enormous audiences worldwide, especially at the three football World Cup finals in Italy (1990), the United States (1994) and France (1998).

ABOVE: Kiri Te Kanawa has become one of the most famous sopranos in the world. She is seen here giving one of her popular solo concerts.

Other Voices

God giveth speech to all, song to the few.

Walter Chalmers Smith

Many composers, particularly in modern times, have sought to use the voice as an instrument in new and unusual ways, whether by extending its range outside the normal compass or by incorporating vocal sounds other than singing into their music. The style called *Sprechgesang* that Schoenberg used in *Pierrot Lunaire* (1912) falls between singing and speaking. Humming is a device that is often used in choral works, and sometimes in solos: Villa-Lobos's *Bachianas Brasileiras No. 5* uses a solo soprano voice humming a soaring tune, accompanied by cellos. Speech and shouting add new colours to choral writing, and the use of the microphone has opened up many new possibilities for vocal effects, in rock and pop as well as serious music.

ABOVE: *The castrato Carlo Broschi Farinelli (1705–82) sang all over Europe, including a three-year stay in London.*

Castrati

The castrato, whose voice was prevented from breaking by castration in childhood, first appeared in church choirs to sing the high parts that women, who were banned from the church, supplied in secular music. In the late 16th and early 17th century castrati found a role in the new medium of opera, and opera composers began to write special parts for them.

Some castrati achieved great wealth. One of the most famous of the 18th century was the Italian Carlo Broschi Farinelli, whose voice, it was claimed, was able to reach and sustain seven or eight notes above any other singer of the period. Farinelli's artistry was such that when King Philip V of Spain heard him he was so impressed that he commissioned the Italian to sing him four arias a night for the rest of his life. When Philip died, his successor Ferdinand VI awarded Farinelli the rank of prince and a generous pension.

The barbaric practice of castration for artistic purposes eventually died out, and castrati were banned from the papal chapel in 1903. The last castrato, Alessandro Moreschi, who had been musical director of the Sistine Chapel, died in 1922, aged 66.

Jazz singing

An oratorical style of singing that exploits the contours and cadences of speech, jazz singing is concerned with emphasizing the text rather than the tone. Because jazz singers usually follow the dynamics of speech rather than of the melody, their voices tend to be low-pitched; soprano jazz singers are very rare.

In some jazz styles the interest lies in musical effect rather than emotional content, a prime example being scat singing. This is a wordless performance, usually improvised, that uses the voice like an instrument. Although many jazz singers include scat singing in their acts, not many are capable of keeping it up for more than 32 bars. Louis Armstrong's solos in the 1920s and '30s began a vogue for the style.

ABOVE: *Jazz singing has arisen from the traditions of blues singing and popular songs. It usually involves improvisation to fit the lyrics to the music.*

LEFT: *The musical is the modern-day version of operetta. The Phantom of the Opera (music by Andrew Lloyd Webber, lyrics by Charles Hart) is one of the most successful ever staged. Sarah Brightman and Michael Crawford performed with the original cast.*

Human voice orchestra

In the 19th century there were various choral groups that sang not words but sounds. One such was Hoffmann's Organophonic Band or "human voice orchestra". Wearing military uniform, the 12 members, who imitated by voice alone a complete orchestra of instruments, were popular over most of Europe. This type of wordless singing was revived in the 1960s by the Swingle Singers.

Yodelling

Yodelling is the sudden change from chest voice to falsetto head voice and back again in rapid alternation. It originated in the Swiss mountains where it was, and still is, intended to be a joyful sound. In the 1930s yodelling entered American blues music where, instead of being a happy sound, it was turned into a lonesome and sad expression, first typified by Jimmy Rodgers and copied by many others since.

ABOVE: *The French-Canadian singer Celine Dion (born 1967) made the transition from child star to French-language chanteuse to an internationally acclaimed ballad singer.*

RIGHT: *A Tyrolean yodelling party in national costume.*

Glossary

Acoustics: the science of sound.

Aerophone: a wind instrument, such as a flute or trombone.

Air: a simple tune for instrument or voice.

Aleatoric music: music in which chance elements can determine the piece.

Aria: an operatic solo.

Atonal: having no definite key centre or tonality.

Ballad: a narrative song.

Baroque: the musical period from about 1600–1750. From the Portuguese *barrôco*, meaning "irregular pearl".

Basso continuo: an accompanying bass line written in "shorthand".

Bell: the flared or bulbous end of many aerophones.

Belly: the soundboard of a chordophone.

Blues: a slow, sad musical idiom characterized by the fusion of African and European music.

Body: the soundbox or resonator of a chordophone.

Bridge: a wooden member that is either set loosely or glued to the belly of some chordophones to hold the strings away from the soundboard.

Capo tasto: a movable device tied or clipped to the fingerboard of some chordophones to assist in transposition.

Chanter: the melody pipe of a set of bagpipes.

Chanterelle: the melody string of some members of the lute family of instruments.

Chord: the effect that is produced by sounding two or more notes together.

Chordophone: an instrument with strings, such as the harp and guitar.

Chromatic scale: the European 12-note scale of semitones.

Coll'arco: direction to play strings with the bow.

Compass: the range of a voice or instrument.

Concert pitch: the standard of pitch to which instruments are usually tuned. At present the A above middle C (*a'*) is set at 440 Hertz.

Concerto: a composition for one or more solo instruments and orchestra.

Consort: a group of instruments of the same family.

Coquille: the hole through a valve that allows the passage of air from one side to the other.

Counterpoint: the weaving of two or more melodic lines together so that they harmonize with each other.

Course: two or three strings lying close together, sounded together and tuned to either unison or octave pitch.

Crook: a detachable piece of tubing added to a brass instrument to alter its pitch.

Diatonic scale: any one of the major or minor scales of five tones and two semitones.

Drone: a pipe or string that sounds a sustained tone.

Dynamics: variations in loudness and softness.

Embouchure: in brass and some woodwind playing, the mode of application of the lips.

Equal temperament: a system of tuning by which the octave is divided into a chromatic scale of 12 equal semitones.

Fingerboard: the front of the neck where the strings are stopped by being pressed against the wood.

Fret: fixed or movable divisions of a fingerboard which indicate stopping points.

Frog: the part of the bow that tightens the hair.

Glissando: a slide up or down, played, for example, by sweeping the hand across harp strings or sliding the finger along a violin string.

Gregorian chant: solo and unison plainsong choral chants associated with Pope Gregory I.

Harmonics: the fundamental and overtones of a given tone.

Idiophone: an instrument made of naturally sonorous materials, not needing any additional tension as do strings and drumskins.

Jack: a thin strip of wood that carries the plectrum in plucked keyboard instruments.

Janissary music: a style of percussive military music, influenced by Turkish music, popular in 18th-century Europe.

Libretto: the text of an opera.

Madrigal: a polyphonic composition for voices.

Microtone: any interval smaller than a semitone.

Modulation: change of key.

Neumes: a system of musical notation dating from the 7th to the 14th centuries.

Oratorio: a setting of a religious text in dramatic form for solo voices, choir and band.

Ornamentation: the insertion of a note or notes additional to the main tune, for decoration.

Overblowing: the production of overtones on a wind instrument.

Pegs: tuning pins used on a stringed instrument.

Pitch: the "height" or "depth" of a note, determined by the frequency of vibrations producing it.

Pizzicato: direction to pluck strings with the fingers.

Plainsong: traditional ritual vocal melodies of the Western Christian church sung in free rhythm.

Plectrum: a device used for plucking strings.

Polyphony: music with several interwoven melodic lines.

Polytonality: simultaneous use of several keys.

Rib: the side wall of a stringed instrument connecting the soundboard to the back of the body.

Score: written or printed ensemble music with all the parts set out one above the other on the page.

Soundboard: the flat front of the body of a chordophone that receives the vibrations from the strings and reflects them.

Sound-holes: holes cut in the soundboard to connect the vibrating air inside the instrument with the outside air.

Soundpost: a piece of wood fixed inside a stringed instrument, vertically connecting upper and lower surfaces, thus distributing vibrations over the body of the instrument.

Speaker key: a key that facilitates overblowing on certain woodwind instruments.

Tonic: keynote of the diatonic scale, from which the key takes its name.

Transposition: the translation of a piece of music into a key other than that in which it was originally written.

Acknowledgements

The publisher would like to thank the following individuals, manufacturers and music shops for the use of their instruments and facilities for photography.

Felicity Forster (violin), Stuart Hall (*tres*, Cretan *lyra*, *saz* and *kora*), Robert Harbron (English mandolin and concertina), Duncan and Hayley Kerr (bagpipes), Giovanni Sipiano (guitars and percussion instruments).

Folk instruments
Blanks Music Stores Ltd
271–273 Kilburn High Road, London NW6 7JR
Tel: (020) 7624 7777

Strings
David Lipkin and Haim Algranati
L. A. Strings
68 High Street, Barnet, London EN5 5SJ
Tel: (020) 8364 9726

Strings, woodwind and brass
Foote's
10 Golden Square, London W1R 3AF
Tel: (020) 7437 1811

Woodwind
Howarth of London
31–35 Chiltern Street, London W1M 1HG
Tel: (020) 7935 2407

Woodwind and brass
John Myatt Woodwind and Brass Instrument
 Specialists
57 Nightingale Road
Hitchin
Hertfordshire SG5 1RQ
Tel: (01462) 420 057

Percussion
Music Bank (Hire) Limited
100 Clements Road, London SE16 4DG
Tel: (020) 7252 0001

Percussion and computers
Norton York and Colm O'Rourke
The University of Westminster
Harrow Campus
Northwick Park, Harrow HA1 3TP
Tel: (020) 7911 5000

Keyboards and mechanical instruments
Finchcocks
Goudhurst, Kent TN17 1HH
Tel: (01580) 211 702

The publisher would also like to thank the following picture libraries for the use of their pictures in the book (l=left, r=right, t=top, b=bottom, u=upper, m=middle). Every effort has been made to acknowledge the pictures properly, however we apologize if there are any unintentional omissions which will be corrected in future editions.

AKG, London: 16t, bl, br; 17t; 18t, b; 19tl, bl, br; 23br; 32bl; 38bl; 40t, br; 43t; 45bl, br; 47bl; 49tl; 54r; 60t; 63b; 66t, b; 78bl; 81tr; 83bl; 86l, r; 89tl; 108l; 109br; 111b; 114t; 115br; 116br; 133tr; 134b; 135tl, tr; 136bl; 144b; 145tr; 149br; 150b; 154b; 161tr; 172br; 181b; 195tr; 198bl; 203b; 204bl; 208t; 216t; 227br; 229br; 230t; 235bl; 246t.

Arena Images Ltd: 7tr, br; 10tr; 34t; 36br; 37tr, br; 38br; 39bl; 41tr; 50b; 55b; 81tl; 96t; 100bl, br; 101t; 109t; 119bl; 121br; 129b; 130bl; 142b; 156b; 161ml; 176tl; 194t, b; 200b; 203m; 206b; 213b; 216b; 217bl; 220b; 221t; 228m; 245m; 246b.

Art Archive Ltd: 6tr; 8–9; 10bl; 11b; 12br; 17m; 20l, r; 21t, bl; 24t; 27b; 29l; 42r; 46b; 47t; 55tl; 59t, b; 67m, b; 101b; 103br; 111tr; 120tr; 126t; 127l; 129mr; 137b; 147br; 159t; 176tr; 180b; 193tl; 196bl; 200tr; 223br; 227tl; 231r; 233tl; 250l.

Bridgeman Art Library, London: 6bl, br; 7bl; 14t; 22tl; 23tl; 30t; 33tl, tr; 43b; 56t; 57t; 61tr; 62t; 74bl; 92bl; 104t; 105tr; 109bl; 115t; 118bl, br; 123bl, br; 127r; 128t; 130tl; 132t; 133b; 135b; 138br; 139br; 145l; 149tl; 155t; 160b; 174br; 181tr; 190br; 191b; 192br; 205br; 211m; 218b; 219tl; 223tl; 225l, br; 231l; 244t; 248t; *Index* 12bl; 30bl; 54l; *Peter Willi* 11t.

Camera Press Ltd: 17br; 33br; 58t, b, (all flags); 59 (all flags); 61bl, br; 63tl; 71tr; 72t; 74t; 75tl; 76l, r; 77bl; 80l; 83t; 84l; 93tl, b; 97b; 170t; 171b; 184b; 185m; 211b; 247t; 249bl, br; 251t, m, b.

Christie's Images: 23bl; 103tl; 116t; 126l; 136br; 149m; 153tr.

Frank Lane Picture Agency Limited:
Roger Wilmshurst 12t.

gettyone Stone: 23tr; 24br; 31t (3rd from right); 61tl; 68bl, br; 69t; 72b; 94–5; 107t, bl;

110r; 113bl; 119t; 121t, bl; 128br; 131br; 157br; 163t; 164tr; 185t; 189br; 197tr; 201tr; 203t; 209t; 235tl; 241tl.

Horniman Museum & Gardens: 169t; 178t; 179br; 239t.

Hutchinson Library: 14bl, br; 15t, b; 25t; 111tl; 126b; 151m; 157tr; 166b; 167mr; 173t; 183bl; 185b; 191t; 193b; 207b; 235br; 237tr.

Kobal Collection: 233br.

Lebrecht Collection, London: 13t; 22tr; 24bl; 26l, r; 27tl; 28t, bl, br; 32t; 35tl; 42l; 45t; 46t; 48t, b; 49m, b; 56b; 60b; 62b; 64b; 67t; 69br; 74br; 82l, r; 85bl, br; 89tr; 90l; 92br; 102b; 103bl; 106tl; 113t; 114b; 115bl; 122bl, br; 123t; 125br; 129tr; 130tr; 131ml; 132l; 133tl; 145br; 148br; 158bl; 159m, b; 161tl; 163b; 170b; 171t; 172t; 173m; 174bl; 175t, bl, br; 176br; 177l, r; 178b; 179t, bl; 182b; 190bl; 192bl; 211t; 212bl; 219tr, b; 223tr; 225tr; 226b; 227tr; 229bl; 230b; 234bl; 238b; *R. Booth* 134t; 137tl; *Zdenek Chrapek* 56m; *J. M. Cook* 237br; *N. Dyson* 68t; *Mike Evans* 51t; 229m; *David Farrell* 55tr; 79b; 91tl; 139t; *Jim Four* 142t; *Betty Freeman* 87m; *Richard Haughton* 57b; 105tl; *C. R. Henderson* 65t; *S. Lauterwasser* 49tr; 78t; 88b; 91bl; *Nigel Luckhurst* 247b; *Suzie Maeder* 83br; 87t; *Morris* 69bl; *Kate Mount* 51t; 53m; 107br; 221b; *Odile Noel* 50t; 65b; 143bm; 167tl; 189tl; 247m; *F. Noronha* 38t; 138bl; 197bl; 237tl, bl; *M. Peric* 199b; *Pictorial Press* 63tr; 73tr, b; 75bl; 77br; *Wladimir Polak* 91tr; 91br; 117b; 147t; 151t; *Private Collection* 47br; 248b; *Royal Academy of Music* 80r; 106tr; 125bl; 131t; *G. Salter* 7tl; 34br; 52t, b; 64t; 104b; 117tl; 137tr; 152br; 153tl; 155br; 161b; 169m; 181tl; 195tl; 198br; 207tl; 208b; 245b; *Chris Stock* 15m; 92t; 100t; 136t; 143br; 152bl; 163b; 166t; 167bl; 168b; 169bl; 174t; 183t; 189tr; 199tr; 207tr; 212tr; 217t; *Toby Wales* 2; 93tr.

Mary Evans Picture Library: 10br; 13m, b; 17bl; 19tr; 21br; 27tr; 29r; 30br; 33bl; 36t; 44; 84r; 85tr, bl; 124t, b; 125t; 143bl; 188bl; 201bl; 209br; 210b; 222l; 224b; 236b.

Max Wade-Matthews: 169br; 209bl.

Performing Arts Library: 70t; 90r; *Clive Barda* 53t, b; 57m; 63m; 78br; 96b; 97t, m; 113br; 151b; 152ml; 153b; 165tr, b; 199tl; 205bl; 228t; 249t; *Marcelo Benbahan* 202b; *Sisi Burn* 81b; *Fritz Curzon* 35b; *James McCormick* 146t; *Kate Mount* 210t; *Linda Rich* 22b.

Redferns Music Picture Library: 37tr; 51b; 70bl, br; 71tl, b; 73tl; 75tr, br; 77tl, tr; 79tl, tr; 87b; 89b (all in panel); 105b; 112l; 117tr; 121bur; 139bl; 143t; 157tl, bl; 165tl; 173b; 183br; 191bl; 204br; 205t; 212br; 217br; 226t; 233bl; 240b; 244b; 245t; 250r.

Simon Broughton: 25bl, br; 106b; 196t.

Index